Friendship Fictions

I0878261

Rhetoric, Culture, and Social Critique

Series Editor
John Louis Lucaites

Editorial Board
Richard Bauman
Barbara Biesecker
Carole Blair
Dilip Gaonkar
Robert Hariman
Steven Mailloux
Raymie E. McKerrow
Toby Miller
Austin Sarat
Janet Staiger
Barbie Zelizer

Friendship Fictions

The Rhetoric of Citizenship in the Liberal Imaginary

MICHAEL A. KAPLAN

THE UNIVERSITY OF ALABAMA PRESS
Tuscaloosa

The University of Alabama Press
Tuscaloosa, Alabama 35487-0380
uapress.ua.edu

Copyright © 2010 by the University of Alabama Press
All rights reserved.

Hardcover edition published 2010.
Paperback edition published 2018.
eBook edition published 2010.

Inquiries about reproducing material from this work should be addressed to the University of Alabama Press.

Typeface: Bembo

Cover image: © Icefields | Dreamstime.com
Cover design: Michael Kaplan and Todd Lape

Paperback ISBN: 978-0-8173-5938-6

A previous edition of this book has been catalogued by the Library of Congress as follows:
Library of Congress Cataloging-in-Publication Data

Kaplan, Michael A., 1966–
Friendship fictions : the rhetoric of citizenship in the liberal imaginary / Michael A. Kaplan.
p. cm. — (Rhetoric, culture, and social critique)
Includes bibliographical references and index.
ISBN 978-0-8173-1689-1 (cloth : alk. paper) — ISBN 978-0-8173-8351-0 (electronic) 1. Citizenship in motion pictures. 2. Friendship in motion pictures. I. Title.
PN1995.9.C5128K37 2010
791.43'653—dc22

2009032238

To Alan and Mila Kaplan, for more than I can say

Contents

Acknowledgments

Strange as it may sound, I have wanted to write a book since I was six or seven years old. I'm not sure where the idea came from, but I vividly remember daydreaming about the thrills of being an Author. Back then I could not have imagined that this juvenile fantasy would actually come true, let alone that the book itself would be a scholarly work, written in a language I had not even heard yet. Still, in retrospect the book's major themes were already shaping my imagination. For a child growing up in the USSR, citizenship was a pervasive point of reference, while friendship directly sustained material, social, and psychic life, and so occupied a hallowed place in collective consciousness. For a Jewish kid living in Soviet Ukraine, these two pillars of sociality were also sources of often inscrutable and intractable distress. But then my family immigrated to the United States, and both citizenship and friendship became daily preoccupations in an entirely new, and newly illuminating, way. There were enormous gains and notable losses, to be sure, but also the critical distance afforded by the juxtaposition of starkly different cultural experiences. Perhaps from that point on, a book bearing the indelible traces of these experiences was all but inevitable.

But even the inevitable is seldom simple or easy, and this book, while inescapably personal, is hardly the product of solitary authorship to which I once naïvely aspired. Many people, including friends, family, colleagues, and unaccountably magnanimous strangers, offered me generous material, intellectual, and emotional support without which this book could not have come into existence. Their contributions mean that friendship is more than a theme addressed by the book: it is what made the writing of the book possible.

First and foremost, I am grateful to my parents, Alan and Mila Kaplan, for their countless sacrifices in making possible not only my scholarly endeavors but my life as a citizen of the liberal democracy about which I write. Similarly, I would like to thank Regina Katz for her inexhaustible patience with me during the writing of this book and for readily assuming numerous familial responsibilities so as to give me time to work. Many thanks to Dilip Gaonkar, who encouraged my interest in the affinity among citizenship, friendship, and popular culture, and whose mentorship and friendship have been invaluable to me for well over a decade. Likewise, I thank Bob Ivie for his professional mentorship and uncanny proficiency at keeping me calm during periods of stress. Valuable conversations with Keith Topper and Jon Simons impelled me to refine my understanding of liberalism, while memorable discussions with Chris Kamrath propelled me toward new insights into the film *Smoke.* A series of informal workshops held by the Public Culture collective aided me immensely in sharpening my thinking about the discursive constitution of the liberal imaginary, social reflexivity, and the speculative logic implicit in the gift, and in this regard I owe special thanks to Beth Povinelli, Benjamin Lee, Michael Warner, and Serguei Oushakine. At critical moments, Phaedra Pezzullo, Ted Striphas, Robert Terrill, Chris Miller, and John Sloop were enormously helpful in focusing and streamlining both the arguments at work in this text and the text itself. Much more importantly, I am especially grateful to Chris, Phaedra, and Ted for the singular gift of their friendship. Finally, I thank the University of Alabama Press for its adroit stewardship of this project.

A version of chapter 2 appeared as "Imagining Citizenship as Friendship in *The Big Chill,*" *Quarterly Journal of Speech* 91 (November 2005): 423–55. A version of chapter 3 appeared as "Rebel Citizenship and the Cunning of the Liberal Imaginary in *Thelma & Louise,*" *Communication and Critical Cultural Studies* 5 (March 2008): 1–23. I thank the anonymous readers of those manuscripts for their attentive and insightful responses.

Friendship Fictions

Introduction

Rhetoricizing Liberalism

Liberal Democracy and the Limits of Critique

Liberal democracy, its critics convincingly claim, undermines citizenship. In its emphasis on private life over public affairs, it derogates community, diminishes solidarity, and devalues civic virtue, participation, and commitment.[1] In establishing abstract universal norms of inclusion, it systematically excludes, marginalizes, or excessively encumbers women and sexual, racial, ethnic, and cultural minorities.[2] In relegating the distribution of essential resources to market mechanisms, it curtails collective control over fundamental social processes and facilitates systematic exploitation.[3] In its drive to promote personal rights over popular rule, it suppresses political antagonism in favor of administration, clientism, compromise, or spectacle.[4] Consequently, liberal régimes tend to lose their credibility.[5] In sum, since it both discourages interest in civic virtues, bonds, and activities and thwarts democratic efficacy, the liberal model of citizenship is disingenuous, deleterious, dysfunctional, and destined to decline.[6]

Nor are these considerable defects contingent; on the contrary, enormous energy has been expended to demonstrate that liberalism's limits are irrevocably rooted in its rudimentary premises. Even liberalism's advocates tend to concede that its critics are substantially correct, proposing to salvage some semblance of citizenship by recovering marginalized traditions of liberal thought and ameliorating or updating liberalism's conceptual rationale.[7] In short, both the critics and defenders of liberalism concur that, as things stand, its conception of citizenship is inherently vexed, demanding substantive revision or wholesale replacement.

What both critics and supporters seldom consider, however, is the way the discourse of liberalism itself thematizes and contends with these problems in the cultural public sphere, demonstrating rhetorical ingenuity and resilience far beyond what can register in theoretical debates.[8] Modern polities, including liberal ones, are constitutively imagined communities sustained by the publicly circulating discourses of mass media, whose dominant mode is increasingly that of visual entertainment.[9] Consequently, the liberal polity's commitment to its admittedly vexed notion of citizenship is not only doctrinal or institutional but constitutive of, and sustained by, its mass-mediated public culture. As critics focus on the conceptual defects of liberal citizenship, they generally refrain from asking why the liberal polity fails to fail as predicted, enduring and even thriving despite what appear to be irreparable flaws. They are thus impeded from seeing that the most intractable of these flaws are not only obstacles to overcome but rhetorical features that function as productive cultural and political resources. To grasp the momentous consequences of this, it is essential to expand the field of analysis beyond theoretical debates regarding liberal principles and to examine the rhetorical agility of the liberal imaginary in the context of public culture.

It seems evident that, while conceptually and sociologically liberalism appears to inhibit citizenship, in liberal public culture, citizenship is a popular theme. For example, a polity supposed to be indifferent or even hostile to civic identity, attachment, virtue, and practice enthusiastically consumes countless narratives of citizenship in the mode of entertainment. In particular, contemporary visual culture is replete with images and narratives of citizenship. Popular fiction films in which problems of political agency, collective attachment, social membership, national identity, and racial, gendered, sexual, economic, and other conditions of citizenship are imaginatively addressed attract large audiences and extensive attention from other media, often provoking public discussion of their political ramifications. Of course, a common criticism of such films is that they convert complex political problems into vapid entertainment. They are thus disparaged for usurping the place of serious collective deliberation, for distorting the real nature of the problems they address, or for co-opting, circumscribing, and thereby preempting urgently needed genuine critique.[10] But whatever the (limited) merits of these criticisms, the sheer ubiquity and popularity of citizenship as a thematic repertoire for mass entertainment powerfully testify to its salience as a public concern, challenging the consensus view that liberalism marginalizes citizenship.

This tension between liberal derogation of citizenship and citizenship's extensive popularity in liberal culture is the impetus behind the present study. Combining theoretical investigation, critical interpretation, and metacritical reflection, it seeks to understand the irreducibly rhetorical process whereby the liberal imaginary is constituted in American public culture.

Selectively focusing critical attention on the indispensable role played by fictions of friendship in mediating liberal citizenship both in political theory and in popular film, this investigation endeavors to elucidate key rhetorical features and discursive dexterity of the liberal imaginary. Accordingly, it pursues three intertwined trajectories. First, it strives to resituate the diverse range of theoretical and polemical critiques of liberalism in relation to contemporary visual culture while reconceptualizing the political dimensions of this culture—especially as these emerge in popular fiction film—in terms of the negotiations of liberal citizenship it mediates. Second, it proposes a conceptual framework capable of explaining the rhetorical hold liberal discourse has over the contemporary democratic imaginary. Third, it advocates and models a broadly deconstructive critical practice for the task of exposing the limits and challenging the hegemony of liberal discourse.

If citizenship theory has been slow to assimilate the consequences of the insight that the liberal polity is inherently imaginary and decisively dependent on the reflexive addressivity and counterfactual publicness of circulating forms of impersonal discourse, politically driven media and cultural criticism tends to overlook the constitutively liberal character of the cultural public sphere.[11] The burgeoning work emerging from critical media, communication, and cultural studies either disregards liberalism as a discrete problematic or relies on an expedient assortment of its more familiar categories, treating it as one contingent discourse among others, one capable of being supplanted at any moment by some more democratic one. Focusing on a series of specific political struggles—such as those involving race, gender, sexuality, or social class—it is easy to lose sight of the way the liberal project is to supply the very idiom by which these struggles are conceived, conducted, and constrained. One of this study's theses, then, is that the discourse of liberalism, while certainly contingent, is not simply optional, since it represents a distinctive and efficacious rhetorical solution to the problem of democratic governance—a problem that emerges and acquires its legibility and shape from the very discourse proposing to solve it.

The Political Productivity of Depoliticization

Citizenship appears as a problem—even the problem—for the liberal imaginary precisely because liberalism explicitly presents itself as an antipolitical discourse of democracy. If it displaces citizenship, it does not do so deviously or accidentally; on the contrary, the promise to minimize political responsibility and antagonism is an explicit ground of its appeal. Viewed from one direction, this appeal is incoherent—liberalism is a politics that promises to relieve its citizens of civic demands and thus of citizenship itself. But this incoherence is not a symptom; it does not indicate a failure or limit of liberal logic. On the contrary, one of my premises is that it represents the public formulation, within the terms of liberal discourse itself, of the fundamental dilemma of democracy that the liberal project proposes to address.

From this vantage, the antipolitical stance for which liberalism is consistently berated is neither an ideological ruse nor an inadvertent side effect, but the crux of the liberal solution to the problem of democracy. This solution is not only conceptual and institutional but also rhetorical, inasmuch as liberalism does not simply discover but also determines democracy as a problem of a particular, rhetorical sort. Moreover, liberalism is not reducible to a particular enunciated content subject to logical strictures of systematic coherence and noncontradiction, but is an ongoing project that mobilizes diverse modes of enunciation for which the apparently irreconcilable impulses found in liberal theory function as culturally and politically productive resources. And since the liberal solution is advocated openly and is subject to ceaseless and contentious scrutiny, this very reflexivity regarding the apparent contradictions of citizenship must be grasped as integral to the rhetorical infrastructure of liberalism. As a result, liberal public culture is organized in no small part around the paradoxical fiction of citizenship as an antipolitical sovereign stance attributable to a counterfactual *private public.*[12] This, however, means that while the steady stream of cinematic citizenship narratives cannot be dismissed as mere ideological propaganda, the tensions and divergences articulated in these fictions do not amount to an open-ended struggle to hegemonize the meaning of citizenship.[13] On the contrary, the production of such a public struggle is itself internal to the discourse of liberalism and inscribed in its model of citizenship as permanent critique of organized authority. It is by means of this public reflexivity that the openly imaginary liberal solution acquires and retains whatever credibility it enjoys.

This is why, if meaningful progress in citizenship theory requires a more sophisticated grasp of the mediatized character of the liberal imaginary, critical communication, media, and cultural studies urgently require a robust account of the way liberal discourse operates rhetorically to underwrite and overdetermine the political struggles transpiring in the cultural public sphere. Currently, even political projects advanced from perspectives intrinsically hostile to liberalism—especially the broad range of anticapitalist, pluralist, and populist ones—neglect the rhetorical obstacle liberalism poses for them. For the political struggles promoted by critical media, communication, and cultural studies to be effective, their advocates need to take liberalism much more seriously. Just as liberalism is not one of a set of conceptual options, neither is it one of a series of interchangeable discourses. Modifying or dislodging it requires a nuanced understanding of its rhetorical efficacy—that is, of the way it both appears to solve the intractable problem of social cooperation and succeeds in securing its solution as contingent, elective and, in this sense, democratic. In sum, while citizenship theory needs to continue pursuing its recent cultural turn, politically driven cultural criticism would benefit by taking a rhetorical turn. I attempt to address this double exigency by laying the groundwork for and modeling this double turn.

Film Friendship in Focus

If the cultural public sphere is a vital site for the constitution of the liberal imaginary, within this imaginary cinematic friendship narratives disproportionately mediate dilemmas of citizenship. Today, when Americans are prompted to think through difficult political predicaments—ranging from official corruption to social hierarchy to the contradictions of democratic authority—they are urged to imagine their repercussions in the context of elective and affectively sustained personal attachments. So, for example, war and its sociopolitical aftermath, gender politics, homosexuality and heterosexism, class anxiety, the "crisis" of the family, the power and impotence of the presidency, racial tensions, immigration, ethno-cultural diversity, and globalization have all been depicted in countless commercially successful films as events, patterns of action, or structures of feeling mediated by friendship.[14]

This pervasiveness of friendship as a category of popular political reflection is matched by a corresponding prevalence of friendship in democratic theory, from Aristotle to Arendt to Agamben.[15] Democratic thought has from its beginning repeatedly returned to friendship as a privileged figure of civic relations.[16] However, where the Athenian polis appears to have been a "politics of friendship," liberalism purports to be a "politics of strangeship."[17] Put another way, liberalism determines its distinctive conception of citizenship in part through a defining contrast with friendship, which in turn becomes the exemplary mode of the sort of elective and affective sociability that liberal culture promises to promote in order to secure its historically novel scheme of voluntary cooperation grounded in mediated collective oversight of semiautonomous social systems.[18] Yet, political and social theorists repeatedly invoke friendship as paradigmatic of the sort of social bond liberalism supposedly lacks or undermines.[19]

Thus, if friendship is a pervasive and insistent category of liberal discourse on citizenship, it is also a highly improbable one. This is why fictions of citizenship organized around friendship provide a unique vantage onto the rhetorical structure of the liberal imaginary. Taken together, the staggering quantity and variety of popular films narrating citizenship through friendship confront us with a set of mutually exclusive yet coexisting impulses: dismissive of citizenship, liberal culture cannot refrain from imagining it; putatively individualistic to the point of narcissism, liberal citizens eagerly consume fantasies of intimate and generous affective bonds; jealously guarding these bonds from the corrupting influence of politics, liberal culture nonetheless grounds citizenship in friendship.

How is it, then, that fables of friendship have come so conspicuously to mediate citizenship in the liberal imaginary? If liberalism presupposes and produces narcissistic subjects who resist and corrode their own "constitutive attachments" as alien impositions, why should they be interested in even compensatory fantasies of intimate citizenship? Is this simply a case of "the return of the repressed"? If, on the other hand, liberalism aims to depoliticize social relations in favor of purely elective affective attachments, why, and with what consequences, do such attachments become the very matrix of liberal citizenship? Addressing these questions, I argue that the figure of friendship is neither a superfluous theoretical conceit, nor a symptom, nor a gratuitous popular metaphor, but an indispensable category of the liberal imaginary that affords privileged access to a critical understanding of liberalism as a potent discursive formation and cultural logic. The resulting analysis aims to account for liberalism's rhetorical efficacy and resilience in the face of apparently insuperable defects, as well as to provide new critical insight into its actual limits, insight essential for the political task of transforming liberal culture.

Taken together, the case studies offered here map the key ways the liberal project deploys the category and fictions of friendship to secure its own fundamental premises, distinctions, and discursive logics. The argument commences in chapter 1, which poses the problem of citizenship as it emerges in debates concerning liberalism, resituating this problem in relation to liberal public culture. Noting the persistent yet variegated recurrence of friendship in theories of citizenship from classical Athens onward, I argue that this recurrence is best understood in relation to historical context on the one hand and constitutive dilemmas of democracy on the other. I go on to theorize the return of friendship today as a model of citizenship in what appear to be diverging theoretical conceptions of democracy.

In contemporary citizenship debates, friendship emerges with notable urgency in critiques of liberal civic sensibility, where it is invoked to model a noncoercive yet affectively compelling social bond. In response, critics express concern that a politics aimed primarily at securing social cohesion will tend to obfuscate, displace, or otherwise thwart efforts to correct injustice and oppression, effectively reinforcing existing hierarchies of power under the guise of forestalling social upheaval. In these debates, then, liberalism appears to solicit, incoherently, both concern about its very viability and opprobrium for its potent ideological dissimulation.

It is, however, seldom noted in these debates that classical liberal theory itself advocates friendship as the elemental social bond—in pointed contradistinction to politics. Classical liberals such as Locke, Smith, and Hume give systematic expression to a historically unprecedented model of social life partitioned into the domains of "public" and "private." Facilitating this transformation, friendship emerges as the privileged figure of private association. In liberal democracy, then, the affective attachments embodied by friendship become key to an informal moral order no longer sustained by institutional authority, an order that now functions as a check on such authority. In other words, a liberal imaginary is obliged to produce the sentimental attachments of private life as the site of extrapolitical sociality, inasmuch as, paradoxically, their imagined antipathy toward authority effectively renders them paradigmatic of liberal citizenship.

The ambivalent function of friendship in liberal theory is emblematic of a more rigorous ambivalence in the liberal imaginary generally concerning citizenship. The liberal solution to the democratic paradox relies on the gesture of depoliticizing broad areas of social interaction as a way of circumscribing the antagonisms that inevitably erupt when order is understood as a precarious and contingent achievement rather than a reliable inheritance.[20] This gesture is "democratized" by being submitted to public scrutiny and displays of consent, but the result is the familiar liberal attenuation of citizenship. Liberalism thus involves a paradoxical civic disavowal of citizenship to sustain voluntary cooperation—an antipolitical politics mediated by fantasies of a noncoercive yet binding sentimental morality figured by friendship. There is, in other words, an elective affinity between liberalism's legitimating fictions and the figure of friendship, an affinity that emerges with continual insistence in liberal public culture.

Bringing this affinity into sharper focus, I pay extended attention to the work of Hannah Arendt and Jacques Derrida in order to elucidate the key impasses of democratic citizenship and the key features and limitations of liberalism's solution to them. For Arendt and her legatees, democratic citizenship must be oriented by an ethos of friendship, which is to be conceived in very specific, even perplexing, terms. For Derrida, by contrast, the democratic ethos recurrently finds itself both indebted to and threatened by its reliance on friendship, which for him is irreducibly aporetic in its simultaneous insistence on inclusion and exclusion, universality and difference, calculation and the incalculable. Derrida's insight is that the friendship supplement introduces into democracy a politics and a rhetoric that divert and impede the democratic promise. The mutually troubling encounter between these subtle and powerful lines of thought sets the stage for the ensuing case studies, in which the liberal imaginary's negotiation of the impasses of democracy are subjected to rigorous analysis and critique.

Cinema Citizenship

The remainder of the inquiry unfolds through a series of politically inflected analyses of four popular films: Lawrence Kasdan's *The Big Chill* (1983), Ridley Scott's *Thelma & Louise* (1991), Sophia Coppola's *Lost in Translation* (2003), and Wayne Wang and Paul Auster's *Smoke* (1995). Each film, in its reflexive relation to its own cultural genealogy, deploys a friendship narrative to address a nexus of basic dilemmas of liberal citizenship. Each therefore affords access to a discrete range of the concerns commonly invoked in regard to liberal citizenship: the supposed contradiction between liberal individualism and the constitutive attachments of community; the tacitly presumptive social class of liberal citizens and its role in facilitating or disrupting social and political bonds; the disjunction between the liberal principle of universal juridical equality and the socially prescribed subordination of women and homosexuals; the self-canceling effects of structural reflexivity as that which both promises and preempts the possibility of deploying publicly circulating knowledge to manage political, economic, and social processes and subjects; the normative transparency of whiteness as a condition of the liberal civic bond; and the counterfactual premises legitimating the liberal promise of universal autonomy, elective attachment, and procedural justice.

It is probably clear by now that the focus of the study is neither on the "historical poetics" nor on the "ideological" ramifications of the films being examined.[21] Neither formalist nor historicist approaches are adequate to my particular task, although both aesthetic (as it happens, chiefly narrative) form and historical context become indispensable to it at certain moments. At the same time, for reasons outlined above, I do not regard these films as instances of ideological distortion or manipulation. Instead, I approach them, together with major citizenship debates, as sites where characteristic aspects or key trajectories of liberal discourse become visible with particular clarity or force. So, on the one hand, the features of liberal rhetoric I highlight are pervasive and familiar, not confined to film as a medium (where they are nonetheless most common) or fiction as a mode. Yet, on the other hand, outside theoretical reflection on liberalism (and even there), they seldom assume the relatively coherent and engaging form made available—but not invented or directed—by contemporary Hollywood's "institutional mode of representation."[22] Just as it is not my aim to take sides in debates regarding liberal citizenship, neither is it to explain why or how Hollywood cinema promulgates liberalism. Rather, the aim is to examine both sorts of discourse in order to understand the legerdemain of liberal rhetoric as it becomes conveniently (though not altogether contingently) accessible in particular cultural texts.

Am I, or should I be, claiming that there is an elective or structural affinity between Hollywood fiction film and the theme of citizenship, an affinity that, for reasons that would need to be specified, obtains to a notably lesser degree between this theme and other media or modes? The answer is: not exactly. If there is such an affinity, it is not directly between Hollywood cinema and liberal citizenship—which is, after all, a frequent theme and even more frequent subtext in lots of different media texts—but rather between friendship as a metaphor for citizenship and the rhetorical commitments of the liberal imaginary. This can partly be inferred from the insistence of this metaphor in both theoretical and popular citizenship discourse: the recurrence of friendship in both critiques of liberalism and in liberal theory itself; the proliferation of friendship-based, politically inflected film genres (road movies, Westerns, buddy cop films, war movies, women's films,and so on); the vast range of political problems addressed by such films via the narrative device of friendship (race, gender and sexuality, class, ethnicity, nationalism, immigration, cultural diversity, elite corruption, the electoral process, the law, war, environmental risk, globalization, and the like). This affinity seems to eventuate in the proliferation of cinematic depictions of citizenship as friendship for more contingent reasons, such as the significant, though not unique, role of public fictions in generating the liberal imaginary's hypothetical legitimating narratives; the relative cultural preeminence or practical and formal advantages of Hollywood narrative film over other fictional modes, such as the novel, drama, popular music, or episodic television; the "path dependence" of the Hollywood mode of representation; and, given the liberal promise of life unfettered by politics, the unsurprising dearth of explicit public discussion of citizenship apart from concrete political deliberations or controversies.[23]

In short, while the reasons why Hollywood film is a particularly rich site for observing the rhetoric of liberal citizenship are complex, conditional, and largely outside the purview of this study, the richness itself is nevertheless importunate, consequential, and instructive. This, in turn, may help to clarify what it might mean to read Hollywood film rhetorically as exemplary of liberal citizenship discourse. The main trajectory of the argument is surely familiar: it organizes the now-institutionalized dispute among historicist and formalist approaches, ideology critique, and the theory of cultural or discursive hegemony.

The first of these begins with the observation that movies are made under specific institutional, financial, technical, formal, and sociohistorical constraints; their production is costly and resource intensive, and thus carefully planned and executed; and they are highly responsive to prevailing market and aesthetic conditions. Consequently, it seems reasonable to surmise that much of what the largest audiences ultimately see is the more or less immediate product of such responses. From this perspective, each film is best understood in relation to the conditions of its production, and it is simply misguided to seek polemical motives where institutional ones suffice.

Still, the empiricist, historicist, or formalist inflections of this view often converge with some forms of ideological criticism—particularly the currently ascendant critique of "the politics of representation"—insofar as they help explain the formal consistency and political complacency of Hollywood output in quasi-materialist terms. Given the discrete and verifiable factors driving production and aesthetic form, it should not be surprising that Hollywood product reflects or promotes politically conformist points of view. After all, it must be clearly legible, enjoyable, and widely popular in order to turn a profit. From this vantage, Hollywood fare is liberal to the degree that American culture is liberal, and any departures from this norm will most likely be limited and in the service of mostly superficial and potentially remunerative aesthetic novelty.

Of course, both of these accounts must confront the surprising diversity of political positions actually proffered by Hollywood films, and especially the simultaneous circulation of politically incompatible or antithetical stories—including ones that raise probing questions about the conditions of their own production (all subject to a wide and unpredictable range of audience interpretations). This is where hegemony theory comes in, arguing that popular culture is a site of political struggle over accepted meanings and norms of representation, wherein even artifacts produced under quite similar conditions can nonetheless advocate dramatically divergent political views that vie for dominance.[24] In work driven by this perspective, any given discursive formation can only be precariously hegemonic, subject to being dislodged or supplanted at any moment, or at least contending endlessly with fundamentally incompatible alternatives in an irrevocably fractured cultural space that lacks any universal metalanguage for sorting out which discourse should gain adherents. According to this logic, liberalism could only be a provisionally hegemonic discourse subject to constant pressure from genuine rival options.

Liberal Discourse and the Rhetoric of Dissent

My own approach both overlaps with and diverges from all three of these views. While I do regard public culture as a site of disputation, I understand such disputation as itself a key manifestation of the liberal imaginary, and therefore as unlikely easily to transgress the limits of this imaginary. Yet for this very reason, it is the nature and effects of these limits that are most urgently, though usually tacitly, at stake in the political struggles they make possible. Any political project—or, by extension, politically salient popular text—taking shape within the liberal framework of public or notionally "democratic" disagreement will both conform to and chafe against the discursive norms that make it possible while also making its limits palpable. It is by attending to this tension that I endeavor to discern the discursive features of the liberal imaginary itself, as conceptually if not practically distinct from the political projects taking place within its purview. In some projects or texts, this tension will itself be thematized, and in some of these cases, the rhetorical framework itself will become the object of critique or resistance. However, because critique and resistance are themselves normative within the liberal imaginary, such projects (or texts) will from the first be ambivalently situated as both belonging to and disavowing their own conditions of possibility.

Moreover, insofar as it is an active social imaginary rather than a structure or system, these conditions themselves comprise a rhetoric rather than a metalanguage. It is here that questions of form in its rhetorical intricacy and incoherence become significant. A rhetorically productive reading will be one that interrogates the friction among the various "levels" of enunciation: what the text seems to have been designed, according to the usual protocols, to accomplish (the historicist-formalist moment); the political project or struggle in which it participates or intervenes (the cultural hegemony moment); and the ways it does or does not function to respond inventively to these conditions of its own enunciation. In other words, a productive reading will be rhetorical in the deconstructive sense, attentive to the ways a text's internal struggles to meet incompatible demands fortuitously make its discursive conditions of possibility accessible to critical elaboration and assessment.

Accordingly, the most urgent critical question to ask concerning the liberal imaginary is neither whether or how it operates ideologically, nor whether it contradicts its own premises in setting rhetorical limits on democratic politics; rather, it is whether and how it functions rhetorically to provide opportunities to transgress these very limits without thereby undermining the democratic promise on which its legitimacy relies. But in order even to pose this question, it is essential first to distinguish liberalism as a decisive rhetorical force in public culture without reducing it either to a dominant ideology or to one discursive formation in hegemonic competition with others. If liberalism is an ideology, it is an anti-ideological one; if it is a discursive formation, it is one that enframes and confers legible form on the hegemonic rivalry in which it also participates. It is for these reasons that popular texts that seem to offer narrative arguments invoking the rhetorical dimensions of liberalism stand out as exemplary in the double sense often noted by Derrida: at once typical of significant patterns and in some telling way exempt from them.

Tailoring its reading strategy to the particular film, each chapter examines a key feature of liberal discourse by critically engaging a set of major debates in political theory and media/cultural studies. For example, *The Big Chill* serves as an occasion for interrogating the communitarian and republican indictments of liberalism, prompting an encounter with the work of Hannah Arendt and her contemporary intellectual disciples. Similarly, *Thelma & Louise* initiates a complex negotiation with a range of feminist and queer critiques, especially those grounded in Lacanian psychoanalysis, Foucauldian theory of power, and the deconstructive interventions of Judith Butler. Next, *Lost in Translation* offers an opportunity to engage neo- and post-Marxist theories of global late capitalism—especially those advanced by Fredric Jameson and Jean Baudrillard—through competing accounts of reflexive modernity found in the sociology of Niklas Luhmann and Anthony Giddens. Finally, *Smoke* facilitates a nuanced modification—

derived from the work of Jacques Derrida—of critical race and multiculturalist theories.

Building on the preceding examination of friendship in Arendt, chapter 2 offers a detailed analysis of *The Big Chill* in the context of the communitarian and neo-Aristotelian critiques of liberalism. The film was selected because of its continuing status as a pivotal point of reference in contemporary public discourse concerning the wholesale political transformations of the latter half of the twentieth century. A staggering array of social and political phenomena are now routinely condensed under the rubric of the film's title, and its central themes are also those of innumerable popular and academic studies of recent political culture. The film therefore constitutes a unique entry point into the dominant contemporary debates regarding the questionable premises, putative contradictions, and dubious fate of liberal citizenship.

Situating *The Big Chill* in relation to these debates, my analysis brings into relief the rhetorical function of friendship as a political promise of intimate sociability, a central catalyst for the liberal project of neutralizing social antagonisms by imagining relatively bounded spheres where different principles of cooperation can predominate. In effect, I propose to reread dominant sociological accounts of modernity (Weber, Parsons, Luhmann, Habermas, Giddens) from a rhetorical perspective, not as descriptions of social actuality but as observations regarding an ongoing imaginary (re)production of a set of interlocking constitutively discursive structures of cooperation. Whereas, say, Habermas envisions modernity as a partition between "system" and "lifeworld" and accords the latter the task of legitimating and supervising the former, for me liberalism is the social imaginary that makes this partition conceivable and renders it mundane through a complex series of rhetorical operations. It is, as it were, a hypothesis concerning the most effective mode of social cooperation, a hypothesis that immediately posits the criterion of its own vindication and therefore involves a certain inescapable circularity that assumes the form of a certain intrinsic reflexivity. From this perspective, the communitarian valorization of friendship as a "constitutive attachment" opposed to liberal individualism, then, is more than simply misplaced, but itself belongs to the innermost logic of the liberal project. It now becomes clear that liberal discourse actively produces the melancholic communitarian controversy in order to secure the priority of intersubjective attachments against the "corrupting" influences of publicity. Politicizing intersubjective intimacy turns out to be neither a communitarian-republican corrective of liberalism nor a betrayal of the initial liberal promise; rather, it is exposed as the discursive destiny of that promise, revealing liberalism to be a "politics of friendship" in an altogether unexpected, but structurally irreducible and rhetorically fertile, sense.

Chapter 3 takes up the obverse of this promise, commonly stylized as a defiant or heroic politicization of privacy, particularly by feminist and multiculturalist projects. If Marxists and republicans concur in regarding liberal privatization as destructive of citizenship, feminists and multiculturalists derogate it for facilitating the exclusion and systematic subordination of women and various sexual, ethnic, racial, and other minorities. For such groups, private life emerges as a de facto site of political struggle, and citizenship predictably assumes fugitive forms of oppositional solidarity.[25] The privileged popular figure of such solidarity is, of course, friendship, which consequently appears to have a political valence diametrically opposed to that evinced by the communitarianism of *The Big Chill.*

Yet on closer inspection, it turns out that such insistently politicizing deployments of friendship are equally overdetermined by the logic of liberalism, giving articulate form to what might be called liberal "rebel-citizenship." An exceptionally visible and extraordinarily self-reflexive instance of this trope is central to Ridley Scott's 1991 controversial hit *Thelma & Louise.* A monumental media event, it was perhaps the most widely debated film in several decades. The multigenre story of female rebellion against patriarchal authority prompted hundreds, if not thousands, of conference papers, journal articles, books and book chapters, master's theses and dissertations produced across the humanities and social sciences. It focused enormous public and academic attention on the institutional problem and media representation of gender as a category of political membership and obstacle to political agency. As such, the film sits at the intersection of a vast network of critical discourses concerning the politics of gender.

Yet despite the stunning volume of writing about the film, little notice has been paid to the friendship at its narrative and thematic center, and less still to its sophisticated and distinctively liberal rhetoric of citizenship. Responding to this surprising inattention, my analysis situates the film in relation to its multifaceted critical reception, interrogating the inadvertent complicity of the most typical reading protocols with the liberal project. In *Thelma & Louise,* friendship is the figure of liberal rebel-citizenship, and the film's cunning gesture is to posit a specter of patriarchy as the incarnation of state power, to be resisted in consonance with liberal antipathy toward organized authority and preference for sentimental attachment supposed, like mercurial "woman," to exceed the restrictive grasp of public rationality and discursive phallocentrism. Friendship, then, emerges as a key to grasping the film's liberalism, as well as liberalism's apparent immunity to feminist and queer critiques of gender-based subordination. Indeed, the film is emblematic of the signature liberal strategy of deploying a structural inequality as a rhetorical resource. Through the figure of female friendship, the rhetorical calculus governing the film's narrative not only salvages liberal citizenship from the potentially vexing implications of feminist and queer cultural politics, but installs it as the very model of feminist and queer political agency.

The figures of the rebel-citizen–friends give form to the liberal disavowal of power, which paradoxically demands citizens whose political agency consists in defying their own citizenship. *Thelma & Louise* marks, and remains caught within, this impasse of citizenship construed as oppositional critique or resistance. By contrast, Sophia Coppola's 2003 hit art film *Lost in Translation*—the subject of chapter 4—thematizes this impasse directly as a key entailment of the social reflexivity undergirding the liberal project as such. Through a close rhetorical reading of the film, I engage the twin problems of globalization and postmodernity as theoretical metaphors for an emerging crisis in what might be called "social cybernetics." This is the project, coextensive with modernization itself, of submitting social processes to more or less direct social control, mediated by publicly circulating expert knowledge and large-scale institutions and technologies. As an integral dimension of modern social cybernetics, liberal democracy shares its premises, which is why it construes citizenship as both reflexively oriented and skeptically disposed. Yet the structural reflexivity of liberal modernity, which proceeds by staging various political critiques and alternatives, itself produces a paradox: the more thoroughly society is socialized, the more it acquires the features of Baudrillardian simulacra.

The result is the experience of a loss of the very reality reflexive modernity would sustain, as well as a corresponding diminution of agency. This is the central thematic concern of Coppola's film, which situates its protagonists in a disorienting and debilitating hyperreality and follows their struggles to overcome the profound alienation of global late capitalism. Their ambiguous success comes about when Bob (Bill Murray) transforms Charlotte's (Scarlett Johannson) transferential love toward him into friendship. In effect, the ennui produced by the relentless reflexivity of the social objectivity in which they find themselves is alleviated by Bob's own reflexive intervention into his relationship with Charlotte. The response to hyperreflexivity is thus more reflexivity, which here assumes the form of friendship. This, in turn, means that while the film astutely identifies a constitutive limit of the liberal model of citizenship, its solution can only beg the question it is proposed to resolve. The figure of friendship renders this performative contradiction rhetorically potent, preempting the discovery of alternatives to even overtly failing liberal reflexive citizenship.

In *Lost in Translation,* we confront the self-defeating tendency of reflexive modernity. The elemental process by means of which modern liberal societies endeavor to govern themselves turns out to undermine its own condition of possibility—the definitive distinction between the act of observation (or distinguishing) and the social reality this act produces as its own appurtenance. Yet while this aporia of reflexivity emerges with laudable clarity in the film, its figuration as a problem capable of being solved by the bottomless enigma of affective intersubjectivity only defers this aporia. We seem to be confronted, then, with an obdurate limit of the liberal imaginary: bound ineluctably to deconstruct its own logic, this imaginary appears incapable of escaping the resulting cul-de-sac. Yet the self-defeating efficiency of reflexive sociality—a key manifestation of the democratic paradox within the very imaginary committed to overcoming it—need not necessarily assume the shape of a vicious circle, just as the unobservable, inherently indistinct secret need not reproduce the structure of knowledge relocated to the private space of friendship.

This is because friendship is also self-deconstructing: this is the theme of Wayne Wang and Paul Auster's 1995 film, *Smoke.* As the denouement of the narrative shaping the book, chapter 5 considers the possibility of taking liberalism's legitimating fiction seriously as a starting point for imagining a politics of attachment no longer bounded by investments in contractualist and autological notions of justice.[26] Focusing on the film's nuanced revision of the prevailing theoretical and popular representations of the interplay between race and liberal citizenship, I perform a Derridean reading of the film, situating it in relation to the influential and continuing debate concerning the gift economy as an alternative to capitalism, demonstrating how the narrative troubles the logic of reciprocity upon which liberal culture is based. This logic structures both political and affective relations, and its internal impasses emerge in the form of persistent tensions between those relations. This partly explains the productively ambivalent function of friendship as both a telos and an unsurpassable limit of liberal politics, as figures of exchange appear as the ruling metaphors of sociability in the liberal political imaginary.

I argue that *Smoke* endeavors to lay bare and resignify this structure by developing a network of narratives in which the practice and rhetoric of contractual exchange are tested to the point of failure, brought about by their own inevitable reliance on intractable forms of excess. This failure, however, is not a disaster but the very condition of community: the excesses are excesses of generosity that escapes any form of intentionality; what cannot be contained by the economy of equitable exchange is the giving of gifts and the proliferation of stories that both obligate and emancipate those they affect. What emerges is a liberal community of friendship based neither on elective attachments nor on compulsory ascriptions such as race, but on a virtual "law" of fortuitous gratuity. Here, friendship comes to indicate not the antipolitical politics of elective reciprocity that produce both hierarchical ascription and the project of its supersession, but the proto-discursive bonds presupposed by any sort of universality, equivalence, and reciprocity. The film is thus a rare instance of popular deconstruction of the liberal imaginary, and its value lies in the light it throws on the democratic potential inherent in the liberal circumscription of democracy.

Rhetoricizing the Paradoxes

The book concludes with a retrospective overview of the foregoing analyses and findings that reinforces my central claims regarding the structural affinity between the figure of friendship and the liberal project; the misperceived sources of liberalism's resilience and the overlooked loci of its instability; and the superiority of an interdisciplinary and chiefly deconstructive approach to the project of transforming the liberal imaginary in the direction of greater justice. Liberalism, it appears, is resilient because, in positing discursive struggle—that is, rhetoric—as the privileged mode of social cybernetics, it "depoliticizes" this struggle. This is a basic point I make in different registers through my readings of *The Big Chill,* where friendship emerges as the intersubjective locus of politics that effaces the antagonism constitutive of social life, and of *Thelma & Louise,* where friendship is a site of resistance that is already the presumptive form of citizenship in the liberal imaginary. By contrast, in *Lost in Translation* the reflexivity valorized by liberalism is exposed as an obstacle to itself, demonstrating that the route to transformation cannot be more antiliberal argument, whether such argument is staged in popular discourse or in academic criticism. Only in *Smoke* do the ruses of liberal reason confront their own limitations in a way that does not end in a cul-de-sac or a compromise but suggests an opening to a democracy-to-come. The film thus challenges the dominant premises of contemporary cultural criticism, too often unwittingly suspended between ideology critique and social constructionism.

Neither is adequate to the task of challenging a hegemonic politics itself grounded in antifoundationalist and reflexive critique of social authority. The political advantage of deconstructive rhetoric lies in its capacity to provoke a productive confrontation between liberal discourse and its own impossible but compulsory promise.

1
Imagining Citizenship as Friendship

Citizenship and the Friendship Supplement

Neither the theory nor the practice of democratic politics, it seems, can get very far along without friendship. When Aristotle ventures to delineate the norms of citizenship in the polis, he turns to friendship as the relation that would not only model civic membership but would directly supply its very form. When Adam Smith endeavors to imagine social relations unsullied by the demands of market rationality and uncorrupted by political machinations, he nominates friendship as the epitome and privileged mode of attachment. When Carl Schmitt emphatically rejects liberalism's administrative anemia and advances power as the irreducible stake in social antagonism, he gives the minimal condition of the political as the bedrock distinction between friend and enemy. When, in recognition of the passing of the *res publica* and of the disempowering tendencies of the modern liberal nation-state, Hannah Arendt tentatively holds out the promise of an eruptive politics of "founding," it is friendship that is charged with the paramount task of sustaining the common world of "inter-being" continually threatened with obliteration by "the social" on one side and totalitarianism on the other. When Michael Sandel joins Charles Taylor, Michael Walzer, Robert Bellah, and numerous others in issuing a thoroughgoing critique of the liberal citizen's fictitious autarky, he proffers friendship as the paradigm of a "constitutive social attachment" necessarily preceding and orienting in advance any intentional, subjective choice of ends to be "distributed" politically. When Chantal Mouffe strives to imagine a noncoercive, nonascriptive yet reliable political bond, she combines Michael Oakeshott's notion of *societas* with Schmitt's notion of antagonism to argue for a "radical democracy" that would transform mortal enemies into purely political adversaries—that is, in effect, civic friends.[1] When Jacques Derrida delivers a long-awaited book-length disquisition on the enigmatic implications of his lifelong philosophical project for democratic politics, he calls it *Politics of Friendship.*

From its inception in ancient Greece to its hegemony in liberal modernity and across the long hiatus in between, the democratic imaginary has relied on friendship as an indispensable inventional resource, a supplement to its assorted conceptions of citizenship. If Aristotle's polis took the form of assembly and speech in the agora open only to those few rendered "equal" by virtue of an *oikos* comprising women, children, and slaves, the civic bond and the obligations it entailed could have appeared to the citizens themselves as virtually indistinguishable from friendship. As nascent capitalism began generating antagonism between the royalist aristocracy and an emerging merchant class aspiring to political power, it was the friendship tie that made both thinkable and practical the novel contractual form of political legitimation that came to supplant patrimony and to serve as the basis of the parliamentary structure. When, under what Arendt would call totalitarian rule, Soviet citizens evolved a richly complex private life hinging on a parallel, unauthorized "economy of favors," a system for circumventing the official bureaucracy, and a risky illicit network of dissident political knowledge and resistance, these all depended for their existence and efficacy upon an intricate and nuanced imaginary and practice of sentimental friendship. And today, when Americans are invited collectively to imagine the good life as personal satisfaction secured against social, economic, juridical, or other institutional pressures framed as unjust coercive encroachments, this fragile state of grace is commonly figured as casual, intimate talk among friends, stylized as trusted, affectionate, generous soul mates endowed with compassionate insight into each other's idiosyncratic inner lives.

We seem to be faced, then, not with a fortuitous parallelism between political theory and social discourses and practices, nor with any simple pattern of causality linking them, but rather with a deep and pervasive affinity, structural or elective, between one particular mode of social attachment and the very concept of democracy. According to at least one commentator, democracy "finds its origin in a system of thought in which the idea of friendship is the major principle in terms of which political theory and practice are described, explained and analyzed."[2] The question immediately raised by this observation ought to be: Why should any political practice be thought of in terms of an affective interpersonal bond, and can (or should) democracy, in particular, be thought of otherwise? Horst Hutter hurries past this question when he asserts that the friendship relation is, in itself, "suprahistorical" and is linked to a(n equally suprahistorical) notion of democracy insofar as friendship "tends toward equality."[3] In other words, friendship's persistence as a political trope across historical time and heterogeneous forms of cultural inscription and rhetorical deployment is to be explained by an essential homogeneity between it and democracy "as such."

It is vital to see that the idea of democracy "as such" occludes that which insistently calls for explanation, namely the peculiarity of friendship's historical leap from the Athenian polis to the late modern liberal nation-state. We thus confront a series of puzzles. What would it mean for "democracy as such" to depend on friendship? If democracy implicates friendship in its very notion, then this notion ought to be rigorously reexamined in light of its constitutive metaphoricity. How must friendship be conceived to make this supplemental relation possible or desirable? Both the Athenian polis's reliance on friendship and friendship's reappearance within the liberal imaginary demand a historically alert explanation. Hutter inadvertently hints at the scale of the problem when he notes that while "the idea of friendship [as a model for citizenship] has . . . been supplanted by the idea of market exchange . . . the concept of reciprocity cannot exhaustively explain the *content* of a friendship relationship."[4] On the one hand, late modern liberal citizenship is explicitly constructed as a form of contract, even as it is everywhere *imagined* as friendship; on the other hand, friendship appears to *exceed* citizenship's minimal requirement of reciprocity. It is, then, a distinctive determination of friendship that is advanced within the liberal imaginary, and it is advanced precisely in the guise of "friendship as such"—so much so that it is easy to misrecognize this particular determination as friendship's ontological, "suprahistorical" notion. Thus Hutter is entirely correct to link liberalism, friendship, and contractual reciprocity, yet far too eager to promote the inner mystery of friendship as the nostalgic solution to the very alienation of citizenship in which a certain liberal determination of friendship is already complicit. Put another way, if friendship appears to tend toward equality and thus to promote a certain democratic ethos, this appearance may itself be sustained by a certain predetermination of what friendship "is in itself," a predetermination that already relies on a tacit privileging of liberal equality, with its autarkic subjects and elective contractualism. Thus today we may be confronting in the *very notion* of friendship a certain figure of democracy, and there is every reason to think that this figure does not issue from democracy "as such" but incarnates its late modern liberal avatar.

Friendship in Liberal Theory

Explicitly seeking to deflect the familiar critique of liberalism as producing alienated citizens able to relate to each other solely on the basis of contractual reciprocity, Allen Silver calls attention to the pivotal role played by friendship in classical liberal theory.[5] In his account, liberalism's philosophical progenitors conceived of a historically unprecedented way of dividing social life into the domains of "public" and "private," with the ideal of friendship, reimagined in an novel way, becoming paradigmatic of private relations. This "domain of the private . . . is . . . a distinctive creation of the impersonal order central to modern economies and polities. The private sphere understood as the ideal arena of love, tenderness, and 'kindly services' requires the very impersonality of the public world of bureaucratic administration, contractualism, and monetized exchange against which it is culturally distinguished." Early liberal theorists "argue that 'commercial society' introduces a historically unprecedented distinction between self-interested relations and personal bonds that are normatively free of instrumental and calculative orientations. . . . A newly 'private' world of personal relationships . . . is . . . made possible by the new 'public' world of commerce, contract, and impersonal administration."[6]

The "exemplary significance of friendship," in this view, is that it "is a prototypically 'private' relationship": "[A]n ideal of friendship so quintessentially 'private,' so contrary to the forms of association that dominate the 'public' domain, is distinctive to our times . . . [wherein] friendships are judged of high quality precisely to the extent they invert the ways of the public domain." Consequently, "[s]ympathy" becomes "key to an informal moral order no longer sustained by religious, economic, and political institutions.[7] In effect, then, the sentiments ascribed to, and encoded as, friendship are henceforth charged with sustaining the novel structure of social cooperation—that is, the politics—characteristic of liberal modernity.

In his spirited defense of this early view, Silver describes the emergence of a dichotomous social arrangement in which the newly imagined private sphere is the locus of moral order. The new relation between the public and private introduced by liberalism is asymmetrical. The worlds of commerce and politics are subject to natural law, and in them human beings function as self-interested agents, relying on institutional arrangements to ensure fairness and justice. In the private sphere of intimate relations, on the contrary, individuals are bound by moral law and are expected to set aside what here appear as *base* or amoral motives of power and profit. Such a configuration of "public" and "private" thus embodies a hierarchy of motives that is reproduced in the constitution of the liberal subject and its constitutive attachments. While public life emerges as indispensable, it is private life that is now the site of fully human sociality and moral authenticity. Yet this new hierarchy is neither a simple ideological ruse, as Marx contends, nor an epic error, as civic republicans and communitarians insist. The "depoliticization" of private life and the new delineation of "politics" are mutually contingent elements of a political innovation: they belong to a radical new solution to the newly urgent problem of socializing political authority.

Nor is the logic delineated by Silver confined to the work of early liberal theorists. Some of liberalism's most sophisticated contemporary exponents outline an entirely homologous structure. Jürgen Habermas, for example, builds his entire theory of postfoundationalist democratic legitimation on the distinction between "system" and "lifeworld."[8] In this Parsonian schema, systems form a domain of social action in which instrumental rationality is dominant and which broadly corresponds to what Smith understood as the economic and political spheres, complete with the corresponding "steering media" of money and power. The lifeworld, by contrast, is a domain in which communicative rationality is primary, inasmuch as action here aims at social integration grounded in commitment to intersubjective understanding. For Habermas, as for classical liberals, the integration achieved in the lifeworld supplies the legitimating ground for the processes taking place in the political and economic systems. This is possible because in at least one important sense the communicative action of the lifeworld is extrapolitical: it aims, implacably even if only implicitly, at mutual understanding, which for Habermas is logically anterior to any possible conflict of instrumental interests. Unsurprisingly, it is just this conceptual move that "radical" democrats such as Mouffe and Rancière reject as "displacing" political antagonism.[9]

Indeed, Mouffe understands this move as inherent to liberalism itself, and not just as the contingent error of one theoretical account.[10] Yet even as she claims to reject what she takes—mistakenly, I think—to be liberalism's refusal of antagonism, she recommends under the rubric of "radical democratic citizenship," in effect, nothing other than liberalism itself: "What binds [the citizens of radical democracy] is their common recognition of a set of ethico-political values. In this case, citizenship is not just one identity among others—as in liberalism—or the dominant identity that overrides all others—as in civic republicanism. It is an articulating principle that affects the different subject positions of the social agent (as I will show when I discuss the public/private distinction) while allowing for a plurality of specific allegiances and for the respect for individual liberty."[11]

Not only is this description all but indistinguishable from Habermas's "constitutional patriotism," it also requires recourse to the figure of the friend.[12] Mouffe reintroduces Schmitt's friend/enemy distinction into liberalism in order to mark the necessity of antagonism, but immediately preempts the obviously antidemocratic consequences by insisting that the "radically democratic" approach to antagonism is to convert the political enemy into an adversary—in effect, a kind of friend.[13] For all her avowed radicalism—indeed, because of it—Mouffe cannot go all the way with political antagonism, reverting to the liberalism she would renounce via the figure of civic friendship as a relation that is neither simple "prepolitical" community nor outright hostility. Perhaps, then, liberalism cannot so easily be dismissed as erroneously, insufficiently, or cynically committed to political neutrality. What Mouffe seems unable to recognize is that the friend/enemy dichotomy is not simply suppressed within liberalism; on the contrary, as I hope gradually to make clear, liberalism represents a discrete solution to the problem encoded by this dichotomy.

While Mouffe vacillates between abandoning and salvaging liberalism, Danielle Allen directly recommends reforming the liberal paradigm, which she thinks can be pursued by leveraging—what else?—friendship.[14] Allen argues for what Arendt would recognize as civic friendship in what Habermas would call the lifeworld—a move that might perplex a civic republican no less than a radical democrat, but that, it would seem, is entirely consistent with the liberal thesis that politics is predicated on the logically prepolitical mutuality established among members of a society. If for Smith this mutuality was made possible by "moral sentiments" cultivated among friends, for Allen it is the correlate of trust built through reciprocal acts of sacrifice among strangers, who thereby become political friends.

The point not to be missed is that this "private" lifeworld of affective mutuality performs indispensable political labor, which is made possible only by the rhetorical gesture of recoding the processes of social integration as pre-, extra-, or even antipolitical. Indeed, this is the condition of possibility for the liberal solution to the problem of antagonism. For this very reason, however, it is not to be regarded either as a conceptual error within liberal doctrine or as a cynical ploy in the service of a hidden sectorial interest (though of course this may be one of the effects).[15] On the contrary, if, as theorists from Hobbes to Marx to Laclau have maintained, the very ontology of the social is riven by irreducible antagonisms produced by sociality itself, this liberal partition must be regarded as a historically novel—and stunningly effective—strategic approach to maintaining incredibly complex and extensive forms of cooperation that rely upon the very antagonisms they generate.[16] From Smith to Habermas to Allen, liberal doctrine simply formalizes the rhetorical strategy of liberalism as a discursive solution to the "democratic paradox." Consequently, liberalism is better understood as a productively contradictory project in which friendship becomes a privileged synecdoche for the principles of moral accountability, solidarity, and binding elective attachment as specifically nonpolitical attributes of a universal humanity in need of protection against the encroachment of, and capable of acting as a *politically legitimate* check against, "systematic" forms of power and authority.[17]

In this way, the liberal imaginary transforms the "ontological" paradox of democratic cooperation into the "ontic" discursive contradiction of coding fundamental political presuppositions as extrapolitical and "displacing" the rhetorical processes of maintaining them into what becomes the "cultural" public sphere. Among the considerable benefits of this solution are what Marx famously derogated as capitalist alienation and fetishism. That is, the liberal partition makes it possible to establish vast regions of cooperative endeavor that seem to require little substantive agreement of the sort valued by Habermas and Marx alike, and indeed commonly engender surprisingly extensive forms of heterogeneity. Markets, after all, are decision systems charged with allocating the collective surplus. Their political legitimacy, which is routinely contested and thus far from ideologically assured, stems directly from the fact that they are designed to work "behind the backs" of those whose welfare is subject to their operations—this is Marx's chief objection to the "invisible hand" of market decisions. His "alienation" thesis holds that, as the production and distribution of the collective surplus is relegated to impersonal market processes, citizens surrender collective control over the conditions of social life. For Habermas, as for liberal economists and so-called Third Way theorists and politicians, this problem can be ameliorated if economic and political "systems" are more actively supervised by way of democratic deliberative processes so as to gain the benefits of efficiency they bestow without surrendering collective control over the damaging externalities they inevitably produce. It is in this context that the problematic of legitimation takes shape, so it is erroneous to dismiss liberalism as an ideological veil destined to secure the unfettered expansion of capital. On the contrary, liberalism explicitly advocates and relies on market mechanisms to secure levels of cooperation inconceivable if pursued through either deliberative processes or coordinated coercion. The argument is almost tiresomely familiar: it is because markets operate "behind the backs" of citizens that they can deliver the staggering surpluses characteristic of capitalist societies. Coordinating action by way of competition, markets appear not to require nearly the degree of discursively achieved agreement presupposed by deliberation; on the contrary, they make collectively productive use of forms of plurality and disagreement that could only undermine the efficiency and legitimacy of deliberative procedures. Indeed, Smith's elaborate theory of "sympathy" openly postulates the "alienation" implicit in capitalist social relations.[18] From this vantage, far from being the dirty secret obfuscated by liberal ideology, markets constitute a vital element of the liberal political project. This is what explains the unceasing public discussion regarding the appropriate extent of reliance on markets to address a variety of collective problems, as well as regarding the effects this reliance produces, including the recurrent failure of market mechanisms themselves. Within liberal polities, little is less invisible—or politically contentious—than the hand of the market.

In sum, the critiques of liberalism as an erroneous or cynical "displacement" of politics are inadequate. In its Marxian form, the displacement thesis gives too little credence to the actual political tasks to which liberalism obligates itself; in its several republican forms, this thesis misconstrues or gives too much credence to liberalism's vociferous disavowal of politics. The result is an incoherent image of liberalism as both politically pernicious and politically impotent. Yet this incoherence is not the result of a simple conceptual or empirical error on the part of liberalism's numerous critics. On the contrary, it reflects the irreducible ambivalence concerning citizenship around which the liberal imaginary organizes itself rhetorically and which gives rise to quite complicated discursive articulations of the liberal project across contemporary public culture.

Envisioning Citizenship

In popular friendship fictions, in particular, politics is often coded as the antithesis of everything to be valued in human relationships, since the liberal imaginary commits itself to the rhetorical production of an extrapolitical elective sociability ruled by the "moral sentiments" of friendship. Popular friendship narratives can thus be approached as sites where this imaginative production takes place. But if films insistently tend to depict friendship under duress, and if their proliferation is continual, it is because the private intimacy that is the avowed telos of liberal culture is vexed from the start. As a rhetorical project aimed at securing contractual relations by appearing to oppose them, it is inherently contradictory, and this contradiction is inevitably what friendship films both occlude and mark. While modeling the liberal ideal of privacy with its superior forms of subjectivity and modes of sociality, the figure of friendship as a response to political duress simultaneously underscores the artifice of this model, rendering every narrative victory provisional and hollow and necessitating the propagation of more narratives.

The proliferations of friendship films is thus part of the cultural procedure of *secreting* the "private" domain of intimate authenticity. If liberalism as a political imaginary is founded upon a specific normative distinction between public and private, this norm functions as a pivotal rhetorical vector in liberal political culture and practice. The "democratic ethos" of liberal culture corresponds to a disposition *to produce* the private sphere, to *precipitate* it out of the messy mixture in which the public and private are always already commingled together. Liberalism as a strategy for organizing political life can be regarded as a kind of mechanism for manufacturing the private, insofar as the teleology of liberalism is the *surpassing* of politics. Silver's endorsement of the earliest formulation of the public/private distinction by liberal philosophers lends itself to just such a reading. It is no accident that friendship is the key trope for these thinkers in their attempt to imagine the good life secured by the liberal construction of citizenship. Friendship offers a model of private life that appears able to get along without politics, relying on moral law and the conventions of personal loyalty and trust. On the other hand, cultural anxiety over the impossibility of getting beyond or away from the political drives the imaginative production of private space. Or, more powerfully, this imaginative process is a principal way liberal public culture both *generates* and *fulfills the constitutive promise* of liberalism. The private sphere can never be secured through "real" political contest; the walls are always coming down, and in any case the walls are themselves the objects of political struggle. The private is thus supplied allegorically; although, even here, it is always haunted by the politics it is supposed to displace.

Hannah Arendt and the Political Dilemma of Friendship

To observe the efficacy of this discursive maneuver, it is instructive to attend to the work of Hannah Arendt, the major twentieth-century exponent of a politics of friendship whose trenchant critique of liberalism has recently launched a veritable cottage industry of scholarly commentary. In criticizing what he sees as an "antidemocratic strain in Arendt's work," Sheldon Wolin remarks: "It was not accidental that she excluded the sentiments of fellow-feeling—compassion, pity, love—from the political realm, or, more important, that she was silent about 'friendship' (so central to her ancient Greeks) and 'fellowship' (so basic to Hebraic and Christian conceptions of community)."[19] What is strange about Wolin's observation is that while it is certainly true that Arendt banishes sentiment from the public or political world, she does so in significant part by reinserting friendship into the heart of politics. Far from remaining silent on the subject, she takes great care to delineate and refine a specific role for friendship in civic life, and she does this in large part by derogating "sentiment" as a constitutive aspect of friendship. It is difficult to see how Wolin could have noticed this derogation without noticing Arendt's recourse to friendship.

On the other hand, Wolin is not alone in dramatically underappreciating the importance of friendship in Arendt's political philosophy. Indeed, to risk a sweeping claim, given the extraordinary amount of scholarly focus on Arendt in recent years, it is remarkable how little attention has been paid to the role of friendship in her work, something that becomes particularly telling when one notices that Arendt represents a point of passage in ongoing debates among liberals, civic republicans, communitarians, public sphere theorists, feminists, multiculturalists, and radical democracy theorists. Given that this debate concerns the relationship among citizens within a polity, and given that each camp makes some effort to assimilate Arendt's work to its theoretical program, it is perplexing that the aspect of her thesis most directly relevant to the theoretical claims advanced in the debate is almost systematically overlooked.[20] Although Arendt mentions friendship infrequently, it both occupies a pivotal place in her theoretical edifice and marks that edifice's moments of incoherence.

The conventional view of Arendt's project, neatly summarized by Craig Calhoun, is that her "critical engagement with modernity centered on the ways in which emergent social conditions—notably what she called 'the rise of the social,' but also the related development of totalitarianism—undermined a needed distinction of public from private."[21] From this perspective, typical of scholarly writing on Arendt, her work is oriented toward delineating a conception of political practice capable of fostering freedom. "The related development of totalitarianism" is treated, as Calhoun's syntax and grammar aptly suggest, as an *exemplary corollary:* totalitarianism, broadly conceived, appears as a constitutive tendency in modern liberal nation-states and is a political form that condenses and intensifies the constraints on freedom obtaining in the everyday life of contemporary societies. Arendt scholarship thus sets about explicating the major categories comprising her political theory as these emerge from her searing critique of modern barriers to free action. Thus we have invigorating and fruitful debates concerning her views of the public/private distinction, political judgment and agency, freedom, plurality, and so on. In the process, scholars repeatedly find it necessary to turn to the question of Arendt's Jewishness and to her views on friendship as opportunities to clarify ambiguities in her conception of, say, "judgment" or "publicness." But it is invariably the general problem of politics that drives investigations of the particular issues of ethnicity and friendship. I would like to suggest that there is much to be gained from reversing this analytic relationship, posing the question as follows: What sort of politics would be required to produce the form of friendship that could have withstood the pressure exerted by Nazification?

Thus reduced, perhaps too violently, to its basic coordinates, Arendt's project aims to explain how Germans could participate in, collaborate with, or permit the systematic state-sponsored murder of their Jewish friends. When, reflecting on the Nazification of Germany, Arendt writes that "the problem, the personal problem, was not what our enemies did but what our friends did," she should be read as foregrounding the basic ("personal") dilemma orienting all of her political thought.[22] This may appear to be a narrow, tendentious, or even absurd way to summarize her considerable and far-ranging body of work, and it is certainly a motive that, in critical reception of this work, is treated as heuristically important but not theoretically pivotal. But perhaps this hypothesis can be made to appear less reductive. There can be no doubt that "the Jewish question" concerned Arendt a great deal; all I would like to suggest is that her efforts to grapple with it in a variety of texts and contexts should not be viewed either as more or less sophisticated "applications" of her otherwise freestanding theory, or as idiosyncratic excursions explicable by biographical factors.

Arendt's expansive and powerful critique of modernity seeks to elaborate the conditions under which the Nazi horror could plausibly take place, but this in itself would hardly make her work unique. What does differentiate it from other, equally ambitious explanatory projects is the shaping influence on her theory exerted by the vexing incongruence between the singular experience of friendship that Arendt thought she had known in Germany and the genocide that interrupted and, in retrospect, seemed to invalidate it. For her, neither notions of anti-Semitism nor theories of social control (intimidation, propaganda, ideological misrecognition of any kind) are adequate because they fail to explain the sudden transformation of friend into enemy. Hence she rejects or modifies psychological, ideological, sociological, materialist, and other accounts. Such theories can explain ethnic hatred as well as why states foster it; they can explain how people come to accept ethnocentric prejudice and to act upon it. But such explanations presuppose a more or less permanent, even if subterranean, rift between those who hate and those who are marginalized by hatred, a rift that under the right circumstances produces violence. Faced with a clear-cut case of what by any account appears to be abiding, intimate friendship across the ethnic divide, however, such explanations fail to satisfy. We need only to recall the recent enigmatic horror of Rwanda to apprehend Arendt's befuddlement.

To account not only for the historical emergence of ethnic conflict and its political causes and repercussions but for the inexplicably sudden turn from personal friend to ethnic mortal enemy, then, would necessitate a thorough reexamination of all the received meanings of "nation," "friendship," "politics," "history," "rationality," "humanity," "love," "power," "agency," "judgment," and related others. This is what Arendt sets out to do, and her redefinition of "friendship" in light of its historically momentous failure teleologically inflects all the other terms in the series. Her theory acquires its peculiar features partly because it aims to salvage an image of friendship that Arendt would endorse while making it possible to dismiss the German-Jewish friendships that were betrayed as in some sense inauthentic—without implausibly accusing countless individual Germans and Jews of either disingenuousness or witlessness.[23]

Arendt's Rhetoric of Friendship

Margaret Canovan and Lisa Disch offer strikingly similar accounts of the way Arendt's peculiar notion of friendship influences her determination of judgment in the Lessing Address.[24] In this speech, delivered in postwar Hamburg as she accepted the Lessing Prize, Arendt labors to shift the standard of political or civic responsibility away from humanist universalism on the one hand and Romantic notions of personal authenticity on the other.[25] To do so, she finds it necessary to delineate a certain version of friendship: "Just what does Arendt mean by friendship in this context? She does not mean to recommend a relationship based in the humanist ideal of respect for man in the abstract. But neither does she mean to recommend a communitarian vision of brotherhood."[26]

Arendt's aim in generating her model of friendship is to secure a properly political practice of judgment, which she develops as a modification of Kant's aesthetic judgment and in express opposition to his "inhuman" and "coercive" moral philosophy.[27] On the other hand, "[i]n opposition to the seductive vision of fraternity with all its warmth and closeness, Arendt sets a much cooler and more distant relationship which she calls 'friendship.' . . . This 'friendship' . . . should not be understood in terms of the post-Rousseauian ideal of intimates opening their hearts to one another, but as a relationship mediated by talk and argument about public affairs, a sense better understood by the Greeks."[28]

Despite her sympathetic tone, it should be noted that Canovan places Arendt's term "friendship" in scare quotes, indicating her own discomfort with this choice of appellation. Disch, too, finds it misleading: "Arendt calls it friendship, but it is in the service of partisanship for the world."[29] This "'sober and cool' friendship . . . allows and requires space between people," and thus "room for disagreement and dispute about the affairs of the common world."[30] Both Canovan and Disch plausibly attribute this disdain for excessive closeness to Arendt's view that "[f]raternity of this sort . . . is produced by conditions of persecution and does not outlast them."[31] Arendt's concern here is biographical as well: it is her sense that "excessive" affective intimacy blinded the Jews of Europe to the "political facts" that eventuated in the Holocaust. That is, a misleading—and, for Arendt, inauthentic—sort of friendship among Jews and between them and their German (and, by extension, Polish, French, Russian, and so on) neighbors deprived them of the capacity to exercise political judgment.

At the same time, Arendt's objection to the legacy of Kantian humanism is the paradoxical "inhumanity of Kant's moral philosophy."[32] That is, by grounding moral and political judgment in an abstract imperative constitutively indifferent to historical context and social particularity, Kant produces a cold, calculating, and coercive model of judgment disastrous for the virtuous conduct of human affairs he seeks to secure. Arendt's account of friendship is meant to counter this particular model without annihilating the space of political pluralism. Arendtian political judgment, then, is inconceivable without friendship to model the middle course between coercive objectivity and debilitating fraternity. By the same token, this "worldly" form of judgment secures her "cool" model of friendship, which can in turn be juxtaposed with what in retrospect appears as mere camaraderie or fraternity among German Jews.

One heuristic advantage of approaching Arendt's political theory through the problem of friendship is that doing so sheds light on key ambiguities in her work. Thus, for example, when Eli Zaretsky summarizes Arendt's analysis of the ideological origins of racism in *Origins of Totalitarianism,* he characterizes the book as "brilliant, impassioned, loosely organized and self-contradictory" to the degree that it simultaneously accepts and rejects Marx's analytic framework.[33] Arendt views race as a means of staging the (false) appearance of a social bond in capitalist societies whose members are deracinated by Hobbesian competition. This Marxian insight possesses far greater explanatory power than the "vulgar" Marxism of Arendt's day could generate, and it is more than coincidence that Arendt achieves it by attending to a problem her Marxist contemporaries did not find compelling. That is, the discourse of race tells Arendt something vital about the structure of sociability under capitalism, and she turns to rehabilitating friendship in order to supply an alternative to ascriptive social membership.

At the same time, Arendt's frustrating ambivalence concerning the prospects for political agency in modernity is likewise structured by her overriding concern with the dilemma of friendship. Scholars persistently debate the location of "action" for Arendt. On the one hand, she often insists that genuine politics can transpire only in a distinctly marked public realm; on the other hand, she frequently suggests that politics comes into existence through certain kinds of action. Consequently, she is both excoriated for limiting the scope of politics in advance and celebrated for presaging the "cultural turn" of political engagement. To a significant degree, this ambivalence inheres in Arendt's investment in friendship. The underlying question concerns the passage from a personal attachment to vigorous engagement with political reality. On the one hand, friendship seems to depoliticize social relations as friends withdraw into personally fulfilling but socially oblivious intimacy, which ought to be denounced for complicity with oppression and abdication of political responsibility. On the other hand, friendship, insofar as it cultivates the capacity to criticize without abandoning and to assist without abrogating autonomy, seems to incubate a sort of germinal mode of publicness that ought to be defended as the last hope against oppression. How, then, is political agency to be specified—as belonging to a realm of activity that is the precondition of freedom, or as the direct eruption of free action itself, capable of positing its own realm? Arendt cannot but remain scrupulously ambivalent on this issue because either alternative entails unpalatable consequences for friendship: if friendship in the absence of a public realm is inherently debased, it cannot sustain the hope of resistance that Arendt would have liked to demand of her German friends; if friendship retains a critical political dimension, then its failure under Nazi rule remains an enigma—or worse, requires that friendship be abandoned as a basic, "suprahistorical" human value. From this vantage, Arendt's diligent effort to salvage friendship from irrelevance is a decisive impetus of her work.

Why, however, does Arendt want the term *friendship* for the type of social relation she is describing? Why not call it something else—say, "respect" or "vigilant partisanship," which is apparently what she is after? After all, Arendt's definition seeks explicitly to exclude components that appear to be essential to friendship as it is most commonly understood or represented.[34] If intersubjective identification, emotional intimacy, intense loyalty, and personal familiarity are displaced in favor of "political facts" and "inter-est," just what would impel people to feel committed *to each other* in the way we typically understand friends to be? Arendt's "friends" may be strongly committed to their common world, but this world does not seem to require—although it may privilege—the participation of specific individuals: if I am loyal to the "in-between," the individuals with whom this is comprised matter relatively less, except in a way mediated by the "in-between," which, however, acquires the character that compels my loyalty in virtue of being the product of interactions among specific persons. Thus I am loyal to these people because I need them to maintain our world; I am not committed to them as individuals irrespective of the particular conditions encountered in the world. Rather, for Arendt, the degree to which I am interested in persons notwithstanding the world is the degree to which the world is in "dark times."[35] Thus what is most commonly understood as elemental to friendship is excluded from it by Arendt: the intense personal commitments shared by people under worldly—that is, political—duress.

Clearly, Arendt requires the affective force of "friendship" even as she refuses intimacy, and this conflicted desire produces a number of difficulties in her discourse. After all, choosing this term over others suggests that there is an element of this term's standard connotative cluster that fits Arendt's theoretical and rhetorical project. So while she meticulously "corrects" what she views as fundamental misconceptions about friendship, she is not simply recuperating the term. Again, does the mode of attachment she describes answer to the name "friendship" as it is conventionally understood? We know it does not, precisely because it is the elements of this understanding that Arendt devotes so much energy to "correct." And if it does not, why undertake the labor of revising and annexing this *particular* term?

Even a cursory reading of the Lessing Address supports the view that "friendship" names the very problem Arendt is trying to address by way of a thoroughgoing rereading of political theory. At a pivotal moment in the text, Arendt explains the "way of thinking governed by neither legal nor moral nor religious strictures," so that the question of whether or not it is justifiable to exterminate a race convincingly demonstrated to be inferior "would have to be posed thus: *Would any such doctrine, however convincingly proved, be worth the sacrifice of so much as a single friendship between two men?*"[36] Friendship is clearly of decisive importance here, displacing all other criteria of ethical and political analysis and judgment. But note the way the question is phrased. A "single friendship between two men" invokes an image markedly different from the transpersonal "world" in the interest of which Arendt's redescription would deploy friendship. It suggests a singular, selective bond between individuals, directed by each toward the other in its uniqueness and intensity. The friendship Arendt wants us to imagine here is at odds, at least to some degree, with the friendship she so carefully distinguishes from intimacy. That "civic" friendship, modeled on the ancient Greeks (though not identical to either Aristotle's "utilitarian" or his "virtuous" version), seems to operate in a different register of affect from that implied here.

At the conclusion of her reading of the speech, Disch turns to Arendt's generous effort to aid the correspondence between Karl Jaspers and her husband, Heinrich Blücher. She explains that "Arendt's writing of Jaspers's letter is . . . not an act of 'world'-travel but one of friendship," through which Arendt "respects a distinction that feminists continue to affirm and contest, that between public appearances and private life."[37] But this assessment flies in the face of what Disch spends much of the essay arguing, namely, that Arendt herself contests the view of friendship as an essentially private relation in favor of redefining it as an issue indissociably linked to "political fact." And certainly Disch is correct in pointing out that Arendt would have been highly sensitive to the political facts at issue in her friend Jaspers's assessment of her. What she does can indeed be read as an act of friendship, but one that privileges the personal relation over the very political complex she indicts as inhuman on the grounds that it violates the primacy of friendship. Her actions support her words even as they contradict them: in practice, she explicitly excludes the political, thereby privileging the very personal bond she would enlarge to include the political. This ambivalent or even aporetic moment does not simply reassert an Aristotelian or Habermasian distinction between public and private. Rather, it repeats the ambivalence and ambiguity in Arendt's own view of such a distinction—which differs from the two others—introduced by her account of friendship, which inevitably transgresses it.

Arendt's singular focus on salvaging friendship produces, in addition to the aporias already discussed, a telltale blindness concerning the polemical function of friendship in modern politics. Her argument that friendship should serve as the model of citizenship is intended to supplant ascriptive social membership—especially race and ethnicity—as the privileged mode of attachment. Race is, in her view, a stopgap or supplemental corrective to a *fundamentally untenable* form of sociality—liberal-capitalist modernity (which she notably conflates with post-Enlightenment idealist humanism). For Arendt, modern politics *has failed* or is (always, as it were) in the process of failing, and the symptoms of failure she enumerates include the collapse of public space into an undifferentiated "social"; racism, or what has since come to be called ethnocentrism and "identity politics"; the rise of totalitarianisms; the demise of properly political discourse in favor of self-serving power contests; citizens' alienation from the political community; and other unwelcome developments. However, while her analysis of these problems is insightful and trenchant, she does not consider the possibility that what she views as inadequate *substitutes* for *authentic* politics and citizenship are rather the specific *modes of sociality* liberal culture actively produces.

If this is the case, the (liberal) politics of modernity has not failed at all—just the reverse. Moreover, the *rhetorical efficacy* of liberalism depends on a specific social imaginary of friendship to secure the very privatization of citizenship and foreclosure of "republican" civic space that Arendt laments. Thus Arendt identifies the basic elements but misconstrues their actual relationship, so that her ambivalent solution suffers from what appears as a sort of tautological naïveté. What she regards as fatal flaws in the modern construction of excessively intimate friendship are better understood as its defining features and keys to its hegemony, ones not easily amenable to change through philosophical fiat.

Attempting a sort of philological recuperation of friendship, Arendt stops short of realizing that its meaning is rhetorically overdetermined within a discursive formation performing the monumental labor of social maintenance and reproduction. She does, however, have a strong intuition about the political character of friendship's modern meaning; this is why she insists, counterintuitively, on the primacy of happiness as the shared emotion most indicative of genuine friendship. For Arendt, the closeness fostered by duress creates solidarity that falsely appears as friendship, since it is only under conditions of individual freedom that true friendships can form. She is clearly groping for a distinctiveness abiding within the friendship relation that would dissociate it from the "distorted" or "debased" form witnessed in modern liberal capitalist polities. As a consequence of her investment in recovering *a forgotten truth* of friendship, she posits as its precondition what she is trying to secure as friendship's chief effect—the surpassing of "dark times" and the enduring possibility of happiness. Moreover, from this philological perspective it is difficult to see how the practice of friendship can generate political space, since under existing conditions individual subjects are perforce not free to engage in modes of attachment independent of the duress produced by liberal modernity. That is, lost in "the social," individual citizens experience the alienation that forces them into the inauthentic friendships Arendt derogates.

What remains unresolvable in Arendt's formulation, then, is the relation between her critique of liberalism and her articulation of civic friendship. Given her position, the recommendation of friendship seems impracticable. Let's return for a moment to her contradictory insistence on both a distinct public realm and a latent politics of friendship. Jacques Rancière singles out Arendt when he critiques political philosophy for positing as the precondition of politics that which can only be the (provisional and unstable) outcome of political struggle—the "partition" of society and activity into the political and the nonpolitical, or the predetermination of the political dimension of life: "What is proper to politics is . . . lost at the outset if politics is thought of as a specific way of living. Politics cannot be defined on the basis of any pre-existing subject. The political 'difference' that makes it possible to think its subject must be sought in the form of its relation. . . . If there is something 'proper' to politics, it consists entirely in this relationship which is not a relationship between subjects, but one between two contradictory terms through which a subject is defined."[38]

At this stage, it may appear that Rancière's position comports nicely with that of Arendt, who insists on the political as a relation in which the subject discovers what he or she is. On the contrary, however, it is precisely Arendt's solution to the tautological procedure of political philosophy that Rancière goes on to reject:

> This problem is in no way resolved by reverting to the classic opposition between two modes of action: *poiesis,* on the one hand, governed by the model of fabrication that gives form to matter; and *praxis* on the other, which excludes from this relation the "inter-being" of people devoted to politics. . . . In Hannah Arendt's work, for instance, the order of praxis is that of equals with the power of *archein,* conceived of as the power to begin anew. . . . Once Arendt defines both a proper mode and sphere of action, a vertiginous short-cut is formed that allows one to posit a series of equations between "beginning," "ruling," "being free," and living in a city-state.[39]

Despite its apparent proximity to a view in which the subject of politics is the outcome of engagement in political action, such a partition presupposes the political equality of citizens as the substance of their freedom. It is doubtless the case that freedom necessarily entails equality; however, it is just as clear that within the limits of the Arendtian view, the struggle for equality ceases to count as politics. Arendt's solution to this dilemma, as Bonnie Honig and others like to point out, is that participants in such a struggle achieve and exhibit both equality and freedom in and through the gesture of "founding."[40] Their self-authorizing revolutionary act performatively stages a new political realm within which they are equal and free.

Such a solution is not without problems, however, since it implies that Arendt's public realm can come into existence *only* at such moments of "founding." This is undoubtedly a view closer to Rancière's own, but it is doubtful Arendt would endorse it. For her, "founding" is exceptional insofar as it restores politics where some form of oppression has diminished it. Otherwise, in an Arendtian democratic state or polity, political action would be an ongoing practice of free and equal citizens.

Rancière would reverse this account. For him, the struggle for freedom and equality defines politics, and any existing partition of society into the political and the nonpolitical exists only to forestall or silence such a struggle. Such a partition always masks a condition of inequality and unfreedom; it is never the consequence of their achievement. From this perspective, Arendtian "founding" is the properly political moment par excellence—it is the "state of exception" that alone merits the name "politics." A central corollary of this view is that the gesture of designating the realm of politics, its mode of action, and its subject(s) is a ruse of power aimed at depoliticizing its own operation. This procedure Rancière calls *police:* "The police is not a social function but a symbolic constitution of the social. . . . Its essence is a certain manner of partitioning the sensible."[41]

If friendship is to "save" the political in a world defined by its eclipse in "the social," then friendship cannot simply be a *feature* of this world. As a supplement to politics, it must usurp politics. If politics remains a live possibility in such a world in the form of the refusal to sacrifice "so much as a single friendship between two men," then Arendt's own scheme tacitly eventuates in Rancière's formulation: the Arendt of the polis is the Arendt of the police; whereas the Arendt of friendship and founding is the Arendt of politics as rupture:[42] "The essence of politics . . . is to disturb [police partition] by supplementing it with a part of no part identified with the community as a whole."[43] According to such an analysis, the refusal to sacrifice a friendship amounts to a paradoxical universalization of the very particularity violently excluded by the police partition: if belonging to the "German" portion of the Nazi partition of the races means sacrificing one's Jewish friends, then politics must amount to asserting *each* such friendship as the universal principle of the German nation. It is the irreducibly excessive, "private," or "intimate" particularity of the friendship relation—in opposition to its putative "worldliness"—that renders it public and political in such a case.

So there is an inescapable irony in Arendt's project that is instructive for any effort to grasp the rhetoric of friendship as a figure of democratic citizenship. Her lifelong labor is motivated by an understandable suspicion that the fate of the Jews under Hitler was an emblematic symptom of liberal modernity. Drawing heavily on Marx's critique of capitalist alienation, Heidegger's critique of modern instrumentalism, and Schmitt's critique of liberal political anemia, she develops the thesis that liberalism undermines the specifically political dimension of collective life, including the distinctly political bond that obtains in the world of "inter-est" and sustains the possibility of action in concert—that is, of authentic freedom conceived as "natality," or the capacity to produce unanticipated new forms of common life. The disappearance of the political bond (in favor of administration, necessity, technics, and so on) compels compensatory gestures, such as race-thinking, intimacy, and the emergence of abstract, rigid, and politically obtuse morality, eventuating in, on the one hand, totalitarian projects and, on the other hand, a sheer political impotence. In the end, only politically effete compensatory strategies, such as affective mutuality based in intimacy, remain.

The solution Arendt proposes is to recover the natality still discernible at revolutionary moments. This recovery would consist principally in promoting friendship as the paradigmatic social bond, one that would retain the political dimension without supplanting it with administering necessity on the one hand (the liberal pseudo-public realm of the market and the state) or affective intimacy on the other (the liberal "private" realm of affective intersubjectivity). Friendship would also supply a distinct, unequivocally political, criterion of judgment, entailing a reflective decision (modeled on Kant's aesthetic judgment) concerning the maintenance of the world of inter-est as a constitutive part of every exercise of judgment. The test this bond is designed to pass is that of furnishing compelling, yet still democratically responsible, reasons to side with the Jews in Hitler's Germany (or indeed to preclude Hitler's rise altogether), reasons that cannot be derived from universal moral algorithms and are more likely to result in political solidarity than is affective attachment alone.

Clearly then, friendship bears enormous weight in Arendt's theoretical edifice. It amounts to nothing less than the architecture of democratic citizenship as such, solving a wide range of complex problems characteristic of liberalism. This investment in friendship opens Arendt's account to interrogation on a number of distinct but interrelated fronts, starting perhaps with the substance of her critique of liberalism. One might begin by asking whether the problems she identifies are attributable directly and exclusively to liberalism, or whether they can be traced to what has variously been called the aporia, impasse, or paradox of democracy itself. Liberalism, after all, recommends itself rhetorically as a solution to the problem of cooperation, a problem Arendt barely acknowledges and even dismisses, along with Marxian class struggle, under the rubric of "necessity." Indeed, it is for this reason that Arendt can discern in intimate liberal friendship only a poignant token of compensatory pseudo-solidarity and thus fails to register liberalism's own complex politics of friendship. It would seem, then, that Arendt's critique of modernity fatefully conflates what she construes as characteristic inadequacies of liberalism with the limits internal to democracy as such, and does so in a way that undercuts the coherence of her approach, obscuring the way her own highly original contribution to the theory of democracy is itself both haunted by these very limits and predicated on the historical emergence of liberalism as the discourse that submits the whole of social life to a politics grounded in nothing other than society itself.

More to the point, however, one might ask whether friendship really can effectively mediate the solution Arendt proposes. Her recourse to civic friendship requires her to specify what this will be, but it never occurs to her that the content and function of civic—or private—friendship are themselves stakes in political—that is, rhetorical—struggle. In this way, her model presupposes what it would produce—an enabling form of elective attachment that will sustain the polity as a discrete solution to the problem of democratic governance. In a poignant irony, Arendt's monumental effort to reinject politics into "the social" leads her to put the cart of civic friendship before the political horse: civic friendship would be an achievement, not a precondition, of republican democracy. Indeed, determining how attachments—intersubjective, civic, national, economic—will function is the political problem par excellence. To stipulate, by theoretical fiat, political friendship as the uniquely democratic bond is to depoliticize democracy by securing a concrete form of cooperation in advance. Ironically, a champion of rhetorical performance as the substance of democratic life overlooks the possibility that the content of democracy is nothing other than the rhetorical struggle over its meaning—a struggle in which the figure of friendship repeatedly acquires central importance. As Derrida demonstrates, the problems haunting democracy are the very ones haunting friendship itself. This is no accident: neither one is possible in its very notion, insofar as each must presuppose the very bond it is supposed to produce. This is one of the main implications of the title of Derrida's book: there is an irreducible "politics of friendship" that precludes it from operating as the untroubled ground of democracy.

In the end, both Arendt's tendentiousness and her inevitable ambivalence are instructive. In mistaking a rhetorically overdetermined form of friendship for a regrettable but reversible side effect, she inadvertently highlights—in having her argument thwarted by—the fact that the apparent excessiveness of sentimental friendship is a productive fiction integral to the liberal imaginary. Yet Arendt's biographically prompted intuition that friendship is intimately linked to the historical determination of a political imaginary merits just the degree of scrutiny she gives it. Moreover, the aporias of her own analysis mark the sites demanding the most careful critical examination. If it is finally impossible to decide whether a politics determined by an ethos of friendship can emerge from a friendship already constituted by a prevailing political project, then this apparent circularity itself ought to become the site of critical intervention. This is the task Jacques Derrida undertakes. Where Arendt, in her effort to break out of this impasse, is driven to posit antithetical alternatives (that is, a public realm to produce civic friendship and a friendship capable of inaugurating the public realm), Derrida interrogates the political presuppositions of friendship—and, indeed, the social bond apparently presupposed by any possible democratic politics.

Derrida's Democracy: Beyond Republican Friendship

If for Arendt, whom Derrida does not read, there is a (political) danger of excessive intimacy in friendship, this very excess testifies, for Derrida, to the impossibility of regulating sociability, of submitting it to the rule of law and its corollary axioms of proportion, calculation, and good judgment.[44] Beyond any pathological cathexis, the very possibility of both this pathology and its normative obverse is sustained by the play of *différance,* which underwrites the radical disproportion that is the paradoxical precondition of all mutual obligation. If, on the other hand, Arendt discerns within friendship a subversive capacity to generate political resistance "in dark times" along the axis of affective solidarity, this capacity is not only (à la Foucault) the dialectical correlate of oppression, but also the incarnated force of the radical responsibility imposed by the promiscuous play of *différance.* If, in liberalism, friendship is to be strictly opposed to politics even as it functions, both normatively and subversively, as the extra-political site of citizenship, then these overlapping contradictions of the liberal imaginary are possible only on condition that a certain politics of friendship logically precede its liberal determination. Thus, while Derrida does not substantively address liberalism as a distinct democratic form, his work in general is pivotal for grasping the rhetorical limits of the liberal imaginary.

In *Politics of Friendship,* Derrida significantly extends and elaborates his project of rethinking the meaning and implications of the political as a relation that exceeds any particular system, régime, or program. This project is motivated by Derrida's lifelong commitment to extricating the possibilities of ethical responsibility and justice from their logocentric determinations (in both their transcendentalist and empiricist, "conservative" and "progressive" versions). The book is oriented by the observation that in the canonical texts of Western democratic thought, friendship plays an unexpectedly decisive organizing role—that is, that Western democracy seems always to have been a politics of friendship in one or another sense. One implication of this is that if democratic thought turns to friendship for its model of the political bond, it is because democracy as such is unthinkable as a purely structural, institutional, or juridical form. Investigating the trajectory of friendship as a democratic precept from Aristotle through Cicero, Montaigne, Kant, Nietzsche, Schmitt, and Blanchot, among others, Derrida sets himself two overlapping tasks. First, he labors to expose the limits of democracy entailed by its reliance on friendship, especially in light of the long-standing republican tradition of conceiving friendship, and thus citizenship, in terms of fraternity. These limits turn out to contradict the very concept of democracy that the recourse to friendship would sustain, so that democracy's reliance on friendship turns out to be both necessary and self-defeating. Second, he endeavors to elicit from the aporias structuring the very concept of democracy—for example, the conjunction of universal equality with respect for singular particularity; the simultaneous requirements of inclusion and exclusion—the possibility of a friendship, and thus of a political relation, that exceeds these limits, opening every democratic régime to what he has called "democracy-to-come."

To highlight the aporetic structure of democracy as friendship, the book is organized as a lengthy, recursive meditation on the phrase "Oh my friends, there is no friend" across its multiple iterations in heterogeneous texts. For Derrida, it is the very paradoxical character of friendship—its resolute recalcitrance to any simple and coherent determination as a ground of extrapolitical homogeneity and noncoercive integration—that ironically makes it a suitable model for democracy-to-come. Although, unlike so-called radical democrats, Derrida does not reduce democracy to hegemonic struggle, he does imagine it as a form of relation—or disposition or ethos—rather than a type of régime. It is what is at stake in such an ethos that the aporetic structure of friendship indicates for him: it is a relationship the defining features of which invariably indicate their own impossibility.

In the wake of Derrida's abundant and momentous interventions in democratic thought, however, the specific role friendship plays in the liberal determination of democracy remains a largely open question. Though his work offers incomparable resources for analyzing the rhetoric of liberalism, and though there are strong indications that Derrida himself considered liberal democracy an indispensable inheritance that cannot and should not simply be set aside as a kind of historical faux pas, he leaves mostly tacit the question of the relation between liberalism and the ethos of democracy-to-come.

In an exchange with Geoffrey Bennington shortly after the publication of *Politics of Friendship* in English, Derrida stipulates that "I think that there is inequality and repression in the traditional concept of friendship such as we inherit it. It is in the name of more democracy that I think we have to unlock, to open, to displace this prevalent concept, and this is not my initiative, not the initiative of someone operating in a deconstructive manner; it is what is happening today. Today this model of brotherhood, man, friendship is being deconstructed in the world."[45]

So the "displacement" of "this prevalent concept . . . is happening today": that is, we are living in a time when the friendship/democracy couplet is deconstructing itself. Responding to a question from the audience, Derrida acknowledges that the engine of this process is the series of developments generally subsumed under the rubric "globalization," which he himself cautions against using. He similarly resists overinvesting in any specific régime as particularly congenial to democracy, or to democracy-to-come. Nonetheless, it is a short step to recognizing that the historical elaboration of a liberal imaginary has itself been responsible, to a significant degree, for facilitating the self-deconstruction of the canonical notions of democracy and friendship.

Derrida's concern with the republican reliance on fraternity would appear consonant with a commonplace in political theory that attributes the function of sustaining attachment in liberal democracies to forms of ethnonationalism. So, for example, for Arendt the substantive social bond missing in the liberal polity is supplied by the nation-state form hypocritically predicated on "race-thinking." Yet, in a fashion perfectly consistent with the liberal tradition, Habermas posits "constitutional patriotism" as a purely political mode of allegiance explicitly independent of any supposedly anterior extrapolitical identity. Similarly, Michael Walzer speaks of an obligation to live for the state and of "American" identity as grounded in commitment to liberal principles over and against ethnic, religious, cultural, or national bonds.[46] Indeed, the lack of transparently nonnegotiable bonds is not simply a problem from which liberalism suffers; it is an achievement of the liberal insistence that all attachments be submitted to explicit choice. That is, within the liberal imaginary friendship does not encode fraternity as a supplement to civic ideals; it does not function only as a kind of immanent proxy for filiation, masculinity, race, ethnicity, or the autochthonous nation. On the contrary, liberal friendship encodes a discrete, productively ambivalent form of citizenship premised on modern stranger sociability, the contingency of and skepticism toward power, reflexive autonomy, elective rather than pre-given solidarity, and so on. If, as Derrida shows, the canon of democracy is inextricably intertwined with a determination of friendship that would secure as natural the boundaries of the polity, the virtues and privileges of citizenship, and the stable homogeneity of the community, this is emphatically not the case in the liberal imaginary, which is normatively committed to an expansive (if not unlimited) pluralism and relentlessly subjects to public scrutiny all forms of authority, restrictions on agency, and norms of inclusion. If the link between democracy and fraternity is everywhere under pressure, liberalism is surely central among the sources of this pressure.

Unsurprisingly, then, popular narratives of liberal citizenship seldom imagine citizens dying for the nation; instead, "private" subjects *die for their friends.* For all the patriotic bluster in the rhetoric of the institutional public sphere, liberal citizens do not desire to die for the state, or even, directly, for the nation—witness the widespread resistance to public images of war dead (as compared with the reverential public display of dead warriors in the Athenian polis or republican Rome). But in popular fictions, we repeatedly imagine friends *dying for each other.* This imaginary willingness to die for another is the "substantive" social glue supposedly missing from liberal citizenship and cultural logic, but it is certainly not a figure of any sort of natural bond. Far from functioning as a metonym of kinship, race, or nationality, friendship is construed as a worthwhile bond in contradistinction with these.

Nonetheless, this "test" of friendship has a paradoxical character. The test must be death, but death cannot be reciprocated. Given the liberal promise and presupposition of purely elective attachment, the motivation to die for the friend is itself perplexing in its excessiveness. If my relation to my friend lacks a pathological ground—that is, it is not homoerotic attachment, narcissistic codependence, or some other psychic cathexis—then our friendship is perfectly democratic: we are mutually elected equals.[47] How does such an attachment produce the gesture of self-sacrifice, which would necessarily be *in excess* (beyond the perceptible terms) of our equality? In other words, my willingness to die implies a dimension of my love for the other that *affects* me with a *force* beyond my control. Even framed as an ethical response to the call of the Other, it is a *duty beyond the call.* This means that either the pure relationship is a myth and there is always a "perverse" or particular—and thus impermissibly, or "ideologically," motivated—bond attaching us (in direct contradiction to the liberal rhetoric of reflexive autonomy), or, even in its transcendental dimension, the call of the Other always already destabilizes liberal logic (not by introducing a particular content, but via the excess of universality itself).

The good life of liberal private citizens spent in the company of friends is what would be disrupted by the call of national feeling. This is a corollary of the "socialization of society" thesis.[48] The positing and representation of society as a more or less integrated whole available to knowledge and management makes it possible to solicit subjective identification with its image, but only insofar as it is tacitly acknowledged that, paradoxically, it is the autonomous "pre-social" subject who so identifies, as if from outside this social totality. Again, this subject chooses its attachments deliberately and strives to purify them of any aspect not so chosen. It is for this reason that the choice of social membership itself must be staged and justified by affect: "If you could choose the polity, you would do so because you *love* it."[49] Nonetheless, both the choice and the love are visibly virtual and must remain so, lest the autonomous subject becomes a fanatic eager to destroy all his fellow citizens to safeguard the phantom polity against them.

Does this mean, however, that the apparent excessiveness of self-sacrifice for the sake of the friend can be explained as encoding a commitment to sociability as such that is implicit in any friendship? Am I willing to die for my friend because, in addition to being my friend, he or she represents my membership in a socius that exceeds and sustains me? This is the implication of, on the one hand, Levinas and Derrida and, on the other hand, theories of ideological interpellation. Am I dying for the ineffable quasi-universal principle of sociability, or for the particular nation or culture that has produced me as (its) subject? If universality is the condition of possibility for particularity, the answer is rigorously indeterminable. The Derridean point, however, is that what calls to me through my friend is *both* my "own" socius *and* the "quasi-transcendental" law of infinite responsibility underpinning it. When, in an ethical gesture beyond recompense, I respond to the ethical law, the particular community to which I belong benefits. When, in a fit of patriotic fervor, I respond to the call of my nation, this response is possible only on condition that *différance* be operative.

Yet, again, I am not supposed to die for my country but *only for my friend* (for whom I am supposed to die over and over again). If my friend metonymically stands in for the socius, it is because, pace Habermas or Walzer, the *polity* is not to die for, at least not directly as such. Attached to my friend, I do not perceive her as emblematic of the Arendtian "world"—this is a precondition of our friendship. At the same time, the figure of the friend retains and reinscribes the ambiguity of the play of *différance.* Insofar as it exceeds and occludes its function as proxy for the constitutively missing social totality that motivates my sacrifice, the gesture retains the trace of the law of sociability, so that my act, while it may be pathologically patriotic, is nonetheless also ethical in a way that contravenes or undermines this patriotism.[50] What is thus unexpectedly discernible in the fiction of "pure" friendship is not only its impossibility in the absence of a pathological substrate, but also the *dependence of any such substrate* on the quasi-universal law of sociability. This is what makes it such a potent figure in liberal culture: as a supplement to elective reciprocity, it unexpectedly voices the excessive dimension securing reciprocity itself.

If, dissociated from republican fraternity, liberal friendship no longer functions in any simple sense as a mechanism of domination or exclusion—and when it does, it is in the context of communitarian and republican fantasy—neither is it simply a metaphysical or foundationalist ruse. It is, or at least aims to be, overtly and purely conventionalist in its insistence on the exclusively intrasocial sources of binding authority, particularly "the people" as a special, sovereign case of indeterminate, counterfactual publics of impersonal address. Accordingly, neither the utilitarian nor the deliberativist turn to rationality is supposed to supplant a priori transcendental guarantees, since each acknowledges the possibility of irreducible conflict among rational parties—that is, collective action problems (in rational choice theory) and the competing universalities (in deliberative theory) to which they give rise or from which they develop. Put simply, liberalism does, contra Schmitt, explicitly presuppose the inevitability of *polemos*. Yet liberalism, too, despite the claims of communitarians and civic republicans, relies on friendship as a rhetorical supplement to its inherently ambivalent model of citizenship. And while Derrida has worked tirelessly to mark the aporias haunting the liberal imaginary, the consequences of this reliance for the fate of democracy in modernity remain to be examined.

A few other authors attempt to fill this gap, at least in part, but since Derrida's interest is in the ethos of democracy as an experience of justice, it is sensible that no systematic account either critical or supportive of liberalism should have issued from his work.[51] What has issued, of course, is a legendary series of remarkable analyses of signature categories of both ancient and modern democratic thought, especially the law, the concept of right, sovereignty, violence, the bounded state, the social contract, and justice. These studies are indispensable for any attempt to understand liberalism in relation to the metaphysical and anti- or postmetaphysical trajectories of modernity. Just as important, no one more than Derrida has marked the limits of democracy itself, so that a basic question emerges from the totality of his work: Just what is the relation between the liberal imaginary whose elementary premises he has deconstructed and the aporias of democracy as such? Given the pivotal role friendship plays in the democratic canon, and given its return as a trope of citizenship within the liberal imaginary, it would appear that analysis of contemporary public friendship fictions is valuable for any effort to address the question of liberalism's fate.

Democracy's Dilemma

As Hobbes made clear at the threshold of liberal modernity, the problem of democracy is nothing other than the problem of collective self-authorization. This is because democracy is the direct historical manifestation of the irreducible aporia of cooperation: the permanent, irretrievably paradoxical question is whether, and by what effective and legitimate means, social cooperation can be sustained once it is stipulated that only social cooperation itself can ground both effectiveness and legitimacy. Put another way, if politics must tacitly presuppose that which is its chief task to produce, democracy is the sort of régime that precludes this presupposition. The democratic aim of intrasocially grounded yet binding authority is constitutively aporetic, so that democracy is, in effect, impossible in its very notion.

It is with this problem that every democratic régime must contend. Liberalism responds to it by positing as the elementary unit of political attention a normatively autonomous individual agent. Now, this premise is strictly heuristic; by itself, it does not commit the liberal narrative to an anthropology, psychology, epistemology. It does imply an ethics, but this ethics is itself functional: despite appearances, the autarkic individual is not itself the ultimate concern of liberalism; on the contrary, liberal discourse must endlessly insist on its primacy because it is the rhetorical vehicle for securing a noncoercive mode of cooperation with what subsequently appears to be only minimal agreement. Centering the individual is a chief means of securing this agreement by offering each citizen an incentive to cooperate in the guise of competing for relative advantage. The point is that the preeminence of autonomy is driven by a political project framed and legitimated in collective terms: competitive individualism is tediously defended as uniquely efficient in delivering socially shared benefits. The liberal imaginary commits itself to the rhetorical task of producing the persons, modes of attachment, and political dispositions that liberal theory purports to describe. By stylizing the antagonism intrinsic to social cooperation itself—what Marx calls the "class struggle"—as a natural predisposition of human beings and submitting it to market competition, liberalism converts a fundamental obstacle to integration into a form of coordination. It is therefore no less a mistake to attack liberal individualism on empirical, ethical, or logical grounds than to point out its contradictory structure: liberal individuals are not *simply* hostile to either community or authority; their normatively imagined antipathy is the rhetorical condition of possibility for both distinctions.

As we will see in relation to *The Big Chill,* the republican theme of friendship reimagined by Arendt and deconstructed by Derrida returns in a particularly revealing way in the guise of a communitarian imperative inherent in—rather than opposed to—the liberal imaginary. When the film's sophisticated deployment of friendship is situated in relation to the rhetorical predicament implicit in the liberal project, it emerges as neither a repetition of republican fraternity nor as a communitarian rebuke to liberal atomism, but as a signature rhetorical gesture of liberal discourse. The liberal solution to the democratic paradox and the antagonisms it entails involves producing fictions of friendship coded as extrapolitical elective attachment and a corresponding privileged domain of "moral sentiments" uncontaminated by formally organized authority—that is, by the relations of power proper to politics but inadmissible for collective self-authorization—a gesture *necessarily* (and not just ideologically) impelled to dissimulate its own political character. In this regard, a communitarian nostalgia for pre-political "constitutive attachments" would appear integral to the production of this code—that is, to the "emancipation" of citizens from their political obligations and to the reduction of the semantic scope of "politics" itself. As a liberal rhetoric, communitarianism is thus radically opposed to both Arendtian and Marxian republicanism. To this degree, liberalism is immune to much of Derrida's critique of republican fraternity. Yet this will turn out to have been only part of the story, which proceeds to encompass the obverse of the liberal "displacement" of politics—an obverse legible in the overwhelmingly, though mostly tacitly, liberal feminist critique of the logic of fraternization, and exemplified by the immensely influential feminist friendship film *Thelma & Louise.*

2
Friendship and the Politics of Community
The Big Chill

> To the degree to which the pure relationship becomes dominant . . . a relation of equals, organized through emotional communication coupled to self-understanding, becomes possible. Emotional democracy . . . promises a great deal for the reconstruction of civic ethics as a whole. Individuals who are at home with their own emotions, and able to sympathize with those of others, are likely to be more effective and engaged citizens than those who lack such qualities.
>
> —Anthony Giddens

The Vanishing Revolution

The debate concerning the political consequences of the sixties is a cliché comprising an interminable series of other clichés. Surely nothing is more tiresome than the old argument about whether the baby boom cohort "sold out" its political principles when it opted for professionalization as the safe route to middle-class respectability. Every facet of this claim has been explored both in the popular press and in academic literature, to the point that the endless narration of baby boomer travails has itself come to stand for the generation's putative arrogance and narcissism. It is surely evidence of this narcissism that too frequently the period's many heterogeneous political projects and their socially diverse advocates are synecdochically represented by the white, middle-class, collegiate minority whose ascension to yuppiehood prompts the very charge of "selling out." Yet this reductive locution's salience is not itself reducible to the visibility and supposed cultural hegemony of the demographic segment it impugns. The much more sophisticated cultural critique taking place across the human sciences since the sixties has been motivated in no small part by equally sophisticated versions of this banal question: If something like revolution (that is, thoroughgoing, leftward social and political transformation) appeared imminent at that time, what are the features of contemporary democratic politics and culture that so effectively precluded it?

The question concerns the nature of this "revolution." For example, in Anthony Giddens's account, we are here confronted not simply with a demand for *emancipation* (say, from the undemocratic trespasses, within and beyond the nation, of a warlike state edifice; or from cynical corporate rule; or from patriarchal oppression), but also, and more primarily, with a *shift* from emancipatory toward cultural or "lifestyle" politics.[1] This is a transition in which emancipation is presupposed as both necessary and, by itself, insufficient. Surely, it would be facile to identify this shift with the sixties; it is perhaps more accurate to venture that "the sixties" names the moment when the character of the shift—which, as an effect of growing mediated reflexivization of modernity, had been developing over a longer period—became clearly comprehensible, with the consequence that the logic and project of emancipation came abruptly to appear as a *lost politics.* This appearance of loss would supply the form the shift assumes *within* a cultural space organized by the political primacy of lifestyle projects.

Which is not to imply, as Giddens does, that the shift is itself politically neutral. On the contrary, the case has been forcefully made that a politics revolving around the reflexive project of self-development or identity formation is inherent to the logic of late capitalism.[2] Accordingly, the debate concerning the democratic prospects of "lifestyle" politics is the foundational controversy within cultural studies and between cultural studies and others. Hence, for example, Wendy Brown's lament concerning the leftist abandonment of what she calls "politics of freedom" in favor of litigation over status recognition.[3] Such identity politics is a correlate of a quasi-Foucauldian privileging of microresistance articulated as a "project of the self," which corresponds to the basic coordinates of the political as a relation of recognition between the liberal individuated or "private" citizen and the state. Even if—or perhaps insofar as—this is the case, however, no "return" to emancipatory politics is either possible or sensible, and the nostalgic veneration of such politics should itself be regarded as a product of the contemporary episteme. If empancipatory politics seems in retrospect to have been linked to a sense of community forged in solidarity and legitimated by reference to now-suspect "grand narratives" of *egaliberté,* the emergence of a new species of reflexive citizenship lacking even such imaginary guarantees presupposes a certain fantasmatic loss.[4] That is, to force a marriage of Arendt and Baudrillard, what is "lost" is the imaginary itself—the (always illusory but rhetorically indispensable) *appearance* of durable or rational authority grounding judgment and action.

From the perspective of late modernity, the sixties' feminist dictum "The personal is political" has come to be understood as "The political is personal" and regarded not as a polemical challenge but simply as a descriptive observation. As a result the palpable internal contradiction inherent in this formula has emerged as an urgent theoretical challenge and pervasive theme, persistently framed as a question concerning what constitutes democratic politics and where in social life it is, or ought to be, located.[5] At the same time, this question has come to register powerfully within the cultural public sphere.

The Rhetoric of Liberal Communitarianism

Lawrence Kasdan's 1983 comedy/drama *The Big Chill* concerns precisely the proper location of politics in liberal late modernity.[6] Widely recognized as a loose remake of John Sayles's 1980 landmark independent feature *Return of the Secaucus 7,* the film is a rare case in which the question "Did the sixties generation sell out?" is fairly explicitly posed, something not lost on reviewers at the time.[7] Media critics of the film on both the left and the right understood it to be addressing this exigent question, the difference usually being that leftists despaired of the affirmative while conservatives derided the very gesture of posing the question as lefty self-indulgence.[8] Given this clarity of focus, two features of the film immediately present themselves as notable. First, the rhetorical strategy by means of which the film addresses the problem of "selling out" is to transpose it into a question of the proper or relevant *site* of politics. Second, the contradictory site proffered is friendship.

When, in a 1993 article, James Jasinski offers a defense of the film against both leftist and conservative critics, he shifts the accent of their arguments, claiming that leftists "read the film as an exercise in conservative nostalgia," while conservatives "attacked the film for its valorization of sixties culture and politics."[9] While both criticisms are palpable in the sources he cites, the concern about "selling out" dominates discussion. The contrast between receptions of the film oriented by this polemical concern and Jasinski's reappraisal of it as an allegorical narrative about the prospects of "communal reconstitution" explored through the heuristic metaphor of friendship is only the most immediate effect of the film's rhetorical strategy, which is to obviate the question of the fate of collective action aimed at structural reform in favor of an investigation of intersubjective practices and personal virtues.

In a way, this gesture appears quite plausible. After all, forced to acknowledge, in the eighties, that the sixties revolution never came off, its veterans would seem to have little alternative but to seek satisfaction elsewhere. But the rhetoric of political displacement is a pervasive, even dominant, phenomenon in contemporary American public culture. Extending well beyond appraisals of a given historical period or conjuncture, the strategy is prevalent in narratives concerning race and gender relations and has been advanced as a centerpiece of neoconservative social policy.[10] It can even be identified with liberalism itself, since it derives, however circuitously, from the classical liberal conception of the private or intimate realm as the privileged site of human authenticity. From its inception, the liberal project has aimed to circumscribe politics in relation to a valorized private sociability modeled by friendship.[11] However, that the political relentlessly "returns," in the liberal social imaginary, to the site of privacy from which it is normatively excluded is conspicuous and revealing. Insofar as the priority of privacy over politics is axiomatic for the liberal order, there emerges an overdetermined affinity between the banal topic of "selling out" and the theme of friendship in popular narratives. *The Big Chill,* then, is exemplary because it integrates and exposes to analysis the signature stratagems of liberalism and its critiques on this point. The film's recourse to allegory (rife with untimely bonhomie and underscored by a brilliantly insidious soundtrack) as a means of asserting its distance from what it construes as merely polemical skirmishes over the legacy of the sixties itself aims to depoliticize what persistently appear within its diegesis as ineluctably political anxieties.

The narrative commences with seven friends gathering for the funeral of Alex, an erstwhile member of their group who has unaccountably taken his own life. As we learn later in the film, Harold, Sarah, Meg, Karen, Sam, Michael, and Nick had attended the University of Michigan with Alex in the sixties, where they had been actively involved in the political movements of the time. Nearly two decades later, having kept in touch only intermittently, all have abandoned their political activities for other pursuits. Harold, who owns a chain of athletic shoe stores, is now married to Sarah, a physician, who once during their marriage had had a sexual liaison with Alex. Sam has become an actor and stars in a television detective series. Karen is a housewife raising two children; Meg is a real estate attorney; Michael writes for *People* magazine; and Nick is a cynical former radio therapist turned peripatetic drug dealer. For his part, Alex, who is described as the most intellectually gifted member of the group, had since college pursued a series of occupations, none of which appeared to hold his attention. Just prior to his suicide, he had moved into a dilapidated house on Harold and Sarah's property with his much younger, psychically traumatized girlfriend.

Alex's function in the narrative is akin to that of Seymour Glass in J. D. Salinger's stories: he is a kind of hyperbolic "vanishing mediator" whose absence acts as a diegetic presence necessary to drive the narrative by supplying the screen upon which the animating anxieties of the other characters are projected.[12] His (dis)appearance catalyzes within the diegesis the transition from "failed" or "misguided" collective emancipatory politics to the emerging politics of personal authenticity.[13] His death is a shock not only because it comes as a surprise, but more so because, as the apparent culmination of some inscrutable trajectory, it puts in question the postcollegiate life paths of all the other members of the group. If the one among them endowed with the greatest potential to bring about meaningful change in the world had failed to find meaning in his own life, there must be little to justify their own, less altruistic endeavors. It is this anxiety that permeates and orients all the interactions among the friends as they spend the weekend following the funeral at Harold and Sarah's home. Each represents a distinct, evolving perspective on the meaning of, and questions raised by, Alex's suicide. As the film progresses, the conversations among the friends make it clear that an inexorable preoccupation concerns their inability to sustain their political commitments and, more centrally, to live lives that comport with their once-inalienable political ideals.

In his reading of the film, Jasinski not only rejects the proposition that the film rationalizes "selling out," but insists that this is simply the wrong critical question to pose: "rather than urging quiescence and adopting an apolitical stance, *The Big Chill* offers a critique of what can be termed 'the politics of intimacy' and adumbrates an alternative form of politics grounded in the virtues of friendship." The film's critics, he argues, are blinded by their own ideological investments and fail to grasp the import of this critique, which "eludes easy ideological categorization." In other words, the film is not a polemic rationalizing the abandonment of civic commitment but a systematic critique of self-defeating political practices prevalent within the liberal framework. Here, then, is how Jasinski conceives the problematic addressed by the film:

> As the film develops, we are told that the seven old friends, in an earlier period of their lives, fashioned a *sense of community* that seemed capable of providing *moral sustenance.* But that sense of community, we are also told, had begun to erode as the group made its way in the larger society: values changed, beliefs faded, characters failed to maintain the practices that originally sustained the group, and the bonds of affiliation deteriorated. Alex's suicide—his apparent utter rejection of who he (and by implication his friends) had become—brings

this disintegration to the surface. The group's challenge (articulated most directly in the minister's funeral speech) is to rediscover hope by (re)constituting their community.[14]

Pursuant to his reading of Hannah Arendt, "intimacy" is to be opposed to the "space that relates and separates" friends, a space she deems indispensable for the formation of an authentic public world. Eros and intimacy are, for Jasinski, synonymous and antithetical to philia and publicity, which are also synonymous. These identifications and distinctions form the conceptual frame of Jasinski's reading of the film, which he understands as a narrative about the relative advantages of philia over eros in creating and sustaining a vibrant political community.

More specifically, the film is to be understood as "a complex disjunctive argument in which alternative 'persuasive communities' are constructed and juxtaposed."[15] From this perspective, the film's plot stages a linear progression in which these alternative communities are compared and through which characters evolve in accordance with the principles governing their respective interpretive norms. As a result, the audience is in a position to grasp the differences among these communal frameworks and to witness the consequences they entail. The aim and rhetorical effect of this diegetic strategy is to foreground what for Jasinski is a distinctly Arendtian faculty of judgment as the key to sustaining friendship as a form of civic bond and a privileged—or perhaps, from an Arendtian perspective, the only remaining—locus of civic virtue.[16] Thus we are faced with "three persuasive communities. Each . . . is . . . centered on one of the central male characters: Sam, Nick, and Harold. As the film unfolds, the norms of each community (their values, beliefs, and practices) are disclosed. Sam and Karen constitute a persuasive community based on the norms of intimacy, Nick (initially) adopts the anti-community stance of the stranger, and Harold, Sarah and Meg establish a persuasive community grounded on the norms of friendship."[17]

In this contest among norms of "intimacy, estrangement, and friendship," the proper norms and privileged status of the last will have been embodied by Harold and Sarah and articulated by a decision and corresponding act performed by each at the film's denouement. Paradigmatically, Jasinski asserts: "In the end, Harold, Meg, and Sarah come to embody an alternative communal possibility—one capable of restoring (if only on a small scale) lost hope—constituted by the values, practices, and norms of *philia*." Thus he concludes that "*The Big Chill* counsels us that recognizing the limits of politics does not entail political resignation," since "[t]he realization that politics . . . is an imperfect medium . . . does not lead . . . to 'complacency' or quiescence, nor does it relieve us of our obligation to act."[18]

It is my contention that Jasinski misses the decidedly liberal, antipolitical impetus driving the film's rhetorical strategy, which aims to resolve the characteristically liberal tension between the requirements of personal autonomy and those of continual political vigilance by relocating the "authentic" site of the political to the sphere of the personal.[19] If *The Big Chill* is to be viewed not as a polemical response to what appears as the abdication of sixties social movements in favor of eighties sociability but as an allegory in which friendship functions as a kind of laboratory for testing alternative forms of citizenship, this allegory cannot and does not remain merely heuristic. On the contrary, the disavowal of polemics is itself polemical, aimed at transforming the very meaning of "politics" in a way fully consistent with the liberal accent on modes of social attachment at the expense of concerns with the structural conditions governing the distribution of power. The film's reliance on the figure of friendship evinces—and serves to reinforce—the strong elective affinity between the intersubjective conception of political agency and the liberal model of citizenship (so trenchantly critiqued by one of Arendt's most influential yet disavowed interlocutors, Marx). This allegory thus reinvents for its historical moment the liberal logic it appears to repudiate—indeed, it does so by means of the gesture of repudiation itself. The choice of friendship as the metaphorical vehicle of civic pedagogy is far from contingent, functioning to obscure the effects of a paradigmatically liberal displacement of politics.

Friendship, Judgment, and Liberal Guilt

In responding to the film's invitation to be read as a kind of Arendtian "critique of judgment" accomplished through her distinctive conception of friendship, Jasinski astutely focuses on the way procedures of "character evaluation" index the friends' capacities to make politically salient distinctions. For example, during the after-dinner conversation on the group's second evening together, the topic of their collective history elicits the theme of their respective political commitments. We learn that Michael once taught in Harlem, where his girlfriend continues to teach, and that Meg "was going to help the 'scum,' as I so compassionately refer to them now." For Jasinski, "Harold discloses an essential aspect of his character when he replies 'some of them *were* scum.' For Harold, making judgments or 'distinctions' is an essential practice."[20]

We are then offered an extensive analysis of this brief exchange, necessary because it evinces the logic governing Harold's practices of judgment, practices we are emphatically enjoined to understand as paradigmatic of the "alternative form of politics grounded in the virtues of friendship" advocated by the film. As the sole privileged practitioner of judgment in the film, Harold comes to be involved in two acts of friendship that demonstrate his eventual mastery of this "politics of friendship": at the conclusion of the film, Harold is able to "help" Nick—the stand-in for the enigmatically unhelpable Alex—by inviting him to stay and work on the old house with Chloe; and he "helps" Meg by impregnating her at his wife Sarah's request. In order to understand the implications of these two acts of friendship, it is necessary to locate them within the trajectory of the film's—and Harold's—rhetorical development, something Jasinski does not attempt to do, as he confines himself to tracing Harold's evolving understanding of "the emerging distinction between helping and saving."[21]

It is with his remark about Meg's former clients, then, that Harold first begins to emerge as the embodiment of the Arendtian virtue of judgment. However, what is striking in the dinner scene is less his capacity to *recognize* the quality of another's character and more his sheer willingness to *assert* his evaluation as the *proper warrant for political action or subjective stance.* That is, if, as Jasinski notes, "Meg appears embarrassed . . . making this value judgment," Harold is not, and this absence of embarrassment indicates less Harold's superior faculty of judgment than his greater self-assurance in deploying it.[22] Until the end of the conversation, Harold resolutely rejects what he explicitly recognizes as the emerging consensus around the table about the value of the group's lost political ideals, ultimately referring to his friends, with clear exasperation, as "bleeding hearts." The film's endorsement, in this scene and in general, of such self-assurance functions to submit complex political dilemmas to the test of personal authenticity, construed as the capacity to act in accordance with one's reflexively produced disposition.[23] This gesture is emblematic of the liberal logic impelling the film's rhetoric, which it opens to a number of critical questions.

Why, after all, is Meg embarrassed? And why does she convey her embarrassment by ironically characterizing her own view as (less than) compassionate? Jasinksi suggests that she is embarrassed to *make* judgments. But this seems dubious: after all, she has already called them scum in an earlier scene, and openly admits to making a practice of it. Nor is it likely that she lacks assertiveness, since, in addition to amply demonstrating it throughout the film, she certainly requires it as a successful corporate attorney. It can only be the case that she is embarrassed about what her judgment in this case reveals about her. She is reluctant to assert it directly, distancing herself from it by recourse to irony calibrated both to convey her desire to disavow it and to solicit her friends' reassurance, undoubtedly because it might indicate to them a violation of their erstwhile "communal norm." This other, apparently defunct, norm, far from militating against judgment as such, counsels caution in exercising it to sort fellow citizens, in recognition of the hierarchy between the social location of those in a position to judge and those typically subject to such judgments.[24] Was this norm not the very one she had intended to follow when she originally decided to help the underprivileged? Doesn't her current evaluation of them as "scum" betoken her own failure to retain the perspective that enabled her to judge not individual *persons* but the meaning and valence of their actions in light of sociopolitical circumstances, or what Arendt calls "political facts"? In sum, does her willingness now to consign an entire population to the category of "scum" not amount to a *loss* of the capacity to judge? There is strong evidence to support this reading: if Meg is embarrassed to have arrived at this judgment, why doesn't she simply revise it? The problem seems to be that she feels incapable of doing so: although she fully and explicitly understands that it is not "politically correct," she feels constrained by it, as if it *imposes itself* on her consciousness beyond her capacity to resist it. This is the other implication of her rhetorical irony: it expresses her dis-identification with a view she nevertheless continues to retain.

On the one hand, her embarrassment simply masks her guilt: if people such as her former clients continue to merit her assistance, why has she abandoned her responsibility toward them? From this perspective, she *merits* guilt, so that Harold's response simply amounts to a kind of therapeutic rationalization: if "some of them" really "*were* scum," Meg has nothing to feel guilty about. It is vital to perceive accurately the logic of this rationalization. Even if *some* really were scum, the valorized capacity to make distinctions nevertheless ought to enable one to select those meriting help. But this is not what Harold's comment entails. Rather, the unambiguously asserted "fact" that some do not merit help simply means that Meg is not completely unjustified in failing to provide it. This is the substance of Harold's practice of friendship in this case: to assuage Meg's guilt by relocating its cause from the shortcomings of her character to "objective" features of those she (mis)judges. Ironically, then, we are confronted here with Harold's diabolical *refusal* to practice judgment. It is not simply that he effectively endorses Meg's failure to identify correctly those meriting help; rather, he fully absolves her of the responsibility to make such distinctions in the first place.

On the other hand, even Meg's guilt is not, as it were, simply her own, but is an effect of systemic imperatives and their structural transformations. Meg feels constrained to pass this judgment (and is simultaneously guilty about its content) by her current position within the social hierarchy, from the perspective of which, as Harold puts it, they effectively *are* scum. By contrast to many of her former clients, her new ones are "only guilty of raping the land," and representing their interests implies even to her that she has embraced them. Since she has consciously turned from asserting the rights of the systematically disenfranchised against the disciplinary apparatus of the state to asserting the prerogatives of capitalist elites under the aegis of the state, she has assumed the position of enunciation she once renounced as unjust. Not only does this fact entail her guilt, but it clearly marks the radically problematic status of judgment in a context where the range of possible stances in regard to "political facts" is constrained from the outset by utterly indifferent forces.[25] Whether those Meg once helped "really were" scum is not a simple datum to be discovered and asserted as such, but is necessarily a perception constrained by the social location and access to power of the judging agency. Meg's guilt is thus double: beyond simply changing sides in the political struggle, she effectively has abandoned or lost her capacity to recognize (that is, judge) the *politically overdetermined ground of the struggle itself.*[26] Harold's rationalization addresses chiefly this guilt: what he effectively asserts is less the objective character of Meg's former clients than the possibility of exiting the terrain of political antagonism as such.[27] If Jasinski is right that making distinctions is an essential feature of Harold's character, then we are invited to presume, as Harold does, that judging is a function of that individual reflection that serves to individuate us as liberal subjects—an essential, proto-social capacity we share as human beings "pure and simple" and a constitutive responsibility we have as "private" citizens or, more specifically, friends. And it is this gesture of disavowing questions of power and subjective investment in existing social hierarchies as conditions constraining judgment that, via the exemplarity of Harold, forms a key element of the liberal rhetoric on display in the film.

Friendship and the Place of Liberal Judgment

This scene of the group's first dinner together performs vital narrative labor, establishing the specific differences among the points of view assigned to each character. The choice of airing these differences around a dinner table is also significant, designed to indicate the unity of this diversity: it is the literally nourishing space of friendship that enables each character to

1. Film still from *The Big Chill:* © 1983 Columbia Pictures

disclose the distress accompanied by reflection on the past that Alex's absence now provokes. Yet filming the conversation presents a tricky technical challenge, since the group is arrayed around a large table. The scene opens with an extended master shot that uses the wood-trimmed opening from the darkened living room to the warmly lit dining room as a frame for the large table accommodating the group of eight. Lingering in the middle distance for some ten seconds, the camera refrains from breaching the interior of the conversational space as we hear snippets of repartee. The duration allows viewers to note the location of each diner in an only partly effective attempt to compensate for the somewhat disorienting editing of the conversation itself. The film cuts among the participants in mostly single shots, greatly complicating the usual shot/reverse shot choreography. Framing each speaker individually—with the occasional exception of a double shot to stem the potentially dizzying proliferation of angles—clarifies the correspondence between character and viewpoint, setting up later developments in both.

In addition to requiring much more labor to maintain shooting continuity, this strategy also notably complicates audience orientation within the profilmic space, as the sequence of shots palpably excludes cues that could be provided by the contiguity of nonspeaking characters. As a result, it is easy to lose track of the spatial relationships among the friends. So, for example, unless one commits to memory everyone's position in the master shot, it is all but impossible to realize that Nick is sitting next to Harold, a proximity that, given the emerging complexity of their relationship, could have yielded a number of productive juxtapositions had the scene been shot differently.

The substantial logistical and cognitive price exacted by the scene attests to the considerable narrative value of the strategy of individual framing. But this strategy yields a further advantage that reaches beyond narrative requirements. The far simpler approach of shooting larger sections of the table from, say, two overlapping camera angles would have meant denying individuals their own unencumbered frames and confining them to relatively cramped segments of the group. This, of course, would emphasize the collective character of the group's experience in a way actively precluded by the disjunctive contrast between the serene yet distant master and the subsequent flurry of single and double shots. As things stand, we are either outside the group or laboring to keep up with the discourse of each of its members; there is never an opportunity to experience the group's interior.

Of course, segmenting the group might suggest complicating alliances or tensions, and this could undermine the narrative's fastidious tracking of representative personal attitudes. But that's just the point: the narrative device of activating and following parallel developments is itself congenial to, if not grounded in, the normative premise that social space consists of autonomous individuals who select and pursue independent social strategies and whose interactions assume the form of elective reciprocity. As a result, a straightforward pragmatic adaptation of a mundane formal procedure (shot/reverse shot) not only responds—with incomplete success—to a narrative requirement but also incorporates at the level of form the liberal premises of the narrative argument.[28]

Accordingly, the dinner scene conforms to the principles already implicit in the setup of the story, which takes place at Harold and Sarah's enormous house—in fact, a former plantation mansion—outside a small town (an unnamed Beaufort) on the South Carolina coast. The choice of location is both productive and telling, since it isolates the group in a capacious but self-contained space and enables careful control of its every exposure to the world of "political facts." Not surprisingly, every stranger who enters this space serves only as a prosthesis facilitating the internal dynamics of the group. So the minister advances the group's collective self-examination; Karen's husband provides a foil to their solipsism; and the traffic cop prompts a prefigured confrontation between Harold and Nick. Tellingly, a number of scenes involving outsiders were shot but never made it into the final cut—most notably some interactions at the funeral and a flashback that included a living Alex. Even occasional forays into town transpire without encounters with the locals: Nick joins Harold for a run on an empty morning street; Harold and Sam drive to pick up Chinese food, and the film cuts from the Jeep to the dinner table. Meanwhile, the home sits on a vast estate, far from any neighbors and surrounded by fields, islands, and wetlands. Yet the house itself is spacious, well appointed, and comfortable, decorated in the hallmark eighties eclectic style, right down to the pink sofa, Sub-Zero refrigerator, and small wine cellar. The overall effect is that of Jeffersonian myth: Harold is a country gentleman of wholly independent means and matching upstanding character, the virtuous citizen of a republic *that is nowhere to be seen* but is replaced by an assortment of comfortably familiar guests who, incidentally, joke at the film's conclusion that they mean never to leave this cocoon. Evidently, the optimal approach to dealing with the disappointing, disorienting, and discomfiting world of political facts is to exit from it. And the promise of exit is, of course, a central rhetorical gesture of the liberal project.

Political Friendship without Nostalgia?

The contours of this project's influence on the film emerge still more sharply if, at this juncture, we compare *The Big Chill* to its forebear, *The Return of the Secaucus 7*. In the earlier film, the question of judgment is thematized in the context of a different "politics of friendship." Early on in the story, Katie is emphatically, if comically, established as the character most directly identified with the faculty of judgment. The group goes to a local playhouse to see a production in which Lacy, an acquaintance of theirs, is to perform. It is made clear that, based on previous experience, none of the friends thinks much of Lacy's acting skills; however, when discussing their expectations just prior to the performance, the prevailing inclination among them is to refrain from expressing any overt criticism, resorting to euphemism or demurral. Katie, by contrast, immediately asserts about Lacy that "she stinks," at which point Frances chides her for being "judgmental." Nonetheless, she continues to berate the actress mercilessly, to the point that Irene declares, "Katie, you're heartless!"

Yet by this point it is clear that Katie's insistence on exercising and voicing judgment is more than a personality flaw. When, a bit earlier, she is cautioned that Irene's boyfriend, Chip, whom she has not met, is "straight," she fires off a series of questions designed to elicit the specificity of this "straightness:" "Prep-school straight? Army straight? Political straight? Boy Scout straight? Plaid-pants straight?" In familiar sixties jargon, "straight" was a polysemic characterization meant to pick out a set of personal characteristics—ranging from dress to musical tastes to abstinence from recreational drug use to conservative sexual practices—presumed to indicate sociopolitical conformity. The sixties critique of conformity was a proxy for the imperative to resist a politically repugnant social structure—commonly referred to as "the Establishment"—and "straightness" was not equivalent to simple nerdiness but rather always implied a politically conservative disposition, or ethos. The group of friends in the film is reuniting at the historical moment when the notion of "straightness" is in the process of losing this political connotation, evolving into a description of personal style irrespective of political bearing. This is why Katie finds it both possible and necessary to qualify the adjective as it applies to Chip. On the one hand, insofar as it is now possible to *mistake* the merely personal for the political, the distinction must be articulated for the sake of clarity. On the other hand, it is a distinction that, notwithstanding the historical shift undermining its critical purchase, remains decisive for Katie and her friends. It is the political salience of Chip's personal style that interests her, and Chip's political profile will constrain the range of possible relations between the two. In sum, in relating to a specifically political characterization ("straight") as it inflects affective modes of sociality, the capacity to make distinctions is invoked by the film in the form of a principled refusal to efface politics "in private"—a refusal much more in line with Arendt's notion of civic friendship as "partisanship for the world."

As the semantic transformation of the designation "straight" demonstrates, what is being lost at this moment is the possibility of apprehending politics as the manifestation of social antagonism, the evacuation of irreconcilable opposition from the space of institutional processes and public argument. Politics becomes devoid of the political—of that antagonism which bears on fundamentally divergent conceptions of the common good—and is supplanted by negotiations over power sharing and administration.[29] One of the possible meanings of "the big chill" would thus be the cooling of properly political passions attendant upon the displacement of fundamental political disagreement. In *The Return of the Secaucus 7,* we are invited to bear witness to the (always already past) moment of transition to a " post-political" age. In *The Big Chill,* the passage is staged as a fait accompli, and what we witness is the friends' endeavor to orient social relations within a "postpolitical" imaginary. This absence is a palpable presence for them—it is the raison d'être of the film's narrative. But this palpability cannot overcome the absence: the missing political dimension persists as an inchoate irritant, and the friends are powerless to say exactly *what* is absent, let alone to bring it back.

One of the decisive differences between *The Big Chill* and *Return of the Secaucus 7* concerns the role of the political in the subjectivities of their respective characters. The very title of the earlier film refers to the sense of group identity the friends have acquired as a result of having been arrested en route to Washington, DC, for a political demonstration. The reunited friends share a disdain for the U.S. government, but this disdain is the inverse of the standard liberal attitude toward the state as a necessary evil to be minimized in order to guarantee maximum individual liberty. Their contempt is not directed toward government as such, but rather toward what they view as a de facto collusion of elites to maintain a grip on power at the expense of the citizens. It is, in other words, an emphatically *political* contempt, a kind of principled populism. While not altogether inimical to the liberal imaginary, it contrasts sharply with the attitude typical of characters in *The Big Chill* in that it is absolutely integral to what might otherwise appear as "private" personality and modes of attachment—including, of course, sexual liaisons. That is, for the Secaucus 7, political bearing is an irreducible dimension of their subjective stances. Far from being displaced from the public to the private sphere, the political entails for them a permanent state of publicness as a constitutive feature of "private" life. This is to be distinguished, too, from the Arendtian complaint that the public and private have hopelessly intermixed, to the detriment of the autonomy of the public realm. Indeed, this is a political orientation that closely resembles Arendt's model of friendship as marked by cognizance of "political facts." Certainly this form of politics is not to be confused with versions of consumer activism, in which it is simply everyday practices that are rendered political in the attenuated sense of responding to corporate behavior. In other words, although it is a form of political subjectivity compatible with liberalism, it is a variant of "personal politics" in which the political retains its distinctiveness both vis-à-vis what Jasinski terms the "intimate" *and* vis-à-vis extrainstitutional forms of activism.

Two scenes in particular attest to the salience of this distinction. In the midst of a heated political debate at a local roadhouse, Jeff responds to a claim advanced by J.T. with the words "Horseshit! You want another beer?" Both the humor and the "social realism" of the exchange depend on the jarring yet familiar contradiction in the respective tones of the enjambed statements. The expletive that expresses skepticism about a political claim is followed immediately by a personal signal of sociability. Not even a fairly passionate political posture is here permitted to interfere—even grammatically—with the discourse of friendship. The two discourses—political and personal—remain distinct even, or especially, when forced together by the hegemony of Arendt's "social." This state of affairs is to be sharply distinguished from the discourse characteristic of *The Big Chill,* in which the topic of institutional politics appears only obliquely in guilt-ridden, elliptical references to individual characters' long-abandoned attitudes and activities.

In a subsequent scene, we see Jeff reciting a litany of his own arrests while being erroneously booked by a local cop for killing a deer. Following Jeff, his former lover Irene recounts her own, virtually identical arrest record, which diverges from his only for the short period they were apart. The import of this brief scene is understated yet nuanced. On the one hand, since all the arrests are political in nature, stemming from instances of public activism, they attest to Jeff's irreducible civic commitment. On the other hand, Irene's involvement in politics might be interpreted as stemming not from any political convictions of her own, but rather from her romantic involvement with Jeff. In such a case, Irene would be guilty of the sin attributed to her generation by neoconservative revisionists of sixties history, according to whom most young radicals of the period had no genuine interest in politics at all, but were "seduced" by the social aspects of the activist "lifestyle." Yet the scene also provides viewers with a chronology of events that bars such a reading. Simply put, given the dates of the arrests, Jeff and Irene had been involved in politics long before they became romantically involved. If there is a direct link between eros and the political here, it runs in the reverse direction: it was, in part, political solidarity and civic friendship that drew the two friends together in sexual and romantic intimacy—not the other way around.

What is still more noteworthy in this scene is the casual yet resolute tone with which the audience is informed of the shockingly extensive record of arrests. Among other things, the list makes it clear that Jeff and Irene were never deterred by the prospect of incarceration; they relentlessly continued protesting and risking arrest. More to the point, if activism had for them become something like a "lifestyle," this term must not be reduced to its trivial or dismissive sense. Jeff rattles off the long list in a relaxed, almost wistful manner, but his memory of the dates, places, charges, circumstances, and dispositions of all the arrests is sharp and exact. It is clear that while his attitude toward having a criminal record is nonchalant, he is scrupulously faithful to the political endeavors to which it attests.

Taken together, these two scenes consider what it might mean to assume a principled political stance in a time when, for better and for worse, "the personal is political." It means cultivating an ethos explicitly linked to friendship, but in no way involves collapsing the boundary between specifically political discourse aimed squarely at public institutions and the idiom of personal attachment. At the same time, this film about a reunion concerns the obviously vexing and perhaps inescapable prospect of certain loss. The friends are about to turn thirty, an age they regard as marking a transition from exploratory to enduring commitments. It is clear to them that the sort of political activism in which they had been involved cannot be among those commitments. This is so not only because "the system" has decisively won or deprived them of their will to struggle, but rather because activism cannot remain a viable "lifestyle." If the system "wins," it is because the pragmatics of ongoing political struggle seem to mandate either entry into official politics (a course unpalatable to those who see official politics as corrupt) or a life of peripatetic dependence on those who have "settled down." In short, radically oppositional politics—premised on an exigent antagonism concerning the collective good—is granted no visible means of support. The steadfast foreclosure of the political dimension that had engendered and sustained their friendship initiates a deterioration of the friendship itself, foreshadowed by the film's nostalgic tone. The anticipatory sense of loss is, of course, the impetus for *The Big Chill*—which in a sense is a remake and a sequel at once—where friendship survives as a forum and repository of rationalization. In the later film, the loss has clearly already occurred, Alex's suicide representing only its most direct and shocking encroachment into the everyday lives of the survivors. However, if in *Secaucus 7* friendship shares the fate of citizenship, in *The Big Chill* it becomes citizenship's alibi.

Loss of Politics, Politics of Loss

The complex itinerary, in *The Big Chill,* of the faculty of judgment as the locus of citizenship in the "dark times" of what Arendt decries as the reign of "the social" should, therefore, be examined in relation to the film's own account of its historical moment. Thus, for example, Jasinski's communitarian reading—insofar as it ascribes to sixties political projects an orientation marked by eros and its drive to "save" everyone indiscriminately framed as in need of saving—implicitly understands the film as staging a kind of immanent critique. The form of immanent critique is itself a kind of rhetorical lynchpin. On the one hand, it opens the question of whether the failure of sixties revolutionary aspirations results from fundamental problems within liberalism itself, inviting the view that another political mode—say, republicanism—ought to supplant it. On the other hand, it opens the possibility of reinscribing liberalism itself as the "solution." Jasinski's view that the film opens the door to communitarian/republican revision is not simply erroneous; what it overlooks is the way this revision is itself the vehicle of liberalism's reinscription. The thematic focus on the republican faculty of judgment, framed within the task of cultivating a community governed by norms of friendship, stages the film's critique of intimacy from a normatively liberal vantage. Philia disavows erotic intimacy, but in so doing it serves to determine the genesis, meaning, and proper context of sociality and judgment in the "lifeworld" terms characteristic of the liberal imaginary.

It is no coincidence, then, that the privileged voice of judgment is Harold, the successful entrepreneur who hosts the group, helps Nick, and serves as Meg's surrogate. It is Harold who, alone, is able to extract the full measure of education from the weekend and consequently to make the distinction between saving and helping, eros and philia. Evidently, successful participation in market competition is either a prerequisite for, or a mark of, this capacity. Just as Adam Smith predicts, the capitalist organization of social space makes it possible for Harold to distinguish his own private life from that of instrumental rationality, friendship from economy. Moreover, Harold is a success within the terms of a particular emblematic narrative of capitalist meritocracy—the self-made entrepreneur guided by his own perseverance and ingenuity rather than benefiting from established (and suspect) social circuits of financial power. We are thus to understand that Harold's transition from youthful activist to mature entrepreneur is an index of his aptitude for making distinctions and exercising judgment. Harold, unlike Sam, Michael, and Nick, never worries about having "sold out"; he is utterly confident that the changes in his life are not properly described by this phrase. This confidence—indicated by the faux self-deprecation of his company's name, Running Dog—demonstrates that he is not susceptible to *doxa:* unlike his three male friends, he does not second-guess his choices from the imagined perspective of others or from within a paradigm (that of sixties revolutionism) no longer operative or applicable. Harold's supposed independence of mind and entrepreneurial success are strictly correlative: they are both archetypal features of the properly constituted liberal subject.

In sum, Harold's apparently republican capacity to distinguish between eros and philia tacitly depends upon his distinctly liberal capacity to prioritize private sociability over market relations. This is clearly evident in his willingness to violate SEC regulations in an effort to "save" Nick by offering him insider trading information. For Harold, the juridical and economic relations implicated in the gesture are merely instrumental, so that recourse to them is legitimated in terms of private loyalty, without any *political*—as opposed to technical or functionalist—regard for the consequences.[30] Unsurprisingly, he never comes to experience guilt about "selling out" simply because, in his mind, whatever goals and activities—even political ones—he shared with his friends in college properly belong to the domain of friendship, and participating fully in the market bears no consequential relation to that domain.

Friendship and the Political Economy of "Free Love"

It is not surprising, then, that if over the course of the film Harold—and, to a lesser degree, Sarah, Nick, and Meg—seem to cultivate their faculties of judgment, the narrative in no way suggests that they might exercise them in a public context, or, more to the point, in any way directed toward transpersonal ends. Nowhere is the shift in the very meaning of judgment more clear than in the development most manifestly designed to demonstrate Harold and Sarah's exemplary perspicacity in discerning philia from eros—their "gift" to Meg. Meg spends the weekend deliberating which of her "favorite men in the world" she would like to father her offspring. She asks Nick, who is impotent, and then Sam, who declines by citing his reluctance to assume the moral obligation, but she excludes the married Harold from consideration. Sarah, who once had a brief sexual liaison with Alex about which she feels openly guilty, decides that Harold should be the one to help Meg.

It is, then, Sarah's "gift" *of* Harold (and, as a blunt symbolic bonus, of his presumptively virtuous progeny) to Meg that comes to exemplify the political import of friendship in the film. Even as Sarah and Harold demonstrate the capacity to make nuanced distinctions in separating purely functional, procreative—as it were, contractual—sex from the kind of erotic desire that might compromise both their family and their friendship with Meg, the context for action is here thoroughly private, intimate and, precisely, affective. It is only because the friends have known each other for many years; have undergone a variety of experiences together; have personally witnessed the development of their overlapping relationships; know each other's characters, desires, and needs as well as they know their own; and, indeed, directly love each other, that they can securely enter into such an arrangement. The kind of judgment displayed here never could be extended to a wider social world that includes individuals to whom the friends are committed in a civic sense—or to impersonal structures governing the context, meaning, and function of their friendship. Harold,

Sarah, and Meg are confident in their evaluation of the risks involved only because they are longtime friends, and the capacity to make this evaluation is a function of their friendship, not a talent or cultivated proficiency. Consequently, the evolution of their faculties of judgment throughout the film is away from the discomfiting activity, imposed by Alex's suicide, of interrogating the social, economic, and juridical presuppositions sustaining their friendships and toward a set of intersubjective practices that positively rely on the transparency of these presuppositions. Accordingly, at the very moment when the narrative argument the film has developed arrives at its conclusion, it demonstrates a distinctly liberal conception of sociality, relying on, and indeed promoting, a zone of private intimacy as the privileged site of authenticity and moral judgment.

It is therefore essential to grasp the distinction between the case of Harold, Sarah, and Meg and a "world" of "inter-est" or "in-between" characteristic of Arendtian friendship. In Arendt's account, friendship functions to produce criteria of judgment that are neither abstract-universal nor merely idiosyncratic-particularistic.[31] Harold, Sarah, and Meg do share a world that supplies them with criteria for judgment that transcend their individuality without becoming portable abstract principles; and indeed the sexual act these criteria make possible does not violate or collapse the distances between Sarah and Meg or Meg and Harold—nor does it introduce a new distance between Harold and Sarah. So it would seem that Jasinski is right to call attention to the distinction between eros and philia functioning in this context. The problem, however, is not the possible collapse of interpersonal distance in erotic intimacy; rather, it is the active exclusion of "political facts" from the friendship relation. Harold and Sarah help their friend without harming either the friendship or their marriage, but the argument staged by the narrative positions the audience not only to recognize the exercise of judgment but also to accept private intimacy as the *proper site* of its exercise. The three friends don't even tell their other friends what they have done.

Moreover, it appears that Sarah's decision to "offer" Harold to Meg is motivated in part by the distance she did introduce between herself and Harold (and between herself and Alex, as well as Alex and Harold) through her dalliance with Alex. In other words, in at least a functional sense, her "gift" to Meg squares her account with Harold. Granted, the two sexual acts have entirely different meanings for all involved; still, as Karen says upon learning that Nick is taking Alex's place at the old house, "there's a certain symmetry" between them.[32] So it is because their meanings almost symmetrically invert each other—the affair is illicit and injurious to all three parties; the insemination is sanctioned by all three and benefits each of them—that the second act "balances" the first. After all, the benefit to Harold, apart from the altruistic satisfaction of helping a friend, is guiltless extramarital sex. He is, in effect, compensated in the only way possible within the contractual confines of marriage for the "loss" occasioned by his wife's infidelity. For her part, his wife is able to allay her own guilt. What surely appears to her as a selfless act, for which she undoubtedly congratulates herself, is effectively the conversion of a debt into an exchange that benefits her anew by retroactively inserting her betrayal into a restricted economy of gain and loss. As a result, Sarah will have gained the (effectively self-canceling) pleasure of the affair itself, the restoration of balance in the sexual economy of her marriage, as well as a measure of narcissistic satisfaction arising from her success in legitimating the pursuit of her own ends by routing it through a performatively successful act of friendship. At the same time, to the degree that Sarah's gift is overdetermined by the psychic benefits in confers on her, Meg actually functions as an instrument in the production of these—and so no authentic gift, no genuine act of friendship, is really taking place, unless friendship is conceived in the quintessentially liberal terms of calculative reciprocal exchange.

A theory of action that privileges the faculty of judgment is dangerously myopic if it discounts the constitutive role that contextual imperatives and structural constraints play in determining not only the scope and practical application but also the modality of judgment. Put simply, judgment is not a formal or technical acumen; what *counts* as judgment is already a rhetorical, not conceptual, question. Even if it were the case that in *The Big Chill* friendship supplies the criteria and cultivates the capacity for making nuanced distinctions between eros and philia, this would not suffice to account for the kinds of actions the friends take in regard to one another or for the subjective meanings and social ramifications of these actions. Sarah's gesture toward Meg is *enabled* by the friends' ability to distinguish erotic sexual acts from functional, reproductive ones—as well as sex from love and love from friendship—but her *motives* are selfish, not derivable from a conception of the good shared with the others. Certainly, she would be no less a friend to Meg if she had not offered Harold's "services." Instead, her act is overdetermined: on the one hand, by private motives that have nothing to do with her genuine goodwill toward Meg; on the other hand, by the ineradicable debt, implicit in friendship, that secures all sociality yet is dissimulated in the liberal imaginary.[33] In *The Big Chill,* then, it is through the trope of friendship that the sixties motto and (sporadic) utopian practice of "free love" enters the circuit of exchange.

As a hallmark of the multiform resistance connoted by "the sixties," the ideal of free love bears a synecdochic relationship to the other emancipatory projects of the period.[34] It seeks to name and disrupt the circuit of pleasure and eroticized prohibition through which capitalist sublimation was, at that moment, understood to work: hence to double valence of "free" as both adjective and verb, description and imperative.[35] Though ranging widely in the meanings and effects ascribed to it, insofar as it sought to extricate eros from sublimatory appropriation, "free love" aimed at least in part to short-circuit the delay/detour through which the withholding of pleasure is transformed into a fetishistic attachment to market discipline. Thus, free love does not simply oppose the "puritanical" regulation of sexuality, but also appears, at a particular historical moment, to threaten to destabilize the libidinal economy of capitalism itself. It is, in other words, a utopian political project aimed against what it construes as the entire hegemonic structure of social relations of its time. By contrast, *The Big Chill*'s representatives of the free love generation—it is made clear that many of the characters in the film had had "casual" sex with one or more of the others—have by the film's conclusion arrived at a point where sex has simply lost its "perverse"—and thus political—dimension. Sharing sexual partners has come to seem perfectly appropriate as an act of friendship insofar as it is akin to sharing possessions. More important, this is reproductive sex, indifferent to pleasure—or at least devoid of the transgressive enjoyment that is the whole point of both "puritanical" sex (that is, sex within the economic circuit of sublimation) and free love sex-as-political-subversion.[36]

The narrative contrasts the sexual act between Harold and Meg with a simultaneous one between Karen and Sam. If Harold and Meg are, despite the sexual nature of the act, engaging in philia, Sam and Karen are pursuing eros—the eros retrospectively attributed to the practice of free love. Here, the narrative deviously evicts the emancipatory dimension of free love by identifying it with the "repressive de-sublimation" driving adulterous transgression. The political aim of resisting, removing, or disavowing multifarious sexual prohibitions was to unshackle the subject's desire from a repressive social order. The point was to de-link pleasure from libidinal regulation, which, in repressive de-sublimation, itself comes to be eroticized in such a way that only two essentially repressive options remain: either the subject obeys the logic of sublimation and channels her desire in socially (re)productive ways; or she derives pleasure from "transgressing" social prohibitions, so that these are reinscribed as objects of libidinal cathexis. The project of free love was aimed at cutting this Gordian knot, situating the libido altogether outside the scheme of sublimation/de-sublimation. The subject would be free when her desire was no longer overdetermined by the blackmail of social prohibition. From this point of view, adulterous desire is, on the contrary, entirely the product of this blackmail, which it only serves to reinforce. And the Reaganite Right's success in effacing the distinction between pleasure derived from eroticizing the prohibition and pleasure sought outside its bounds was among the decisive rhetorical triumphs of the neoconservative cultural offensive.

No doubt the Reichian/Marcusean thesis of liberation contributed to its own defeat by underestimating the role of prohibition in generating desire and sustaining subjectivity. As others—most notably Lacan—have demonstrated, there is no desire or libidinal investment outside the sublimatory circuit of the (imaginary) social totality. The politics of free love was almost certainly doomed from the start. Nonetheless, it was most emphatically not doomed for the reason given by Reaganite revisionists—or the conveniently reassuring explanation endorsed by *The Big Chill.* The rhetoric of free love does not fail because it is mere solipsistic self-indulgence; it is not simply reducible to "perversion." It fails because some minimal libidinal organization—and thus coercive obligation—is the precondition of desire as such, so that, in effect, love can never be "free" of politics and remain love. The polemical reduction of the political impetus of free love to narcissistic adultery is thus reactionary, aimed as it is at converting an inherent limitation of that project into an indictment of those who participated in its utopian dream in good faith.

In the sexual economy depicted by the film, the function of friendship is to depoliticize sex itself, or, more accurately, to reabsorb the excessive "pure" expenditure of sexual pleasure into a new hegemonic cultural logic whose animating gesture is the derogation of politics. No longer governed by "puritanism"—that is, by the now-defunct symbolic norms of sublimative capitalism—libidinal energies are now to be governed through the intimate self-discipline of Adam Smith's "moral sentiments" evinced in friendship, and by the interpersonal commerce of gift exchange.[37] If the rhetoric of free love sought to render visible the oppressive politics sustained by the public/private split, then the problem confronting the liberal imaginary was not simply how to displace politics into the private sphere, but rather how to depoliticize that sphere itself. Though of course a key product of liberal politics, the intimate sphere can only function as refuge from politics if it can be experienced as nonpolitical, so this experience must be *staged* by recoding politics *into the very structure* of intimacy itself, as intimacy's "political unconscious," one capable of producing a normative misrecognition of friendship as the other of politics. This is why Jasinski's reading of this exemplary transaction among the friends, asserted on behalf of a strong critique of liberalism attributed to the film, is finally indistinguishable from liberalism's definitive rhetorical gesture.

Friendship and the Utopian Politics of Skepticism

If, in Jasinski's view, Harold has learned that "[i]ntimacy—'saving' relationships—destroys the 'in-between' critical to public life," it is useful to interrogate the meaning of the term *public* being advanced here.[38] Given that Arendt conceives the "in-between" established by friendship as the elementary structure of the common, public "world," what is the fate of this "world" in the imaginary discernible in *The Big Chill?* When Nick debunks Sam's nostalgic vision of the group's past friendship, he tellingly expresses his skepticism by reference to "the world": "A long time ago we knew each other for a short period. . . . It was easy back then. No one ever had a cushier berth than we did; it's not surprising our friendship could survive that. It's only out here in the world that it gets tough."

This platitude of "adult" discourse is not as simple as it first appears, as it laconically conjoins several pivotal themes in the liberal rhetoric of friendship. In what turns out to be one of the film's few direct references to economic class, Nick here suggests that both the trajectory of the group's political idealism and its self-understanding in terms of "pure" friendship are structured and bounded by the members' social location in ways the rest of the narrative never adequately addresses. At the same time, this misapprehended friendship is sharply distinguished from "the world," so that, given the film's clear implication that the group's political and personal commitments were once coextensive, we are left to conclude that engagement in politics itself is to be distinguished from this new "world." If class privilege had been the invisible condition of both their friendship and their political involvement, the juxtaposition of these commitments with "the world" would imply an unexpected salience of market competition there. A key implication of this view is that, in retrospect, the group's activism must itself have been driven by a kind of compulsory delusion sustained by a tacit investment, occluded by friendship, in an economic system and social logic that would be left undisturbed by their political projects—or would derail these at the first sign of such disturbance.

Insofar as his cynicism stems from a series of incisive observations concerning the relation between politics and friendship, it is inadequate to construe Nick's attitude as representing "the norm of estrangement" within an allegorical reading. The film's polemical dimension is nowhere more clearly in evidence. Far from simply being unconvinced about the prospects for "saving" or being "saved," Nick's dis-identification with the alternate norms of friendship espoused by Sam and Harold conveys vexing political implications. This is what is implied by the ambiguity of "out here in the world." Where, in relation to this "out here," does Nick locate his friendship with the others? After all, he is criticizing Sam's idealized, "naïve" account of their relationship, experienced as it was in a sheltered collegiate environment—an "in there" opposed to "out here." What makes the group's college years a period of naïveté? Is it the founding of activism in unsophisticated, morally simplistic political optimism—that is, thinking they could "save" people? At the same time, why should we accept the cynical invitation to regard idealism and activism as naïve or even, in Berlant's terms, infantile?[39]

At first glance, then, even Nick seems to agree with Arendt: "private" or intimate friendship is superficial; it is only the "world" that can serve as the proper site of genuine friendship. But on closer inspection this agreement dissolves: the test of friendship is, for Nick, the duress that inevitably characterizes "worldly" life. The world Nick has experienced is in "dark times." Arendt, on the contrary, argues that duress generates only ersatz friendship, mere provisional solidarity. Genuine friendship is, for her, known only on condition of full freedom, attainable exclusively in the political realm shielded from the demands of "necessity," whether natural or economic. A further difference is thus evident: Nick's "out here in the world" clearly does not correspond to Arendt's "public realm," inasmuch as he is almost certainly referring to forms of sociality characterized by market relations—the stranger sociability of the job and of consumerism; the instrumental discourses and relations colonizing every corner of the social universe. Nick, the drug dealer, daily encounters the hypocritically compulsory permeability of the normative boundaries among the personal, the juridical, and the economic.

Thus when he expresses skepticism about the prospect of being helped, the scope of this skepticism is not adequately addressed by Sarah's and Meg's avowals of loyalty and care. This is because what "gets tough" are what Marx would call the "objective conditions" of social life under capitalism.[40] His friends can surely aid him, but Nick is quite right that they cannot, in their roles as his friends, do anything to ameliorate the conditions that make the world in which he finds himself so tough. Duress will test their friendship, and they will pass this test; nevertheless, the friendship that passes such a test is, like Nick himself, impotent with respect to the political conditions which that earlier, naïve friendship attempted idealistically to challenge.

If we are expected to accept Harold's discourse as exemplary, it is all the more important to note a key feature of Nick's moribund cynicism. In recounting the story of his radio therapy days, he tells Chloe that he quit as soon as he realized that people with genuine problems actually relied on what he knew to be superficial advice dispensed by him. That is, if Nick is a quitter in the mold of Alex, his rationale is governed by an ethic that exceeds its function as alibi: as with Alex, something in him is "too good for this world." Cynicism is here one outcome of an ethical stance for which there is literally no worldly place. Unlike the case of Sam, we are not dealing here with the desire to "save" people—nor are we dealing with a straightforward "norm of estrangement." Nick is neither naïve nor antisocial; his wish to help others founders on the inadequacy of the means available for doing so. The response proposed by the film, however, is not to address the recalcitrant "political facts" impeding ethical conduct, but rather to overcome the resulting cynicism by dismissing as unrealistic the ethics motivating it. Of course, Nick's political skepticism effectively is unrealistic, since it does not comport with the dominant ethos of late modernity—or, more accurately, it is itself a projection of mediatized therapeutic discourse. This is why the figure of Nick is both necessary to, and intolerable within, the liberal rhetoric articulated in the film. A cynicism capable of marking, however obliquely, the disabling effects of liberal depoliticization is here rendered safely impotent en route to recuperation as its own antithesis—the "hope" restored by friendship.

Yet it is necessary to reject the notion that Nick's skepticism is successfully refuted, both discursively and diegetically, by the emerging distinction between "helping" and "saving" and the corresponding faculty of judgment that enables some of his friends (Harold, Sarah, and Meg) to act in the spirit of Arendtian philia. Again, the shift in emphasis from "world" to "help" entails decisive political and interpretive consequences. The larger point, however, is that *this very shift is itself prefigured* in what Arendt calls "the rise of the social" and what even the earliest liberal theorists explicitly identify as the central accomplishment of capitalism as a cultural logic. Nick's bitterness concerning life "out here in the world" is only one side of the coin that has his friends' capacity to help him as its obverse. What makes the world so tough is, not coincidentally, what communitarians and republicans (among others) decry about liberalism and modernity—superficial, abstract, and instrumental relations among people who are debarred from politicizing their expectation of social obligation, from fully assuming both the civic bond and affectively charged personal commitments. Enduring this world requires friends, but the very gesture of turning to friendship to mitigate the damage concedes that the dehumanized world itself resists collective efforts to change it—that, in effect, democracy is impossible—and dissimulates the fact that the form of subjectivity required to sustain such friendship is what liberal discourse forecloses by means of promising it. Of course, this is the crux of the liberal position: for Adam Smith himself, "out here in the world" of economic transactions, impersonal calculation rules—which is why the intimate world of friendship is far preferable and constitutes the very utopia secured by the innovative partition of social space into the economy, the state, and the lifeworld.

Still, doesn't Nick himself accept the verdict against his cynicism when he agrees to rejoin the "community of friendship" by moving in with Chloe on Sarah and Harold's property? One is tempted here, against current fashion, to emphasize the conspicuously bourgeois nature of this community—after all, its site is literally private and secured by the unchallenged and even agreeable reign of private enterprise. But a more fundamental point to be made concerns the import of Nick's acquiescence, given that he is clearly taking the place once occupied, both diegetically and structurally, by Alex. Is this replacement not also a resignification of the place itself? Clearly, Nick differs from Alex in permitting his friends to help him—that is, his acquiescence underscores the cause of Alex's failure. (Earlier in the film, Michael explains his inability to stay in touch with, and perhaps aid, Alex: "I tried plenty; he resisted it.") We are to surmise that the real trouble with Alex lay not in his inability to find meaning in the dehumanized world of instrumental relations—a trait Nick shares—but rather in his refusal to participate fully in the "community of friendship" available to him ("lost hope"). Nick, we are given to understand, learns from this fatal error.

Friendship and the Politics of Absence

It is important to pause here in order to consider more carefully the place Alex both occupies and fails to occupy in the plot, structure, and logic of the film. Jasinski claims that by the time Nick accepts Harold's offer to stay on his property with Chloe, "[t]he existential question of Alex's suicide has been redefined and the film's moral lesson emerges clearly: acts of friendship—properly understood—are capable of restoring hope and (re)constituting community."[41] The thesis that Alex's suicide initially disturbs the remaining members of the group on an "existential" level obscures the possibility that the anxiety it provokes is from the start moral, ethical, and political, bearing no doubt on the passing of (a certain determination of) *friendship itself.* After all, Alex's absence is overdetermined: it functions in the mode of (a) presence, as the missing/necessary signifier that marks and renders the collection of friends a *collective* (community or polity)—he *must* be missing for the group dynamic to take place in the form it does, yet he must have "really existed" for his absence to generate effects. It should be noted that the dead Alex is played by Kevin Costner, shots of whose face are deliberately excised from the final release of the film, generating one of the film's key indeterminacies in an explicit invitation to the viewer to read the accounts offered by the surviving friends as partial reflections of their own subjective stances.

But beyond acting as a screen or floating signifier, Alex is a *structurally missing* friend, the figure of (always really) missing friendship. Insofar as friendship is, strictly speaking, impossible in its very notion (because, as Derrida points out, the durability, authenticity or, finally, actuality of its bond can never be adequately tested and reliably confirmed without thereby destroying the friends themselves—so that friendship always proceeds "as if" it *will have been* confirmed); and because, within liberalism, friendship names that mode of "pure" or authentic sociality that has been lost but is to be returned through systematic depoliticization, friendship marks a *constitutive absence* within the liberal organization of social life.[42] Alex's absence inscribes both these conditions into the film's narrative structure. The test, initiated by his death, of friendship's efficacy in constituting stable subjects within a functional socius depends upon the evident failure of friendship simultaneously signified by his death. At the same time, the radical implication of this fact (that is, that total ideological closure is impossible) is effaced by the proposition that a sort of "ideal friendship procedure" can be installed that would preclude a repetition of such catastrophic loss. The politically decisive premise covertly posited here is that friendship is not a relation that has the power to confound any existing social arrangements by short-circuiting subjective attachments to interpellative discourses, but is rather the paradigm of autonomic contractualist sociality made possible by the liberal disaggregation of politics and the market from the realm of "sentimental" privacy. Liberal friendship is the only site of authentic sociality, because it occurs within the only space where political and economic encumbrances are imaginatively suspended, and where only conscious free choice warrants entry into relationships. Friendship proves fatally inadequate not because, in its very notion, it forms the site where liberal discourse verges on incoherence, but only contingently, when it fails to obey the liberal prescription for robust sociality. Liberalism proposes itself in the mode of a promise to "return" to the subject his capacity for the kind of free association modeled by friendship. This promise not only dissimulates the discursive production of the kind of subject it presupposes and requires, but must universalize a particular version of friendship as both paradigmatic and (always already) lost. This means, in effect, that liberalism arrogates the radical impossibility of friendship and presents it as contingent. Yet it counts on this radical impossibility to guarantee that the authentic friendship it promises to restore can never be restored—and that this failure will not appear as the failure of liberalism itself. In *The Big Chill,* Alex's death and effacement thus function not simply as cinematic devices that appear transparently and only pragmatically necessary to the narration, but also as the places of inscription for the overwriting of structural radicality by polemical contingency.

At the funeral early in the film, the eulogizing pastor, who never knew the deceased, struggles to impose narrative coherence upon the "seemingly random series" of events comprising Alex's life. This scene both informs the audience of the stakes of the narrative to come (that is, can the rupture evidenced by the suicide be reinscribed within a narrative that would successfully account for it?) as well as to the stakes of narrativization itself. Jasinski argues that the function of narrative being foregrounded in the scene—and the film as a whole—is its capacity to constitute what James Boyd White calls "persuasive communities." However, the minister's comical effort is more complex and ambiguous.

How are we to understand the satiric tension of this moment, which inheres in the minister's attempt to mime a knowledge of Alex he never had? On the one hand, this effort is a foil: we are to contrast the absurdity of a stranger trying to explain the life of another with the presumably more authentic efforts of his friends—though it seems that if we are to take seriously the minister's suggestion that our task is narration, then in a sense he has got Alex right. On the other hand, beyond the question of personal knowledge or friendship, in classical Freudian terms psychic failure itself is a failure of narrativization: Alex's life will not have made sense to his friends, or to us, because it did not make sense to him. Of course, the coherence of any such narrative is always retrospective. Rhetorically, then, the ironic staging of the funeral scene pertains not only to the diegesis and the friendship dynamic detailed in it, but also to the uncertain coherence of the filmic narrative itself. Not only are we instructed that our task is to "make sense" of Alex and the group, but we are simultaneously, and by the same formal gesture, alerted that the project of making such sense involves our own active retrospective labor, so that the film's diegesis is from the start only an artifact of this labor. Put simply, though we ridicule the minister and privilege the perspective of Alex's "true" friends, our situation is akin to the minister's own. Moreover, the suicide indicates that even Alex's true friends had only mimed a knowledge of him. As Nick, the former radio therapist, caustically remarks, this gap in our knowledge does not concern some existential abyss of Alex's psychic agony. Rather, it concerns coherence as the contingent and provisional effect of a struggle, one that fails to appear in its properly comic dimension only when it succeeds in appearing as the product of true knowledge.

Alex's failure consequently models the impasse of modern liberal subjectivity that registers in the convergence between Giddens's account of reflexive modernity and Appiah's account of liberalism as involving the active structuring of personal "lifestyle" across a preconstituted lifespan.[43] The signal challenge in this model is reconciling one's own responsibility for constructing coherence on the basis of publicly circulating expert knowledges with the presumption that only spontaneous coherence originating in the intimate self is permitted to indicate authenticity. In this sense, Alex is the subject who fails to become a modern liberal—that is, the structurally missing "failed" or transitional subject who must be imaginatively posited if the true liberal subject is finally to emerge. Alex's failure of narrativity is not directly a failure to achieve coherence; it indicates a peculiar form of subjective legitimation crisis—an *incapacity to misperceive* the extimate content of intimate subjectivity as his own, which would permit coherence to appear authentic or autarkic. The literally unaccountable series of heterogeneous occupations suggests a compulsive, increasingly desperate repetition of an effort to exercise authentic agency, which must only have underscored the artifice of the exercise. In short, he felt like a fake.

This analysis is vindicated by the way Nick comes to assume Alex's place, marking the passage—and its consequences—to fully liberal reflexive subjectivity. Like Alex, Nick is cynical, in part, insofar as he also feels like a fake: this is the reason he offers Chloe for having quit his radio show. It is thus no coincidence that Nick enters the narrative as the impotent voice of therapeutic self-deception, of the (literally) self-canceling "how-to" project of reflexive self-fashioning and the disavowal of, on the one hand, unconscious motivations (radio therapy presupposes the rational self-transparency posited by liberalism) and, on the other hand, politically overdetermined ones (staging the individual as a self-transparent agent in charge of her own well-being, functionalist psychology is a key mode of liberal discourse).[44] Nick is also the sole member of the group who explicitly understands their common history in terms of disillusionment and "selling out." His cynicism is to be contrasted with Michael's compulsive rationalizations and Sam's narcissism, and *it is this cynicism that the narrative functions to disable.* Nick is the only character whose subjective stance turns into its opposite; he embodies the overcoming of liberalism's immanent critique. If the youth politics of the sixties measure American democracy's distance from its own avowed goals of equality and freedom, surrendering the struggle for them is a betrayal of liberal-democratic citizenship itself. This is the disavowed potency of Nick's cynicism: in resenting this surrender, he vacillates between indicting his own generation and expressing skepticism about the very possibility of success in such a struggle. Given all this, doesn't his transformation redeem political hope? No: Nick relinquishes his cynicism in favor of a thoroughly depoliticized form of sociality, perversely figured by his desexualized monogamous bond with the infantile future citizen, Chloe.[45] His newfound willingness to engage will take the form of *personal* self-fashioning, appropriately sited on a private estate in a space segregated from politics, history, and even strangers—and secured through Harold's utilitarian friendship with xenophobic local police officers.[46]

Thus, unlike Alex, Nick finds a way to delude himself through the detour of friendship, which will now function to disguise the extimate sources of his intimate self. Put another way, what we can surmise to have kept Alex from transitioning into liberal modernity and its attendant modes of subjectivity and politics is his naïve investment—once shared, but, as we have seen, abandoned by Meg—in the polity and the state as the proper addressees of political litigation. Alex thought direct engagement in collective struggle could challenge and transform conditions of injustice; like the rest of the group at one time, he was, in Giddens's terms, an emancipator. The tragedy of his subjective legitimation crisis stems from his investment in what Nick knows to be a defunct standard of authenticity. Hence his fatal sense of guilt (which can now be grasped as correlative to Meg's). Reflexive subjectivity demands consistency with personally selected criteria; it does not presuppose the authenticity of the criteria themselves. This was the difficulty haunting Nick during his days as a radio therapist, the reason radio therapy appeared fake and repugnant to him. Unlike Alex, Nick effectively learns that his criteria of authenticity had been misplaced when Chloe tells him that, despite—or perhaps because of—the generic publicness of his advice, he had in fact "helped" her in their pseudo-intimate encounter reflexively mediated by broadcast technology and therapeutic jargon.[47]

The observation that late modern authenticity is grounded in extimate, impersonal, mass-mediated expertise does not suffice to render it inoperative, since the subject normatively concerns itself only with its own capacity to set in motion the life narrative it has constructed for itself. Chloe's obvious youth and apparent shallowness place her within a generation for which these new rules are transparent. Her attractiveness to Alex, Michael, and Nick derives less from her freedom from historical encumbrance than from the fact that history itself is no longer, for her, an index of depth or authenticity. Alex is unable to accomplish what Nick does—to subjectivize Chloe's rules of sociality.

In the process by which Nick comes to appropriate Alex's place, friendship plays a pivotal role as the metaphorical vehicle of displacement. If, following Jasinksi, "helping" supplants "saving," this displacement does not suggest a way out of the socialization of politics. On the contrary, "helping" is here an index of this socialization, insofar as helping one's friend takes the place of structural change or collective social action, both of which are presumed to be impossible. But the point not to be missed is that this is not a choice made by the subject; we are not, after all, dealing with a straightforward case of "selling out." Rather, we are faced here with the displacement of the proper locus of political agency, such that it simply no longer makes any sense to speak the language of emancipation. Such speech lacks a proper addressee. Consequently, the lesson learned by Harold and Nick is not only the right one, but is prefigured as the cardinal development of the transition to reflexive socialization of politics. It is this prefiguration—this reflexive appropriation of the projected "lifespan" of the film—that is itself figured in the eulogy address. This, in turn, means that if there is more political agency within the space of friendship than Arendt allows (inasmuch as friendship is much more than simply a reservoir of future political possibility), there is also less (inasmuch as the promise of this future is fanciful). The two are yoked as two sides of one coin: friendship is the new site of the political because we are in a post-political or pseudo-political universe.

It is in this sense that *The Big Chill* concerns the question of the locus of politics in the liberal imaginary, and as such displays the tensions animating this question. Is the strategy of situating politics at the micro level as an emergent possibility within friendship an adequate answer to the Arendtian critique? To neoliberal personalization of political responsibility? To the leftist critique of privatization? Are we to read the film as taking one or another position within the range prescribed by critiques of liberalism, or are we to see it as registering the impasses that occasion such critiques? The film is finally ambivalent despite its proto-utopian conclusion, which strives to highlight what Jasinski calls a politics of philia—the introduction of a certain reflective distance into intimate attachments—while retaining a distinctly liberal conception of subjectivity and sociality.[48] This emphasis on a minimum of separation is all that would distinguish the film's model of politics from the standard liberal gesture of depoliticization through friendship. Because it is a gesture of political hope that depends on endorsing the liberal model, it would be prudent to dismiss it as belonging to liberalism's rhetorical ambit. Still, given the various post-structuralist accounts of late capitalism, the notion of micropolitics seems to be among a very small number of possible forms of resistance to what appears as an inexorable socialization of politics. If liberalism is the reigning political imaginary, it is because, in order to reduce to the absolute minimum the prospect of antagonistic struggle, it has largely succeeded in rhetorically depriving "the political" of anything like a "proper" domain. *The Big Chill*'s modest proposal, despite its complicity with liberal logic, at least purports to insist on a certain irreducible political dimension available even in the heart of private affectivity. If this dimension remains cynical within the film, it is because too much has been ceded to liberalism in it. Hence the impetus for the sort of sanguine defense offered by Jasinski. The film's micropolitics is surely doomed, but it is for this very reason that the film is of interest.

Conclusion: Friendship as (A)Political Community

I have been arguing that, in the course of a sophisticated polemical defense of a form of citizenship modeled on friendship, *The Big Chill* makes visible an elective rhetorical affinity between the republican critique of liberalism and liberalism's own communitarian temptation.[49] Understood rhetorically rather than conceptually or normatively, the republican fantasy of civic friendship emerges not as a plausible alternative to the putative erosion of political judgment in the liberal order but as a presupposition of the liberal imaginary's own communitarian promise. It is no accident that *The Big Chill* (re)positions philia in relation Arendt's private/public distinction so as to reinscribe, in the mode of communitarian critique, the logic governing liberal citizenship. The film's communitarian republicanism categorically requires liberalism for its own discourse to attain minimal coherence: the thesis that friendship can reinvigorate the political within "the social" depends on the continuing, untroubled hegemony of the liberal imaginary and its attendant forms of sociability. The film's emphasis on "(re)constituting community" foregrounds social bonds in a way that construes political practice as an instrumental supplement, useful primarily for sustaining communal life. The "friends" who are to develop faculties of judgment remain liberal subjects motivated chiefly by their reciprocal contractual ties with one another, without significant reference to any wider polity and without purchase on social or political arrangements. Indeed, even to register as a heuristic allegory of citizenship, their *friendship depends* on this abdication. It thus becomes evident that, far from *lacking* a civic bond because it privatizes politics, the discourse of liberalism cultivates a rhetoric of sociality designed to *supplant politics.* The fantasy of friendship as a substitute for citizenship thus sustains the "actual" modes of liberal political subjectivity and sociality.

At stake in *The Big Chill,* then, is an animating tension of the liberal imaginary. At a certain moment, the conceit can no longer be sustained that it is possible both to maintain bourgeois social relations and to engage in forms of critical citizenship that challenge the logic governing these relations. Yet, in a stunning reversal, the frustrated politics of intimate sentimentality, rather than giving way to more prudent and canny projects of institutional transformation, is used to *reject* such projects as *themselves* a symptom of naïve utopian solipsism. Thus where Arendt worries about the loss of *publicness,* the film foregrounds concern regarding the loss of *community* as the salient political anxiety allayed by philia. By transferring the obligation to act to the sphere of the private and familial (and it is no accident that all the negotiations concerning intimacy in the film revolve around questions of family and parenthood), the film can side with "action" while guaranteeing that its *public* effects will be indistinguishable from "complacency" or "political resignation." In sum, the faculty of "judgment" Jasinski identifies as the narrative's key heuristic serves to *constitute as liberal* the social field in which it appears simply to operate, in the sense that it performs as a model of intersubjective reciprocity so as to render a wide range of collective and public action politically superfluous.

The Big Chill thus demonstrates that the Arendtian effort to segregate a privileged realm of the authentically political is but the obverse of liberalism's signature stratagem. The confounding and confounded space of "the social" appears both to Arendt and to liberal subjects as the result of a loss for the very same reason. For Arendt, what appears to have been lost is the freedom found in politics; for liberal subjects, it is the freedom found in private authenticity. In both its aspects, this loss is a rhetorical product of the gesture of segregation: the will to "partition" (as Rancière puts it) is compelled by the liberal project of neutralizing the antagonism that constitutes social ontology and engenders the democratic paradox. This effort to foreclose political antagonism can today only reinforce the liberal logic Arendt aims to challenge. The liberal imaginary constitutes itself by projecting a loss of authentic private affectivity, modeled by friendship, in order to institute the liberal partition as the means of restoring this utopia. This promise, in turn, sustains "the social" as the space of its forever-deferred fulfillment. Arendt apprehends this space as a lamentable loss of politics, not recognizing that, far from being a side effect of modernity, the (re)production of this "loss" constitutes the liberal project. In short, "the social" *is* the liberal politics of depoliticization. The drive to "restore" the public-private partition not only posits as empirical a purely imaginary loss, it also repeats, in the very form of critique, the definitive liberal gesture of "emancipating" social life from politics.

Yet if the liberal solution to the problem of democratic cooperation involves producing friendship as an extrapolitical form of citizenship hostile to institutional politics, this very hostility in turn sustains the possibility of another modality of liberal citizenship, one construed as resistance to encroaching forms of power. Thus liberal public culture proliferates countless narratives of political resistance in which the protagonists are friends confronting characteristic forms of predictably corrupt official and unofficial authority, and in which it is friendship itself that both supplies the ground of solidarity and represents the precious form of sociality threatened by the sinister, impersonal calculus of power. In consonance with the normative suspicion of formal authority characteristic of the liberal imaginary, such narratives construe citizenship as rebellion. This cultural tendency seems, however, to pose a problem for analysis: whereas the communitarian model of friendship displaces antagonism, rebel-citizenship clearly centers it—so how can both gestures be regarded as equally characteristic of liberalism?

This is among the key questions to be addressed in the next chapter, in the context of an analysis of *Thelma & Louise* and its reception in feminist and queer media studies. Here, the republican and communitarian pseudocritiques of liberalism unexpectedly find perhaps their clearest obverse. Widely praised for its sophisticated transformative appropriation of traditionally masculine film genres for its project of challenging the systematic subordination, disempowerment, and effacement of women by both conventions of popular representation and forms of institutional discourse—indeed, by the symbolic order generally—the film relies on friendship as a figure of rebel-citizenship to effect this challenge. The critical reception and rhetorical project of *Thelma & Louise* are emblematic of the limits of feminist and psychoanalytic critiques of phallocentric power, which tend to occlude the pivotal role played by the liberal determination of citizenship as critique of organized authority in constituting the discursive field in which the problem of power assumes a form specific to the liberal imaginary.

The film thus serves as an exemplary case of the antipolitical liberal rhetoric of citizenship as rebellious dissent, a model that is central to much of the contemporary politically motivated cultural critique. While it appears more overtly "political" in its orientation than *The Big Chill,* the form of citizenship this figure of friendship underwrites is that of liberal antipathy toward power as an essentially suspect dimension of social life. Indeed, the problem is that the liberal model itself produces the political impotence the female protagonists embody in the guise of gendered disempowerment. The rebel-citizen–friend mediates the liberal solution at the cost of driving it inexorably into a cul-de-sac, producing heroic failure as the only plausible and admirable form citizenship can assume.

3
Friendship, Rebel-Citizenship, and the Feminist Critique of Liberalism
Thelma & Louise

> Men who feel threatened by this movie are identifying with the wrong characters. . . . This is a film about freedom. Anyone should be able to identify with it.
>
> —Geena Davis

The Predicament of Gendered Liberty

We have seen that the republican and socialist (or "radical democratic") critiques of liberal doctrine misconstrue the rhetorical efficiency of the "displacement of politics" in liberal discourse. *The Big Chill* evinces the rhetorical constitution of the liberal imaginary around the promise of extra-political elective attachments modeled by friendship. Yet while this communitarian scheme obviates the republican and socialist objections, it seems to confront a limit internal to its own logic, producing the very problem it would resolve. Specifically, the liberal rhetoric of "exit" from politics in favor of morally privileged affective sociability generates a political antagonism rooted in gender hierarchy. This, at least, is the central thesis of the feminist critique of liberalism.

As articulated by such political theorists as Jean Bethke Elshtain, Seyla Benhabib, Carole Pateman, Nancy Fraser, Iris Marion Young, Kathleen Jones, and Wendy Brown, this critique has centered on such matters as the historical, conceptual, and strategic gendering of the public/private distinction, the emphasis on abstract, disembodied rationality as the privileged mode of political discourse, and the supposed normative hetero-masculinity of the liberal citizen, concluding in each case that liberal sexism has consisted primarily in systematically depriving women of a politically perceptible voice capable of formally contesting their tacit social and economic subordination.[1] Here, extrapolitical sociability is at the root of the problem, not because it displaces political antagonism, but because it directly constitutes a hierarchical, and thus antagonistic, politics of gender.

Of course, mainstream feminist social movements have consistently and quite effectively drawn on liberal principles to press for equality, raising doubts about claims that liberalism is inherently sexist and prompting debates on the question among feminist political theorists that continue to date.[2] Yet these debates overwhelmingly concern liberal doctrine, either as a reflection of or tacit warrant for sexist social practice; they take little explicit notice of ubiquitous popular articulations and representations of feminist claims. On the other hand, cultural analysis concerned with the politics of gender representation takes little notice of liberalism as a factor in the public circulation of feminist rhetoric. Instead, the cultural focus of feminist theory and criticism leads it to another, more "radical" object of critique: the sexism of the modern Western episteme, symbolic order, or discursive régime. Drawing primarily on the work of Foucault, Lacan, and French feminists such as Wittig and Irigaray, this formation understands gender hierarchy as an effect of compulsory phallocentric structures inscribed at the level of linguistic norms, especially in the guise of sexual difference and economy. Still, although post-structuralist feminist cultural theory identifies politics with discursive struggle over normative meaning and signifying capacity, its potentially vexing implications for liberalism are not difficult to discern. As Brown puts it, "the legacy of gender subordination . . . is to be found . . . in the *terms* of liberal discourse that configure and organize liberal jurisprudence, public policy, and popular consciousness."[3] Accordingly, to the degree that political and juridical institutions are instances or effects of a sexist discursive régime, transforming this régime will in due course undermine or even overthrow these institutions.

In short, both the social fact of gender hierarchy and academic feminist accounts of cultural and political phallocentrism would seem to pose formidable challenges to the integrity and efficacy of liberal discourse. The importunate question, then, is how, despite the putatively constitutive intransigence of liberalism to feminist demands, liberal discourse not only endures undisturbed in the face of these demands but even purports to endorse and meet them. Indeed, liberal public culture even manages to put in circulation popular critiques of phallocentrism, which academic feminism welcomes even as it casts doubt on their key postulates. After all, if either liberalism or the prevailing symbolic order rests on a masculinist logic, public exposure and censure of this logic should either prove virtually impossible or bring about revolutionary social change. So, whereas feminist thought understandably continues to interrogate the continued subordination of women (and sexual minorities), it seems no less urgent to ask what the simultaneous persistence and commonplace public repudiation of this subordination reveal about the internal logic and resilience of the liberal imaginary in the face of feminist critique.

What, then, are the rhetorical operations by means of which the liberal imaginary generates the appearance of actively pursuing women's equality, despite itself being premised on normatively masculine subjectivity and citizenship? As Brown's way of framing the problem already indicates, the answer is to be sought not in doctrinal debates but in representative instances of "popular consciousness"—that is, in the discourse of a public culture that functions to disarticulate citizenship from presumptive masculinity without in the least troubling the liberal imaginary. An exemplary instance of this process is Ridley Scott's 1991 film *Thelma & Louise,* a genre-blending story of female rebellion against patriarchal authority that was among the most widely debated American films in decades, prompting hundreds, if not thousands, of popular and academic publications, which continue appearing to this day. Focusing enormous public and academic attention on the institutional problem and media representation of gender as a political encumbrance, the film occupies the nexus of a vast network of critical discourses concerning the politics of gender. It thus offers exceptional access to that nexus and its relation to the rhetoric of the liberal imaginary.

Liberalism, Feminist Critique, and the Valorization of Resistance

In the story, Thelma Yvonne Dickinson (Geena Davis) is an Arkansas housewife married to an imbecilic used car dealer, and her best friend, Louise Elizabeth Sawyer (Susan Sarandon), is an unmarried waitress obsessed with cleanliness. The two decide to take a brief vacation road trip, but when they stop off for a drink just outside of town, Thelma is sexually assaulted by a man named Harlan (Timothy Carhart). The assault is interrupted by Louise, who confronts Harlan with the gun Thelma had impulsively taken from her husband, Daryl, for the trip. Incredulous that a woman would deprive him of what he considers his prerogative, Harlan insults Louise, who shoots and kills him. Louise insists to Thelma that there is no explanation they could offer the authorities that would prevent them from ending up in prison, so they take off for Mexico. Louise, however, refuses to drive through Texas. As the women detour through the Southwest, they encounter a series of male figures who pose obstacles to their plan. In successive attempts to extricate themselves from their no longer tenable entanglements with men, the women progressively relinquish the markers of conventional femininity, until the police finally catch up to them at what appears to be the Grand Canyon. Rather than get caught, they decide to "keep goin'" and, kissing and clasping hands, drive off the edge.

The release of the film prompted a strong, and strongly divided, reaction from commentators in the popular press, followed swiftly by a torrent of academic commentary. Socially conservative critics feigned taking the film literally and chastised it for encouraging women toward violent rebellion.[4] More progressive critics praised the film for giving voice to female discontent. Meanwhile, the film succeeded financially, made the cover of *Time,* and attained the hyperbolic status of "instant classic."[5] It was debated whether the film is excessive in its depiction of women's rage; whether it offered an appropriate model of female agency; and whether it was hopeful or despairing concerning women's prospects in a masculine world. It was even debated whether or not the film was "feminist" at all—as were the character, state, and prospects of feminism itself.[6]

The film compelled such attention because it differs significantly from its feminist precursors: in addition to articulating a nuanced critique of phallocentrism, its poignant conclusion and high degree of reflexivity raise questions concerning the political efficacy of the critical frameworks operative in it. Academic reception of the film has focused on its narrative strategies and effects, fascinated by its consonance with variants of feminist critique and treating it largely as a fortuitously apt popular articulation of theoretical insights. As such readings demonstrate, the rhetorical sophistication of the film's feminism is indeed exceptional; it supports highly complex analyses as if it had been produced in accordance with the very theories marshaled to elucidate it. Yet while generally astute, the reception of *Thelma & Louise* stops short of asking how it is possible for the patriarchal culture depicted *within* the film to develop and circulate the vigorous and popular critique of patriarchy enunciated *by* the film. Focusing on the film's concern with the politics and representation of gender, critics see no need to interrogate the rhetorical premises animating its feminism.

This is unfortunate, since the question of how feminism should best be constructed in practice or represented in the media to facilitate gender justice implies a logically prior question: How might citizenship be imagined so as to deliver on the promise of democratic agency for everyone? And given that several trajectories of feminist thought seem to pose a radical challenge to key elements of liberal doctrine and institutions, how does the liberal imaginary within which feminist projects arise constrain the shape they can and do assume? If other critics have asked what sort of feminism the film depicts or how (well) it does so, I would like to ask what sort of citizenship the film's complex, ambivalent feminism presupposes and endorses—and with what consequences. *Thelma & Louise* represents a sophisticated attempt to produce feminism as an essentially liberal discourse, whereby feminism comes to function not as a forceful challenge to, but as a compelling alibi for, the liberal model of democracy. Acclaimed as emblematic of prevailing developments in feminist theory and criticism, the critique of patriarchy and phallocentrism driving the film's narrative functions rhetorically as a vehicle for rationalizing the liberal form of citizenship. And it is no accident that this rationale depends on friendship as the ambivalent figure of solidarity that integrates irrepressible dissent with political complicity.

The thematics of resistance or subversion that critics consistently discern in the film—and praise as exemplifying various theoretical accounts of gender hierarchy—are advocated under liberalism as paradigmatic of citizenship as such. What appears oppositional in relation to structural phallocentrism is simply axiomatic for liberal citizenship, so absent an explicit articulation between gender and the presumptively liberal discourse of citizenship, the most radical feminist critiques are easily rendered complicit with the liberal model, and there is a triple price to pay for this. First, the elision of liberalism as the matrix within which gender hierarchy emerges obscures key aspects of the film's rhetorical project, preventing analyses of the film from achieving coherence. Second, locating sexual difference at the foundation of the symbolic order and identifying the latter with politics generally—without regard to the rhetorical framework the prevailing political imaginary itself supplies for managing the problem of power—tends to produce an agenda for cultural politics unnecessarily limited in its capacity to meet its own goals. And third, the indifference to the cunning of the liberal rhetoric of citizenship ultimately undermines the very premises of feminist and queer critiques, prompting them to misconstrue liberalism's signature features as terminal flaws.

For the liberal imaginary, subjugation *will have been obsolete*—officially disavowed, normatively precluded, its demise anticipated and thus prospectively accomplished—so that when, in practice, inequality proves widespread, it is to be contested from within a presumptively liberal model of democratic agency, which is thus fortified through an encounter with that which might otherwise productively destabilize it. This speculative temporal economy of liberalism's emancipatory promise is vital to the preemptive cunning of liberal reason. In staging its critique of patriarchy, *Thelma & Louise* enacts the *liberal fantasy of citizenship,* the effect of which is, in part, to forestall the challenge feminism poses to it—a challenge that, though articulated in terms of gender and sexuality, threatens to undermine liberalism's constitutive political cynicism, exposing its internal limits to critical scrutiny.

To understand how the film's supposedly exemplary feminist critique reproduces the rhetorical framework that limits its efficacy, it is necessary to understand the strategic role played by the trope of rebel-citizenship in the liberal imaginary, the film, and its reception. This reception can be sorted heuristically into "media-centric" readings organized around the challenge the film poses to conventional representations of gender, and ones focusing more directly on its challenge to masculine hegemony in the juridical and symbolic orders. Both approaches concern the film's stance on the subordination of women; they differ in the degree to which they accent the mediation of this subordination by cinematic conventions or institutional and linguistic structures. The latter group includes a small but disproportionately important cluster of readings that, following Judith Butler, see the film as advancing a critique of sexual difference itself. Accordingly, I will proceed in three stages. First, I will sketch an account of the liberal trope of rebel-citizenship. Second, by examining key features of these reading strategies and their theoretical underpinnings, I will highlight the constraints imposed by the liberal imaginary on typical feminist accounts of the film and on the principal critical strategies underpinning these accounts. Third, I will at the same time indicate an alternative understanding of the film's rhetoric as an effect of the liberal model of citizenship.

Liberalism and the Rebel-Citizen

In Walter Benjamin's critique of the "philosophy of right" underpinning the liberal notion of sovereignty, the figure of the outlaw appears at once as the "universal" analytic counterpart to the hegemony on violence that is the sine qua non of the state *and* as the historically specific, paradoxical product of liberal democracy.[7] Benjamin argues that the figure of the outlaw acquires its critical force with the emergence of the juridical state. As Jacques Derrida explains, for Benjamin "European law tends to prohibit individual violence and to condemn it not because it poses a threat to this or that law but because it threatens the juridical order itself." Accordingly, "The outlaw comes to exert a certain fascination on popular consciousness because [the outlaw] is not someone who has committed this or that crime for which one feels a secret admiration; it is someone who, in defying the law, lays bare the violence of the legal system, the juridical order itself."[8]

Benjamin gives the example of the "right to strike . . . guaranteed to workers who are therefore, besides the state, the only legal subject to find itself guaranteed the right to violence." Of course, the state does *not* view this right as a right to violence, offering it rather as a placebo that provides a strictly circumscribed space for dissent that sustains the appearance of public accountability without troubling the juridical order. Benjamin, however, perceives a radical political possibility inherent in this concession: "if the strike persists, we have a revolutionary situation." Clearly, "[t]he state can hardly stand this passage to the limit," for it threatens to transform the demand for specific concessions into a wholesale transformation of existing political arrangements.[9]

So, insofar as the establishment of juridical order entails sovereignty as legitimate hegemony on violence, the law effectively produces violence as such. There is no natural violence; violence always presupposes some set of political arrangements. For this reason, the (actual or potential) violence of the outlaw is a disavowed form of citizenship, an irreducibly *civic* orientation fundamental to the very juridical edifice that establishes its legitimacy by opposing itself to it. Liberal democracy is peculiar in directly postulating the citizen *as* rebel or outlaw, so that political demands capable of challenging existing arrangements are reduced to forms of resistance that leave these arrangements untouched.

Whereas autocracy could not tolerate open rebellion, liberalism's innovation is to resignify it, to bring its disruptive force under the purview of political negotiation: demands threatening state hegemony on violence take the form of a political positions within a range secured by this hegemony. Understood from this perspective, the right to strike is not a reluctant concession that risks spinning out of the state's control, but the means by which liberal logic overdetermines the field of political struggle. A liberal order is legitimate because it *disavows all hegemony* on power. The citizens' task is to hold those in power to this disavowal; citizenship consists precisely in the outlaw's function of "lay[ing] bare the violence of . . . the juridical order."

So, one of liberalism's chief rhetorical innovations is to proffer its own discourse as an energetic critique of power, casting doubt on the legitimacy of every institution, structure, and discourse of authority. From a liberal perspective, it is never surprising that a given form of authority is dysfunctional, corrupt, self-serving, coercive, or otherwise suspect. Within the liberal imaginary, any social agent occupying the place of power is ipso facto a transgressor whose hegemony can never be fully legitimate precisely because it is a hegemony. Here we face a fundamental impasse: on the one hand, liberalism seems vulnerable to the revolutionary gesture whereby a partial demand is elevated into a wholesale refusal of the juridical order; on the other hand, it appears this vulnerability is a ruse, an apparently secret, subversive possibility in fact systematically held out by liberalism precisely as a way of enticing potential revolutionaries into assuming their prescribed place within the existing order. The revolution is already built in: neither the civil rights movement nor feminism, for example, has, despite lodging demands that once seemed entirely incompatible with existing social arrangements, come close to subverting the liberal order. How, then, are we to think of political agency in its transformative dimension? Is there a way out of the deadlock embodied by the figure of the outlaw or rebel-citizen? This is finally the problem with which the liberal rhetoric of *Thelma & Louise* confronts those feminisms that, notwithstanding their internal complexities, continue to rely on this figure.

Reception Strategies

While differing on the particulars of *Thelma & Louise*'s genre genealogy, Marita Sturken, Jack Boozer, Steven Cohan and Ina Rae Hark, Manohla Dargis, Marsha Kinder, Leo Braudy, and Peter Chumo agree that the film works within the framework of the American myth of individualism, and that it is by repurposing genre conventions that the film stages its critique.[10] Positing genre as the privileged site of phallocentrism, this mode of analysis determines it as the film's main target: "*Thelma & Louise* . . . overturns the masculinist bias of the road" movie and sundry other genres.[11] Thus Glenn Man claims for the film the post-Mulveyan project of constructing "a new way of seeing, a new bearer of the look" that would "deconstruct traditional male structures" of cinematic representation.[12] And Cohan and Hark cite Timothy Corrigan's account of the road movie as an expression of "masculinist fantasies of escape and liberation."[13] Yet it should be clear that this fantasy is itself constitutive of the American dream's liberalism; the dream is liberal fantasy writ nation-size. Moreover, normative masculinity has never been the genre's untroubled *premise,* but rather a persistent *problem* the genre labors to address. As Corrigan himself points out, road movies concern the "hysterical crisis" of normative masculinity in twentieth-century U.S culture.[14] To analyze *Thelma & Louise* in terms of its presumed challenge to the masculinism and heteronormativity of existing genres it is essential to take account of the political crisis these genres already encode.[15]

The consequences of foregoing such analysis become clear in efforts to read the women's friendship as a figure of ambiguous desire troubling the foundational status of sexual difference. Queer readings of the film view the women's friendship as encoding a homoerotic bond capable of functioning as a ground of political agency. They argue that *Thelma & Louise* is to be read as a lesbian love story that deploys a rhetoric of camp and ambiguity to thematize the cultural leitmotif of associating homosexual bonds with death.[16] Thus Lynda Hart claims that the ambiguity of gender made visible by the paradoxical figure of a biological woman whose desire mimics that of men but cannot be identical to it denaturalizes gender and destabilizes cultural, juridical, and institutional norms that constitute patriarchal social relations.[17] Similarly, Sharon Willis argues that "the film pries gender away from sexuality [and] makes the body into its own costume" in order to "stage a form of drag based on a masculinity that aggressively displays its difference from an anatomical base."[18]

Such readings seek to follow Judith Butler, who, via Lacan and Foucault, construes the distinction between "law" and "power" wherein the former is "discursively and performatively instituted . . . within the terms of" the latter. Butler reproaches feminism for uncritically presuming a subject already produced as sexed/gendered within a "heterosexual matrix" that must be deconstructed if the sex/gender dichotomy is to cease operating as a disciplinary technique.[19] Following her reasoning, to frame the analysis of *Thelma & Louise* in terms of the contradiction between "inside" and "outside" patriarchal law would be fundamentally misguided. By contrast, since the heterosexual matrix achieves the appearance of stability and coherence by rendering a plurality of practices, bodies, desires, and subjectivities effectively illegible, conspicuous displays of gender insubordination undercut the premises of this matrix.

Although attacked for dissolving the specific problem of women's oppression in favor of a broader project of cultural politics, Butler does not wish to displace gender as the focus of political struggle but rather to expand this struggle's scope by locating the exclusionary production of sexual difference at the level of language.[20] Her political interest concerns the production of gendered subjects through historically specific gestures of foreclosure,[21] in light of her view that "foreclosure is the way variable social prohibitions work," where such prohibitions are the primary locus of politics to which discursive struggle pertains: "I . . . regard this horizon as a historically variable schema or episteme, . . . transformed by the emergence of the non-representable within its terms, . . . compelled to reorient itself by virtue of the radical challenges to its transcendentality presented by 'impossible' figures at the borders . . . of its surface."[22]

This critical investment in schemas of exclusion raises the question: What happens when a hegemonic discourse sustains itself precisely by claiming to challenge just this sort of transcendentality? This site of historico-rhetorical variability remains beyond the avowed scope of Butler's project.[23] Put simply, our relation to the law, social prohibitions, or normativity is not fully captured by the content and operation of *linguistic* categories and structures, even if these are linked to particular historical conditions. It is essential also to interrogate the rhetorical framework governing this link. Specifically, liberalism itself purports to offer a rhetoric of dissent and subversion that must be taken into account by any political project launched under its régime. By definition, the public circulation and enormous popular appeal of a female couple contesting the masculinity of the law and the hegemonic construction of sexual difference attest to the "possibility" of such a figure, belying claims of its transcendental epistemic foreclosure.[24] Hence the indispensable question of sexual difference and subordination marks the beginning, rather than the end, of analysis.

Indifference to liberalism produces in even the most sophisticated readings of *Thelma & Louise* distortions that inadvertently mark liberalism's influence. Hart offers the most sustained and nuanced example of a reading informed by Butler. Her aim is "to understand how the lesbian functions as a structural dialectic of appearance/disappearance in the process of making women's aggression visible," since "[t]hese representations carry with them the weight of a culture that has made the lesbian and the female criminal synonymous by *displacing* women's aggression onto the sexually 'deviant' woman."[25] Turning on a Lacanian reading of the women's friendship, Hart's theoretically rich analysis falls prey to the rigid structuralism of its psychoanalytic model and ultimately cannot give a coherent account of this friendship's political valence.

She thus inevitably abandons the implication of her own insight that the figure of the lesbian functions to dissimulate the *political* character of female aggression. When, ultimately, Hart insists that the women's final kiss is "too prolonged for friendship," she allows the lesbian subtext to subsume the manifest text: "Thelma and Louise are not criminals because they shoot a rapist, rob a store or blow up a truck. They are criminals because they are *together,* seeking escape from the masculine circuit of desire."[26] So despite all intervening qualifications and modulations, Hart ends up equating the lesbian and the outlaw, wherein the only possible function of friendship is to figure an otherwise "unspeakable" revolt. Nothing is left of friendship itself, its political possibilities or specific narrative functions in the film. Here, Hart falls into the very trap she identifies and criticizes, substituting lesbian desire for dissident female solidarity. Ironically, the compulsion to "find the lesbian" is itself symptomatic of the psychoanalytic procedure that identifies a de-historicized, structuralist model of heterosexist normativity with its historically specific articulation within liberal modernity.[27] Like Thelma and Louise, this critical strategy cannot escape its own constitutive detour.

The figure of the lesbian is hardly subversive; it rather attenuates the threat of civic agency and the politicization of grievance implicit in the trope of the aggressive woman—the possibility that, as a side effect of feminist and queer critique, citizenship will be disarticulated from the anti-political figure of the outlaw. In its very disintegration, Hart's analysis demonstrates that the lesbian does not disrupt the patriarchal régime of representation; on the contrary, she *supplements* it, providing an expedient integral category to which to consign the woman who resists the circumscription of her agency. Insofar as patriarchy is itself a response to the paradox of liberal citizenship that sustains the illusion of extrapolitical agency by staging a contest over the missing phallus, the function of the liberal imaginary is obscured. The contingencies of gender and sexuality here facilitate and dissimulate the project of recuperating the liberal rebel-citizen. We can discern this process at work in key moments in the narrative.

Liberalism and the Rhetoric of Anachronism

The rhetorical imperative to disarticulate liberal citizenship from the embarrassment of gender hierarchy induces a temporal distortion that has profound effects on the narrative, producing hermeneutic complications that cannot be solved if the figure of the rebel-citizen is elided or construed as pertaining exclusively to phallocentrism. The problem concerns the valence of sexual violence in the film.[28] Here the alternatives are between reading such violence as indicative of patriarchy's persistence in what amounts to a "rape culture"[29] and reading it as part of the "backlash" brought on by feminist progress in hastening the disintegration of masculine privilege.[30] The discourse of liberalism organizing the film's narrative compels it to maintain both, mutually exclusive, premises: patriarchy persists in constituting the socio-symbolic space occupied by both the audience and the protagonists; yet the audience is painstakingly positioned to renounce patriarchy as the defunct discourse of crude, effete imbeciles hysterically clinging to their vanishing privilege.

Nowhere in the film is the ingenuity of liberal discourse more clearly—

and problematically—evident. Accordingly, several critics attempt to historicize the film and its media reception as the site of a cultural anxiety concerning female "identification" with masculine violence and a paranoid fantasy of female revenge supposedly evident in contemporaneous Hollywood fare, such as *Black Widow* and *Fatal Attraction*.[31] But attempts to read the film in such terms reproduce the temporal distortion that undermines the coherence of the resulting interpretations.

How is this "revenge fantasy" set in motion? The key moment is Louise's shooting of Harlan. Why *does* she shoot him? Her act is a silent and silencing response to his provocation. After he defiantly declares, "I shoulda gone ahead and fucked her!" Louise demands: "What did you say?" When he spits back, "Suck my cock!" she responds by shooting. The irreducible *necessity* of her response must not be missed. It is *because she cannot speak,* as it were, that she must shoot. Since the antagonism between them concerns the phallus, it concerns power as a prerogative of representation. Critics consistently praise the film for "offer[ing] a potentially powerful critique of women's everyday experience of rape and sexual harassment [by linking] sexual assault to masculine control over . . . language."[32] Harlan's provocation is clearly double: at the level of enunciation, he insists on monopolizing the right to "name" the women; at the level of enunciated content, he identifies this right with masculinity.

But what are the rhetorical reasons for the insult Harlan hurls at Louise, and what are its effects? The film's implied audience is supposed to disidentify with Harlan, and, insofar as we occupy the spectatorial position offered us, to cheer Louise's response. Clearly, in consonance with liberal universalism, spectators irrespective of gender are invited to assume a position of superiority with respect to Harlan, on two levels. First, "we" are not sexist—or, our sexism is not so *uncivil.* Second, Harlan's crudeness is a marker of inferior social status. What we reject is not simply his sexism, but, more urgently, his presumptiveness. While most of the characters in the film belong to the working class, Harlan's social inferiority with respect to the film's implied viewers is selectively marked by his insistence on asserting what more "sophisticated"—or civil—members of the polity actively disavow.

From the orthodox psychoanalytic perspective, Harlan's incivility is a failure of *sublimation,* which is itself marked by social status: only those in a position to benefit from deferring their ambition by routing it through socially productive forms submit to its discipline. Harlan does not expect an adequate return on his psychic investment; he perceives little benefit in the liberal bargain. His crudeness figures a "return of the repressed" drive toward gendered, and therefore durable, supremacy—a luxury of direct expression ironically more available to those with less social capital to lose in the eyes of the "politically correct," implicitly bourgeois normative order embodied by the audience.

Harlan's incivility, then, encodes a temporal distinction: from the liberal perspective driving the film, Harlan is "behind the times": "we" have long since assimilated the lessons of feminism. Harlan's failure or refusal to emit public signs of gender sensitivity appears *anachronistic,* whether because he and men like him have *yet* to catch on, or because they are deliberately staging a "backlash."[33] The film's critique of "rape culture" thus functions to locate its implied audience in the aftermath of feminism.[34] The *untimely* extemporaneousness of Harlan's insult degrades him in our eyes, making his murder not only acceptable but deeply satisfying. But it also antiquates him and the patriarchal system of which he is construed as a relic. His death is thus satisfying for a second reason: it encourages the presumptively liberal audience to take credit for progressing beyond patriarchy. This transaction exploits the social fact of sexual violence to cement our collective identification with the women: outraged as we are by Harlan, our vicarious endorsement of Louise's response renders us her accomplices.[35] Hence the importance of seeing that this identification is secured by a kind of blackmail centered, ironically, on the audience's investment in the very juridical edifice with which it might otherwise dis-identify on account of Harlan's incivility.

Why blackmail? Because the exchange between Harlan and Louise confronts audiences with a forced choice: to identify with Harlan as the victim of an unjustified shooting would require recognizing in his uncouth person the abstract, impersonal principle of the law, and this possibility is actively foreclosed by the rape scene. On the one hand, his embodiment of an unacceptable form of subjectivity bars identification with his particularity. On the other hand, it precisely obscures the liberal principle of abstract universal equality to be upheld notwithstanding its pathological contingent embodiment. Crucially, Harlan's capacity to obscure this principle by failing to embody or signify it properly is overdetermined within the logic of liberalism. Liberal subjects are not supposed *really to believe* this principle; they are never to identify with it directly. It operates as the court of final appeal only by remaining rigorously formal; hence those subject to its rule are effectively in a permanent state of latent rebellion against it. Consequently, antagonism toward this universal is a defining feature of the liberal imaginary.

For the spectator, then, the process of sublimation is activated through the production of surplus enjoyment in seeing Harlan get what he deserves.[36] The audience has good reason to invest its psychic energies in derogating patriarchy: its investment will pay off by producing effective forms of social agency—the happy consciousness of "good subjects" of liberalism. Hating and sacrificing the vulgar "subject supposed to believe" (because direct belief is what vulgarity means) endorses the official Law of liberal equality that is to support the ironic stance from which the film assails patriarchy. This is the *beginning of the end* (which is therefore the beginning, again) of the film: what will have been found intolerable is the *contamination* of the Law by masculinity—*but not the form of law itself.* The film's critique of patriarchy is thus underwritten by the latter's putative divergence from the liberal ideal of equality: the law is not abstract enough; it secretly smuggles in a positive content.

Of course, feminist and multiculturalist critiques of liberalism interrogate the disempowering effects of abstract universality on subjects burdened by contingent particular embodiments.[37] But the film demonstrates that such critiques are themselves subject to the cunning of liberal reason.[38] The murder of Harlan is to be justified, if at all, by reference to Louise's disenfranchisement and systematic silencing by this logic. According to the familiar feminist/multiculturalist account, it cannot be justified before the juridical apparatus because the law is, in its universality, effectively "masculine" or "phallocentric." This is so either because in place of true abstraction we have a secret particular content that comes to be "read" as its adequate embodiment, or because true abstraction itself is "masculine" insofar as it establishes itself as "abstract" by marking any positivity as "feminine."[39] As a result, Louise sees her fate as sealed in advance: in the context of liberal abstraction, there is no justificatory rhetoric she can produce, since, as a woman, she is already effectively an illegal, (over)embodied subject illegible within the idiom of universality. From the law's perspective, Harlan had done nothing to her, and his place in the interminable series of injurious acts perpetrated upon her under the aegis of liberal universality is a priori insufficient justification for her act. She cannot be excused for attacking a particular agent of an unjust system; at best, she might be excused for attacking the system itself. It is, of course, a bitter irony that there is no discernible form of embodied agency adequate to the task of dismantling an abstract symbolic framework—and thus no form of agentive subjectivity appropriate for Louise's predicament.

So the surplus enjoyment Harlan's murder would produce is an instance of repressive de-sublimation, insofar as it turns on audience disidentification with markers of positivity. In order to accept Louise's act as just and even laudable—that is, as a paradoxical instance of *excess justice*—we must endorse the premises and logic that make her act appear necessary. In hating Harlan, we explicitly renounce patriarchy, even if we remain tacitly complicit with it. This renunciation hinges on the film's metonymic identification of patriarchy with his embodied positivity—his suddenly "ethnic" masculinity saturated by violence, vulgarity, and repugnant particularity. Yet we disavow Harlan in order to identify with a form of embodied particularity we are enjoined to respect precisely for its historical suffering. Our good conscience is thereby affirmed, but only at the cost of endorsing as necessary the *gap* between abstraction and particularity. Liberal universality is thus reinscribed as the criterion according to which we can recognize Louise as an unjust victim of oppression and Harlan as the *contingent transgressor* of the principle of equality. Foreclosed thereby is the possibility—underpinning the predominant feminist critique of liberalism—that such transgression is not contingent but inherent to the abstract principle itself. It is only on condition that we ourselves violate this principle by accepting Louise as its adequate embodiment that we are able to indict Harlan and *enjoy* his murder.

What stuns Louise is not only the breathtaking excessiveness of Harlan's arrogance but also the aptness of this excess. It literally renders her mute: there are effectively no words, no rhetorical resources, by means of which she might challenge the discourse he voices. This development underwrites much of the academic enthusiasm for the film, providing strong support for the thesis that patriarchy operates at the level of language itself. This thesis stipulates that linguistic phallocentrism constrains the available rhetorical resources but never asks how the prevailing rhetorical framework—in this case, that of liberalism—in turn constrains patriarchy. In view of subsequent narrative development, we should consider this early gesture on Louise's part a grave error compelled, despite plausible narrative alternatives, by the polemical requirement to inflate language over rhetoric in the service of a liberal determination of citizenship as resistance to power.

Permitting herself to be interpellated by Harlan, Louise becomes complicit in her own subjection. The women then spend the rest of the film trying to escape and resist both the law and their constitutive guilt as "bad subjects." It is important to keep in view both levels of culpability here—as well as the overdetermined connection between them, which renders the discourse of criminality more than simply metaphorical. The solution would consist in discovering or developing a rhetoric of self-representation, of inventing a way they can speak for themselves.[40] If the women's early failure is a failure of invention, then their subsequent rebellion is a rebellion against their own complicity in patriarchy. Hence the performative contradiction that results when critique focuses on the problem of gender while eliding the efficacy of liberal metadiscourse: within the logic of the diegesis, the women lack access to an adequate rhetoric, but as the film's very existence demonstrates, this lack is articulated from the perspective and in the idiom of liberalism, which thereby precisely constitutes this "missing" rhetoric. The resulting impasse is what leads the film into a diegetic cul-de-sac.

Returning for a moment to the language of psychoanalysis, Luce Irigaray observes that "the girl does not know what she is missing when she discovers her 'castration,'" so that her loss cannot be represented.[41] This claim can be reformulated: what she has effectively "lost"—or, more precisely, what has been *foreclosed* for her—is the power of (self-)representation. Now, it should go without saying that this power is factitious, belonging to no one. Patriarchy is thus a symbolic economy in which men are imagined to have "it" in the form of the phallus; women are imagined to *be* the phallus men "have." So, men "speak" women, but only insofar as this speech obscures the radical absence of this power. It is in this sense that "woman is a symptom of man": she *must* be spoken by him to sustain the fiction of the phallus. (Perversely, this necessity immediately confirms masculine impotence.) The feminist point is that insofar as the phallus is constitutively missing—insofar, that is, as "castration" qua foreclosure is the condition of meaning and subjective coherence—women are subject to a double burden. On the one hand, they must challenge the masculine hegemony on representation; on the other hand, they cannot directly "seize the phallus," as it were. This, however, is precisely the liberal formula: it is clearly understood that the place of power is constitutively empty, so to challenge any occupant of this place is the very definition of citizenship.

Hence, after Louise kills Harlan, she continues to speak to him, saying, "You watch your mouth!" Later, Thelma cannot control her laughter as she recalls Harlan's "reaction": "Did you see the look on his face? He sure wasn't expecting *that!*" The proper object of this comment is not only Harlan, but, more urgently, Louise herself. Despite having the symbol and instrument of phallic power—the gun—in her hand, Louise does not control it. Instead, she is controlled through it by something else, something as alien as it is intimate to her. She remains in its grip a moment after firing, addressing the man she realizes she has killed. This is a full display of Louise's incoherent relation to the symbolic order. In fact, there is nothing in the film to indicate that the women ever cease to "read" the killing of Harlan from *the perspective of the liberal imaginary,* according to which power is always improperly encroaching on the beleaguered individual. This is the passage they cannot accomplish, but not because of any ideological closure wherein patriarchy has colonized all socio-symbolic space. Their fate is sealed when Louise refuses to go through Texas, because this decision prevents them from traversing their fantasmatic relation to the symbolic order by rejecting the liberal bargain.

It is thus important to differentiate the journey each woman takes from that of the other. Louise is the inadvertent instigator whose spontaneous crime automatically involves Thelma, and it is significant that Louise is the jaded one, experienced with the intricate ruses of power. Thelma initially appears as a simpleminded dupe; she does not quite know just how much of a victim she has been. Yet it is Thelma who ultimately "drives" Louise: precisely because she is jaded, Louise is incapable of imagining a different relation to power. It is Thelma, whom Harlan's assault and Louise's intervention alert to her predicament, who will commit premeditated armed robbery and say, "Something's crossed over in me. I can't go back." Henceforth, Thelma's understanding of the women's situation will control the action.

Ultimately, the incommensurability of the women's respective subjective stances at the end of the road allegorizes the rhetorical impasse. After all, why don't they simply surrender? If, as several critics note, the journey is fantasmatic, it is because this "real" journey is simultaneously Louise's fantasy, a fantasy in which she fatefully involves Thelma.[42] That is, the psychic drama in which Thelma has been conscripted is actually Louise's. This is what enables her to retain a distance toward its inexorable logic, enabling her to help Louise through it and belatedly to attempt to rewrite the inevitable final act. Nonetheless, the effort is short-circuited from the start by Louise's insistence on the detour. In effect, the women's suicide repeats rather than overcomes this founding gesture: their leap into the canyon is yet another detour. Far from saving them from the disciplinary apparatus of the juridico-symbolic order, it precludes any possibility of contesting this order's legitimacy—that is, of doing what the film as an intervention into public culture purports to do. Finally abandoning fantasy, the women manage only a limited intervention into the symbolic, in the mode of a mutual affection—an "undying" friendship—that succeeds in escaping colonization. Destined to remain utterly illegible within the diegetic world, their martyrdom can only be addressed to a viewing public as ratification of its own liberal model of rebel-citizenship.

If the true revolution is to take place at the level of representation—if it requires changing the coordinates of the symbolic order—then there is nothing about arrest that would either prevent the women from accomplishing such an act or inevitably reintegrate them within patriarchy. The conception of power conjured as the object of the film's critique demands that they misrecognize the locus and nature of their problem, as evidenced in the way the space they traverse is heavily marked by Louise's fantasy concerning the masculinity of the symbolic order. All the thumping, squirting, and pumping machinery that saturates the physical environment renders palpable Louise's projections concerning the field of power.

Indeed, the film's aesthetic strategy is central to this dimension of its conflicted feminism. The sporadic and laconic exchanges between the women do not quite suffice to account for their choices and actions, and the verbal, psychic, and physical violence to which they are subjected would not appear as effects of a *structure* of domination except as a result of the intricate visual grammar that subsumes all these elements within a more or less coherent *stylistic* system. A number of authors have commented on the tense visual style of the film: the contrast between the crowded, overstuffed interiors—reinforced by confining medium shots and close-ups—that the women leave behind (and that subsequently trap men to comedic effect) and the airy expansiveness of the road; the incongruous domination of what ought to be a natural landscape by hypermasculine objects that undercut its utopian promise; the impossibility of progress conveyed by the contrast between the expanse of the landscape in the wide frame and the diminutive scale of the women within it; the bookend device that invokes the breeziness of the travel postcard or snapshot first to foreshadow the women's tragic fate and at last to salvage hope from it. Needless to say, the same critics link these formal choices to the generic conventions the film invokes and revises and to the phallocentric psychic economy and symbolic order it forcefully critiques.

In contradistinction to the questionable coherence of the narrative, it is this system—this visual rhetoric—that elicits and supports the sort of interpretations that dominate the film's academic reception. The visually coded exhaustive saturation of the physical—and thus psychosocial—environment by signifiers of masculine prerogative renders the masculinity of those who perpetrate violence against the women symptomatic of a larger, anonymous structure that, unlike the men themselves, the women cannot escape. The repeated insertion of grim, surreal, or mysterious elements within exhilarating images—for example, the miles of electrical towers stretching beyond the expansive horizon; the eerily backlit rock formations dwarfing the Thunderbird in the desert; a bird's-eye shot of the absurdly disproportionate number of vehicles ultimately involved in the chase—underscores the psychological toll extracted by the ubiquity of patriarchy.

If the trip is a fantasy, then the mode of its signification is to be approached from Louise's vantage, insofar as her perspective functions as the proxy for women's predicament in a phallocentric order. Yet it is a vantage the audience is incoherently supposed at once to endorse and to refute. We accept it as a truth to which Louise's experience testifies. Yet the very possibility of its public articulation in the mode of social critique refutes this truth—it means the symbolic order cannot be totally saturated by masculine power, and Louise's perception must be partial. This is a "feminism" that takes back with one hand what it gives with the other.

So Louise continues to address the dead Harlan not because she fails to grasp that he is dead, but because she never fully grasped that he was alive. Insofar as she heard him speak the familiar and frightening discourse of sexist power, she never heard him speak at all. Unable to distinguish between Harlan and his discourse, she was in effect shooting his speech. Knowing full well that this target she could not have killed, the continues to address it, insisting that it "shut up." The audience is conscripted into Louise's error—we, too, are encouraged to take Harlan for a subject who really believes, or directly embodies, the discourse of masculine domination.

But this is precisely the problem. From the film's own perspective, this particular discourse is effectively "dead," in the sense that it is *no longer* socially acceptable to enunciate it. Even Harlan resorts to it despite himself. Recall that he begins by trying to seduce the women in accordance with the proper norms of civility. He knows well enough not to assume the position of one who directly speaks patriarchal privilege. In this knowledge he is the perfect counterpart to Louise, whose very suspicion of his "type" presupposes a specific relation between civility and power. For both Harlan and Louise, civility is only a mask, an alibi for underlying "true" intentions, which must be concealed inasmuch as they violate avowed social norms. This comports perfectly with those feminist accounts wherein the democratic promise of equality is a cynical ruse that sustains patriarchy under its aegis.

But why is this duplicity necessary? After all, patriarchal relations could be much more effectively guaranteed by other alibis, such as those traditionally supplied by religion and more recently by projects in the natural and social sciences. Doesn't the democratic ethos rather pressure ascriptive privilege, rendering it per se transgressive? And doesn't this pressure vitiate any ideological advantage to be gained by deploying the veil of equality? It is as if, from the moment liberal democracy announces itself, *patriarchy will have been obsolete.* If it persists, it does so *deviously,* against the explicit injunction of liberal universality. Consequently, it is not that liberalism remains secretly patriarchal, but that it *requires the undead corpse,* the *specter,* of patriarchy to retain its symbolic consistency, its ethical promise. The claim that this promise cannot be fulfilled should therefore be reformulated: what cannot transpire is the recognition that it will have been fulfilled in being postulated. What continues within liberalism is not patriarchy as such, but rather its semblance or simulacrum—not the persistence of an earlier order, but a fantasy of systematic power posited from within the liberal horizon itself as its legitimating rationale. This is what makes it necessary to announce simultaneously the end of gender inequality and the ubiquity of patriarchy. Put simply, liberal democracy would be that which renders obsolete the various forms of disempowering inequality. As such, it commits itself rhetorically to marshaling evidence of this obsolescence, which assumes spectral form: they must be defunct yet remain threatening. If the film is to succeed in its project of salvaging the liberal model, it must position Harlan as the undead relic of patriarchy, to which Louise continues to ascribe absolute authority.

Yet this requirement also exacts a diegetic price. In a telltale passage, Cathy Griggers claims:

> *Thelma and Louise,* as a form of social satire, brings to . . . its *audience's social consciousness* a spectrum of negative stereotypes of men. These . . . include the . . . domineering husband, the . . . narcissistic lover, the rapist . . . , the irresponsible but sexually attractive . . . outlaw . . . , the "officer" (a man invested in authority), the infantile but aggressive truckdriver (the public sexual-harassment offender), the cold and punitive FBI officer (a bad imago of the Father/Law), and the paternalistic Detective Slocum [*sic*]. . . . This type, the sympathetic but paternalistic authority, turns out to be the most dangerous because he believes in his own ability to "do the right thing."[43]

This gloss is exemplary in demonstrating what happens when the grammar of power obscures its rhetorical dimensions. The law might be intrusively paternalistic, but the liberal order presents itself as a *critique* of such paternalism. The privilege accorded such critique within the liberal imaginary is what makes possible this social satire in the first place. Moreover, it is central to the satire's rhetorical project to depict the law as patriarchal in order to determine citizenship as a tragic myth of permanent rebellion.

These stereotypes are not simply ways of exposing the dependence of the corresponding forms of masculine subjectivity upon the systematic subjugation of women. These men do not become comically inept in the absence of women; they are *already* inept, lacking dignity, integrity, and genuine agency. They are masculine only insofar as they live in hysterical attachment to phallic fantasy—and this is evident from the film's earliest moments, irrespective of the women's actions. These two facts—the men's impotence and its priority in relation to the women's exposure of it—enable us to understand the rhetorical function of this "social satire." The women's "revenge" cannot be understood as directed at men as more or less adequate embodiments of patriarchal law. Even the various law enforcement officers—the FBI agent, the highway patrolman, Slocombe—operate as such only through a certain irreducible excess: the first two enjoy their authority too much, while Slocombe thinks his own humanity exceeds the law's mechanical strictures. In other words, the first two rely on the law as the artificial support of, or alibi for, their fetishistic fantasies of potency, while Slocombe acquires his sense of agency by reducing the Law to the series of its specific enunciations. In effect, none of the male figures in the film is able to embody the agentive privilege supposedly granted to men under patriarchy.

Patriarchy, then, is not adequately understood if conceived exhaustively as masculine privilege. It is crucial to see that, under liberalism, we are no longer dealing with a political order in which power is legitimately distributed on the basis of gender difference, but rather with one in which gender difference is but one of a series of normatively obsolete forms of hierarchy given new life as specters—anachronistic structures deployed to produce effects determined by the new logic of power while retaining their prior appearance. Gendered inequality and sexual violence obviously persist under liberalism, but their distinct new function presupposes even as it undermines the old: their determination as indices of a hegemonic power rhetorically ensures the credibility of liberalism as a discourse of resistance. No longer a symptom of power structure, the anachronism of sexual violence ironically lends coherence to a rhetoric organized around the premise of resistance to such structures.

This anachronism simultaneously supports a specific form of ideological dissimulation. Political energy is constantly directed at surpassing these outmoded, outrageous inequalities in the name of democracy, a gesture that sustains both the promise of liberalism and the alienation of political agency. When liberalism reflexively posits the emptiness of power, an essential misrecognition disappears: acknowledgment of the absence of any noncontingent principle legitimating the existing order amounts to the disintegration of this order. What is routinely glossed as "Kafka-esque" about modern legal bureaucracy is its diabolical arbitrariness—the palpable absence of any necessary bond among its demands, gestures, and procedures—which imposes onto the subject herself the burden of positing this bond. This is why the bureaucratic subject is always guilty: completing the juridical order, he or she becomes responsible for its efficacy.

Accordingly, when Louise refuses to go through Texas, it is not simply because of what happened to her there or because of her fear, however legitimate, of getting caught by the hypersexist Texas authorities. Whatever their merits, both reasons serve as alibis for another fear: the dawning awareness that omnipotent patriarchy is a fiction disguising the absence of authoritative order. This is the real reason Louise shoots Harlan: her act retroactively transforms Thelma's rape into an instance of symptomatic, rather than arbitrary, violence. This is why killing him *makes her guilty* in a double sense—on the one hand, it legitimates the law's pursuit of her and Thelma, imputing to it fearsome authority; on the other hand, it links Louise's agency to the effectivity of the symbolic order. We see the consequence of this at the film's conclusion, when the histrionic impotence of patriarchy has become evident. The impasse the women reach is also double: on the one hand, there is the violent response they have succeeded in provoking from the law; on the other hand, there is their own agency in having provoked it. The former serves as the final alibi of the latter: "Let's not get caught" finally means "Let's not acknowledge the impotence of the symbolic order." Death is far preferable to subjective destitution, but for this very reason it fails to rise to the dignity of a transformative political act.

Thus media responses that denounce the film's militancy, far from constituting a "backlash," tacitly cooperate in its nostalgic project of "returning" to a more reassuring form of struggle. The assertion that the film "goes too far" amounts to a call for a return to the imaginary time when "moral sentiments" could legitimately be deployed as the measure of justice. In this, critics are in full agreement with the protagonists. At the same time, the women's insistence—even in the course of their own violence—on respecting the rules of civility protracts the tradition of subjecting positive law to extrapolitical ethical precepts. The insistence on maintaining the appearance of appearance is a gesture destined to consolidate the fantasy of "the *man* behind the curtain."

To secure this basic claim concerning the inscrutable recalcitrance of patriarchy, the film must legitimate Louise's shooting of Harlan. As we have seen, it does so, first, by casting Harlan as vulgar and uncivil, cuing audience dis-identification. The generic category of "patriarchy" is instantiated by a particular figure of inferior status, and this is necessary in order simultaneously to secure the metonymic representation (Harlan embodies a genuine feature of patriarchal discourse) and to legitimate the shooting (for the audience as well as in narrative terms). Second, by casting as constitutive a particular rhetorical ruse of patriarchal discourse: Harlan approaches the women through a redneck version of the chivalric code, which Louise correctly identifies as a lure designed to facilitate and justify the subsequent assault, itself staged as a good-faith effort to recoup the sublimatory "investment" of patiently following the rules in pursuit of that which Harlan perceives as an entitlement.

Staging the encounter between Harlan and the women in this way, the narrative effaces the moment of decision involved in Louise's act of violence. As a number of conservative critics eagerly pointed out, the shooting is unjustified. From the perspective of the narrative, however, the choice is not entirely, or even sufficiently, her own. As a rape victim, as Thelma's loyal friend, under duress and provoked by an act of hate speech she knows to be tacitly legitimated by a broader social and juridical logic of which it is an index, Louise is *compelled* to pull the trigger. Despite the politically unpalatable fact that to legitimate her act it would be necessary to discount her agentivity, a legitimating account might actually succeed in court. Conversely, we are to sympathize with Louise precisely insofar as her hand is forced by the diabolical cunning of patriarchy, and our sympathy is essential to justify the women's subsequent flight from the law. They cannot risk a juridical procedure because the deck is stacked against them from the start. But if there is any way to mitigate Louise's culpability without sheer deception, it would be by reference to "diminished capacity."[44] However, the narrative must at all costs forestall the implication of "diminished capacity" for female agency. Hence the rhetorical conundrum: Louise is justified in her shooting insofar as Harlan instantiates a patriarchal discourse in the face of which she is impotent; yet the claim of impotence is her best chance to avoid punishment by patriarchal law. At the same time, her act counts as *resistance* only insofar as it is in some important sense deliberate. We sympathize with her because Harlan—and patriarchal discourse—*deserves* it.

The narrative thus both *presupposes* and *disavows* Louise's responsibility for this act. Responsibility is essential to legitimate the *killing:* as one who voices and embodies the authoritative prerogative of patriarchal violence, Harlan *should* be killed, and this "should" has the force of an ethical injunction that in turn entails subjective responsibility—*someone* ought to shoot the vile cretin; "we" in the audience would do it if we could, and enjoy a modicum of vindication when Louise does. Yet responsibility for the *act* must be removed from Louise's shoulders, so that it can be traced to patriarchy itself. This rationalization is compulsory, insofar as it instantiates and sustains one of the narrative's central claims—the idea that patriarchy has insinuated itself into the very fabric of the symbolic order in a way that effaces any meaningful distinction between the speech of a particular male and the entire régime of legal representation. This is why Louise feels provoked in the first place: what she *accurately* recognizes in Harlan's "Suck my cock!" is not simply his *own* bilious sexism but the authorizing reverberations of an entire political structure. And *this* structure she does mean to kill. The paradox of agency is here on full display. We endorse Louise's act insofar as we concede the closure of the patriarchal symbolic order, but in so doing we must overlook this act's status as an *act,* by definition irreducible to its causal determination.

This is important because already discernible here, in the moment that inaugurates the narrative and sets the terms of its development and the horizon of its critique, is a kind of self-subversion of the critical procedure associated with Lacanian psychoanalysis. Since commentators repeatedly extol the film for deploying this mode of critique, and for articulating it nimbly in narrative form, this self-subversion indicates an inherent limit of the theoretical framework underpinning this mode, a limit that coincides with the reduction of rhetoric to "language," of the metadiscourse of citizenship to a mechanical grammar of power.

It seems that, in order to generate the women's predicament, the film must pass through—in order to disavow—a moment of genuine agency. A moment of decision is ineluctable: it demonstrates not that the women are deluded in attributing diabolical power to patriarchy, but that a belief in the devious coherence of power is itself ineluctable. Within the film's rhetorical scheme, "patriarchy" secures this belief. Hence the fact that Louise's act entails an irreducible moment of decision raises the question of her own investment in the patriarchal order. Yes, she tries to kill it; yet she knows that this is impossible. She may even suspect that the discourse of patriarchy is *virtually* dead, anachronistic, transgressive of avowed norms. This discourse cannot be killed not because it has successfully colonized the symbolic order, but because this order is structured around the liberal conception of power as an empty place. The women's belief in patriarchy has the virtue of lending this order the appearance of necessity; it seems to name this order's secret operator. By contrast, liberalism's rhetoric of opposition to necessity seems to destabilize any grammar in which to ground agency. It is in order to restore her subjection as a condition of her agentivity that Louise shoots the presumptively dead discourse voiced by Harlan. By annihilating, momentarily, the self-evident facticity of its death, Louise resurrects the specter of patriarchy in relation to which the women can attempt to negotiate a measure of autonomy.

This elucidates the necessity of continuing to observe the strictures of civility. Surely, as outlaws by virtue of their gender, the women are free to dispense with politeness. Indeed, codified courtesy should now appear distasteful to them, insofar as they can no longer escape the recognition that solicitude is part of the patriarchal stratagem. This apparently inexplicable wish to continue belonging to the already distorted category of "humanity," which, thanks to both Harlan and Slocombe, they *know* prefigures them as second-class citizens, is not simply an instance of camp deployed to deconstruct gender categories; it indicates the need to secure the illusion that some coordinating principle of social membership—that is, *citizenship*—stands behind it.[45] Civility implies a *reason* to be civil: it is the locus of the social bond, the discursive materialization of social totality.[46] The idea that this contract is patriarchal both consolidates its efficacy and promotes rebellious dis-identification as the proper stance with respect to it—that is, liberal citizenship.

The women's friendship must therefore be reconsidered. Insofar as Louise conscripts Thelma into her fantasy, the women function as each other's points of transference. Louise will teach Thelma the "truth" about the patriarchal symbolic order; Thelma will make sure the women never risk direct confrontation with the absence of symbolic efficiency. The women's friendship is the matrix of the confusion regarding the relationship between the film's homoerotic subtext and its politically ambivalent manifest text. In its appropriation of genre conventions, the film appears to continue the tradition of determining citizenship as rebellion, so that the women's friendship is to be read in terms of political solidarity and their death as the tragedy of a thwarted utopian hope. Such a thoroughly liberal reading deploys friendship to imagine an alternative principle of community, one that is only reluctantly and indirectly political. Accordingly, critics consistently point out that, in opposition to Hollywood norms, the film "exalts the friendship between its heroines and places their intimate relationship squarely at the center of the narrative"; that in this way "their friendship takes precedence over men, effectively subverting patriarchal containment"; and that consequently their political exemplarity consists chiefly in the fact that they "leave femininity, rely on friendship, and achieve fearlessness."[47]

We are then left to wonder if the diegetic and rhetorical inadequacy of friendship as a political strategy is due to the intractability of patriarchy within liberalism or to the trope of rebel-citizenship itself. In the alternative, read through an appropriation of Butler's theoretical work, the women's friendship seems to encode an illegitimate form of desire that disturbs the smooth functioning of the ideological edifice almost by its very existence. Yet in order to attribute political efficacy to this figure of lesbian friendship, it is necessary to read the film's ending teleologically as a symbolic victory—despite the women's death and the absence of any subsequent change in the heterosexist order. These two perspectives, in turn, intersect in symptomatically aporetic readings of the film to produce the thoroughly ambivalent image of female friendship as a latent form of agency that is somehow both powerful and impotent, both beyond the frontiers of the symbolic order and concealed within them. Owing to a certain cunning of liberalism, for the critical perspectives thematized by the film, friendship as a model of revolutionary politics is a dead end.

Circumventing the Critical Cul-de-Sac

Reception of the film that confines its focus to the problem of gender misses the wider implications of the political project shaping the film, which consists in disarticulating phallocentrism from liberalism and recuperating the latter's antipolitical conception of citizenship. The correspondence between the film's rhetoric and the critical strategies organizing its reception suggests that a revision of our understanding of the former should raise questions regarding the adequacy of the latter. To the extent that the film is treated as a popular articulation of current feminist critique, the limits of this articulation indicate corresponding limits of the critical strategies governing the film's rhetoric. The rhetoric of friendship to which the film has recourse facilitates the production of feminism as a liberal politics of resistance and dissent.

The antipolitical stance promulgated by liberal discourse as an elementary part of its solution to the paradox of democratic governance conditions both the rhetorical form and the very possibility of feminist politics, since the figure of the rebel-citizen encodes less a set of normative features or rules of conduct than a disposition toward structures of power without which even resolutely antiliberal (say, socialist) feminism is rhetorically handicapped. This disposition is advocated but also directly performed by the circulation of popular fictions of friendship whose function is to enact the interrogatory gap between the presumptively liberal public and various forms of authority that these narratives depict. That is, liberal rhetoric is not reducible to a particular enunciated content—or, as Brown has it, a lexicon—subject to logical strictures of systematic coherence and noncontradiction; it is an ongoing project that mobilizes diverse modes of enunciation for which the apparently irreconcilable impulses (such as a public commitment to equality and simultaneous practices of subordination) function as culturally and politically productive resources.

For these reasons, politically driven cultural criticism cannot afford to neglect the way liberal discourse operates rhetorically to underwrite and overdetermine the antagonistic struggles taking place in liberal public culture—including those, such as feminism, that seem or purport to undermine its very foundations. Such struggles require attention to and nuanced understanding of liberalism's rhetorical efficacy—that is, of the way it both appears to solve complex problems of democratic cooperation and succeeds in securing its solution as contingent, elective and, precisely, democratic. Insofar as the liberal project reflexively deploys critique to posit its own presuppositions, distinctions, and discursive logics, identifying and examining popular articulations of (say, feminist) critique can only be the beginning, not the end, of cultural investigation and political intervention.

Among the achievements consistently attributed to *Thelma & Louise* is its sophistication in registering in impressive detail the hegemonic colonization by patriarchal discourse of the socio-semiotic field, including especially cultural and juridical norms of representation and legibility. Yet such a view, clearly operating in the film and widely shared by its academic interpreters, posits another hegemony—that of linguistic structure over rhetorical dynamics. The error here is double: the critical indifference to the rhetoric of liberalism reappears in a homologous obliviousness to the rhetorical dimensions of the narrative. Yet the whole conundrum according to which power inheres in a signifying structure that confronts recalcitrant subjects desperately seeking emancipation from the very conditions of their social existence arises in the context of reflexive modernity and its emergent political imaginary. In such an account, rhetoric arrives belatedly on the scene as a set of techniques mobilized to undo the constraints imposed at the level of linguistic structure; the constitutive role of rhetoric in organizing both this structure and its account of itself is largely forgotten until the last possible moment, when it returns, in the mode of deus ex machina, to trouble in highly ambivalent fashion theretofore unproblematic elements of a diabolical symbolic order. Nor are the implications of rhetoric's return and intervention in the very premises of structure ever permitted to trouble the initial account itself.

This drama of power and resistance, however, is *itself* a rhetorical account—one powerfully reiterated by *Thelma & Louise*—the effect of which is to produce a strategic determination of politics and agency that would legitimate the liberal scheme. Having observed the rhetoric of citizenship as friendship central to this scheme, the limits of republican and communitarian critiques of liberalism and those of psychoanalytic feminist critiques of power should be clear. Taking liberalism seriously as a rhetorical project means, among other things, recognizing its status as the political imaginary of reflexive modernity. The implications of reflexivity for liberalism is the subject of the next chapter, which takes up the problem of social reflexivity as an inherent limit of the liberal imaginary in the context of an analysis of Sophia Coppola's *Lost in Translation*. If, as we have seen, liberalism determines citizenship in opposition to impersonal and imposing forms of power, it is in order to secure the notional supervisory independence of citizens in regard to the very social field to which they belong. Both communitarian and feminist rhetorics reproduce this imaginary relation between private subjects and anonymous social and institutional structures without seriously troubling the rhetoric responsible for producing and maintaining this relation. Yet what this rhetoric thereby encodes is the reflexive self-observation of modern social forms. If communitarian and feminist discourses themselves belong to this reflexive schema, *Lost in Translation* reveals how neo-Marxist and postmodernist critiques of globalizing capitalism emerge as symptomatic of reflexivity's self-undermining effects. Among the key implications of the film is that if there is a limit to the rhetoric of liberalism, it will surface as a consequence of this rhetoric's efficacy.

4
Liberalism, Friendship, and the Predicament of Cybernetic Sociality
Lost in Translation

> An individual in the modern sense is someone who can observe his or her own observing. And whoever fails to understand this intuitively or is not made aware of this by his or her therapist can read novels and project them onto the self—as "uno, nessuno, e centomila."
>
> —Niklas Luhmann

A basic premise of cultural critique is the conceptual, practical, and political utility of reflexive observation on the societal scale—that is, the notion that greater knowledge and better understanding of the historical, contextual, structural, ideological, institutional, economic, technological, discursive, and other parameters of a problematic sociopolitical situation are necessary conditions for effective and justifiable intervention to be undertaken from within that situation by those enmeshed in it. This premise is that of modernity itself, insofar as modernization is the project of submitting social processes to more or less direct social control, mediated by publicly circulating social knowledge and large-scale institutions and technologies. As the dominant political form of cybernetic modernity, liberal democracy necessarily shares modernity's premises, which is why it construes citizenship as both reflexively oriented and skeptically disposed. Understood from this perspective, the liberal trope of rebel-citizenship analyzed in the context of *Thelma & Louise* corresponds to the distinctively modern valorization of social critique—typically manifested as dissent or resistance—over other possible models, such as the collective advocacy of concrete demands, phronesis, the cultivation of civic virtue, deliberative reasoning, rational planning, direct participation, and so on. The "contingent" popular figure of the rebel-citizen in effect actualizes a structural necessity: it mediates the public performance of reflexive social critique that constitutes the modern scheme of social cooperation, whose political form is liberalism. Simply put, as mutually contingent instances of social critique, academic cultural analysis and the film's representation and enactment of liberal citizenship share a basic investment in reflexivity as a definitive presupposition of social cooperation.

Yet this structural reflexivity of liberal modernity, so effective in responding to various political critiques and rival options, itself produces a paradox: the more thoroughly society is socialized, the more it acquires the features of what some have called "postmodernity." Whether understood as a distinctive new form of society as "spectacle," as the collapse of an older metaphysical framework, the disintegration of symbolic efficiency, or as the emergence of "hyperreality," the litany of problems imputed to this state of affairs can be traced back to a sort of "short-circuit" wherein (social) reality and its (popular or expert) representation can no longer be distinguished. While this state of affairs is itself often represented as a historical, affective, or cognitive "loss," the problem it poses for modern—and liberal-democratic—reflexivity is that it undermines the central epistemic premise underpinning the liberal imaginary. As a society's reflexive grasp of its own processes comes to influence those processes, it loses its value as knowledge. Insofar as observation consists essentially in making distinctions, the disintegration of the distinction between the observer and the object observed amounts to the loss of the capacity to observe.[1]

This loss does not, however, eventuate in mere ignorance or blindness; on the contrary, it comes to produce effects of déjà vu.[2] To the degree that knowledge about social life precedes and partakes in the determination of social experiences themselves, these increasingly take on the appearance of half-remembered or already-encountered moments, not unlike television reruns.[3] The analysis of such "hyperreal" experiences is by now familiar—even, as it were, passé. But the political implications of "simulation" have not been adequately understood, since the contentious debate regarding "postmodernity" was extensively shaped by the disciplinary, theoretical, and polemical commitments of its various participants. To be sure, the theory of simulation is in important ways implausible and, if taken as a literal description of the state of social life, perhaps counterproductive if not downright irresponsible. But read as a figure for the predicament of reflexivity, simulation powerfully thematizes a fundamental impasse of modernity as a project of social reflexivization.

Reflexivity itself has, of course, been subjected to vigorous critique in recent decades. Most of this critique has been concerned to specify its various limits: for Marxisms old and new, the mode of production remains opaque or indifferent to analysis; for psychoanalysis, the subject and the socius involve dimensions inherently unavailable to reflective consciousness; for anthropology and sociology, practice unavoidably remains oblivious to the level of structure even as structure fails to govern fully the practices it facilitates; for postmodernism and antifoundationalism, no amount of reflexivity can produce a complete and coherent account of social life, which is riddled by irreducible heterogeneity, difference, antagonism, incommensurability, untranslatability, and other forces of divergence; for deconstruction, reflexivity names a metaphysical or foundationalist fantasy of transparency in the service of politically dangerous, ethically suspect, and conceptually vexed ambitions of mastery. In short, these attacks on what Habermas has called "the unfinished project" of modernity focus on demonstrating its inherent impossibility and suspect political aspirations.

However, some so-called postmodernists (for example, Debord, Baudrillard, Jameson), as well as some of their opponents in sociology and systems theory, have for some time been pointing to a different limit of reflexivity—that of proliferating recursive self-reference. For Baudrillard, reflexivity succeeds only too well, producing a hyperreal régime of simulation in which sign and referent, image and reality, the object world and the mode of its production become indistinguishable.[4] For sociologists of modernity, reflexivity engenders a series of paradoxes. For Anthony Giddens, the systematic application of expert knowledge to technical social processes begins to produce the very problems it was supposed to solve.[5] For Niklas Luhmann, the self-reference of social systems leads them to become caught in paradoxes of self-observation, forever unearthing what they themselves have buried.[6]

From this vantage, if the critique of modernity's Cartesian epistemology has freed critics to pursue the politics of discourse and representation, it has done so at a price. For cultural critique is deeply invested in the project and politics of reflexivity. In effect, denying that full reflexive knowledge and control are possible releases us from the responsibility to examine our own steadfast, if tacit, investment in the project of critical social analysis and consequent intervention. It remains for us to concede that our theories and analyses are inherently limited, and we are free to pursue them as we always have, compensating only by a sort of perfunctory modesty regarding our aspirations and claims. Yet what is it that we *do* as critical scholars of culture? Do we not *reflect* on the discourses and practices we construe as objects of analysis? And do we not do so with more or less *cybernetic* and *democratic* aims in mind? Is not our very place in academe the product of the Enlightenment project whose possibility and dubious politics we (sometimes) claim to dispute? Do we not effectively advance this project even in the course of—indeed, by means of—disputing it?[7]

The answer hinges on whether this project is inherently and irremediably metaphysical or foundationalist; that is, whether in the end it is committed to mastery or totalization.[8] But reflexivity is a process; even if it is pursued with the impossible or objectionable aim of mastery, it operates nonetheless as the very principle of social life. Moreover, as Castoriadis and Luhmann have argued, the project of social *autopoiesis* is neither automatically Cartesian nor irreparably imperialist.[9] Indeed, some of the harshest critics of the Enlightenment, such as Foucault, have themselves turned to forms of reflexivity as the basis of a more palatable form of life. Simply put, the cultural disciplines' commitment to a more democratic future is firmly grounded in the modern project of socializing society. To dismiss reflexivity *tout court* as an ill-fated ruse is to expose democratic politics to the risk of utter incoherence. Nor, as a practical matter, can it be dismissed, inasmuch as the value of reflexivity is ceaselessly thematized in, among other places, the cultural public sphere—itself a privileged site of social self-observation.[10]

In sum, the premise and project of reflexivity survive both the critique of Enlightenment reason and their elision or sequestration by critical cultural studies. And reflexivity returns to impose itself both as an unthought limit to critical practice and as a cultural object demanding and even reflexively miming such practice.[11] Specifically, in recent years, the problem of reflexivity has emerged with considerable urgency within the cultural public sphere in the guise of anxiety regarding simulacra. In particular, a growing series of Hollywood films has taken up the régime of simulation as a prominent theme. Numerous examples include *Groundhog Day* (1993), *The Truman Show* (1998), *Dark City* (1998), *The Matrix* (1999), *Fight Club* (1999), *Ghost World* (2001), and *Minority Report* (2002). Among the most interesting in the present context is Sophia Coppola's *Lost in Translation* (2003), a film that takes up the paradoxically disabling effects of reflexivization and proposes a nuanced response figured, again, by friendship. It thus offers a valuable (and inevitably "reflexive") case study of the limits of cultural critique as a mode of political cybernetics.

The simulacrum is not simply the expression of capitalism's fantasy of omnipotent autonomy,[12] but a symptom of a social imaginary so thoroughly constituted by reflexivity that it must refuse all positive content, treating it as utterly contingent, transient, and therefore merely vestigial or supplemental.[13] Insofar as it is self-annulling, then, the simulacrum marks the place where this imaginary, including the public sphere, the market economy, and liberal democracy, encounters its own internal limit. The aim of self-production is pointless exactly to the degree that it is realized: if the market system could break loose of producers and/or consumers, it would no longer make sense for it to address itself to them, or even to retain them as vestigial supplements always threatening to usurp or disrupt it; if liberalism could produce a subject that is nothing but the infinite self-distance of the Cartesian cogito—or the purely abstract agent without positive qualities occupying the Rawlsian original position—it would thereby obviate the citizen whose normative autonomy legitimates the liberal order.[14] By the same token, the project of social critique, insofar as it fully subscribes to the paradigm of reflexivity, must confront in the simulacrum the structural figure of its own epistemological and political limit.[15] To the degree *Lost in Translation* promises but unavoidably evades this confrontation, it raises the question of whether any other option is discernable.

Bob Harris (Bill Murray), a fifty-something American action movie star on the downward slope of his career, is in Tokyo to shoot a series of Suntory whiskey commercials for $2 million. Charlotte (Scarlett Johansson), a twenty-five-year-old Yale graduate in philosophy hesitantly evaluating her career options, is tagging along with her husband, a rising young showbiz photographer shooting a band in Japan. Bob and Charlotte find themselves mostly alone at the Park Hyatt, combating isolation and anomie. Neither one is able to sleep and it is by no means clear that jet lag is the cause of their palpable restiveness and discomfort. They are both literally and figuratively out of place, estranged not only from their temporary surroundings but no less from their own lives. Bob is married with two children, and whenever he speaks to his wife by phone, it is distressingly clear that he's a virtual interloper in his own family. Charlotte accompanied her husband, John (Giovanni Ribisi), all the way to Japan, but she finds the distance between them growing even during the few moments when he's not away on location. While Bob contemplates the irredeemable price of his career success, Charlotte broods anxiously at the ineluctable prospect of choosing a career to pursue.

After a couple fleeting near encounters, Charlotte chats Bob up in the hotel bar, and the two begin a casual, oblique flirtation. Initially eager to get out of Tokyo, Bob changes his plans in order to stay a few extra days. The two venture out of the hotel together, barhop with John and Charlotte's local acquaintances, visit a strip club and sing karaoke, and even sleep through the better part of a night in the same bed. Just when it seems that marriage to others is the sole obstacle to an overt romance between them, Bob accepts an overture from the hotel's middle-aged American lounge singer, permitting himself to be discovered by Charlotte the next morning. Shaken but without legitimate grounds to protest, Charlotte assaults Bob with caustic remarks during their lunch later in the day, and he responds in kind. The rift between them persists until the next—and final—night, when a hotel fire alarm brings them out into the street. Since no romantic relationship now seems to have been possible between them, in retrospect Bob's "betrayal" appears inconsequential, and the two opt for friendship instead. The next day, they say good-bye in the hotel lobby and Bob departs. Riding out of the city, he sees Charlotte in the street, asks the driver to stop, and chases her down for a final farewell. Whispering something in her ear, he kisses her forehead, and she smiles. He gets back in the car and rides toward the airport as the soundtrack plays the Jesus and Mary Chain's "Just Like Honey."[16]

Déjà Vu All Over Again

The film plunges the audience into the disconcerting enigma of simulation from the very start, when, immediately after the brief title sequence, we see Bob in the back of a limousine riding through the Tokyo evening toward his hotel. The scene cuts between angled close-ups of Bob's tired, incredulous face and point-of-view shots of a wall of neon-clad buildings. The overwhelming and chaotic array of colors blends the façades into one endless and incoherent billboard saturating the frame and extending beyond it upward and to the horizon, creating a hypnotic sense of bewilderment. In a slow point-of-view pan of a fragment of this wall, Bob sees a giant billboard image of himself holding up a glass of Suntory whiskey, an image he will encounter more than once. He rubs his jetlagged eyes, as if in the grip of déjà vu. Indeed, the experience of déjà vu aptly captures the mundane uncanniness of this encounter, insofar as it reflects the fundamental cognitive structure of the régime of simulation. In effect, this régime endows all experience with the structure of déjà vu, a malfunction of memory wherein phenomenal temporality collapses and the present, past, and future appear to coincide. This experiential temporal confusion corresponds to a structural one: it is impossible to determine the order of cause and effect, as well as whether one's own actions generate, or are themselves generated as, effects. From this moment on, Bob will repeatedly confront himself as a commodified image, a pure simulacrum without ground in anything outside the global mediatic code of consumption. The film studiously delineates the entailments of Bob's paradoxical predicament as a professional simulator whose successful self-production coincides with an almost total self-alienation.

Most immediately, to Suntory, Bob is literally a valuable commodity. Though his career is past its peak, the endless recycling of Hollywood fare has meant that his visibility remains transnational. It has helped that his peculiar gift is an expressive yet enigmatic, almost illegible face endowed with a certain malleable, self-distant, abstract affectivity—like a mask capable of changing expression without ceasing to appear masklike. Bob's face is, for this reason, a perfect icon for a product that is already a glibly incoherent yet banal cultural hybrid, the meaning and social function of which can in no way be triangulated by reference to its actual North Atlantic and Asian etiologies but is fully an artifact of their exhaustive commodification. Fittingly, his task is to embody the mythical American-ness borrowed from Hollywood films so as retroactively to endow the Japanese brand with the fictive foreign cachet demanded by the "local" market. To this end, the art director, haughtily oblivious to the farcical absurdity of the TV spot he is filming, incongruously demands that Bob deliver the tag line, "For relaxing times, make it Suntory time," with "More intensity!" No clearer demonstration could be made of Bob's predicament: as a living commodity, he is enjoined to personify convincingly an impossible, self-contradictory image derived entirely from a virtual system of representations obviously unconnected to any frame of reference other than the one they themselves comprise.

To underscore the disorienting effect of this injunction, the director delivers his instructions rapidly and garrulously, but the translator renders them with incongruous brevity, leaving Bob perplexed as to his actual task and to the true substance and tone of his interaction with the director. Visibly disconcerted, he must decipher what his Japanese employers actually require of him. But the failure of communication is not the result of incommensurable linguistic or cultural difference; on the contrary, he soon realizes that what they want is a series of media clichés: as they move on to shooting the still photos for print ads, the art director invokes the Rat Pack as the model he wants Bob to emulate, which Bob does with hilarious deadpan precision. The director then moves on to James Bond films, committing the ultra-square error of specifying the prototype of Roger Moore rather than the "original," Sean Connery. What at first deceptively appears as a problem of intercultural translation turns out to be nothing of the sort: the global, transcultural archive of endlessly circulating simulacra provides an already shared vocabulary of fictional, de-territorialized clichés that Bob himself had a hand in producing earlier in his career. It is in this perverse sense that he is an "authentic," and thus valuable, icon.

Among the film's most instructive ironies is that Bob's apparently exceptional status as a media artifact actually renders him prototypical of subjects caught in the self-referential régime of simulation. The "translation" being registered here is the one elucidated by Guy Debord: in the society of the spectacle, the laboring subject's fate of total commodification meshes seamlessly with the apotheosis of the commodity as mass image.[17] The theoretical account of this transition is a familiar one. During capital's earlier stages, the expropriation of surplus value required the active complicity of the laboring subject, whose belief in capital's legitimacy had to be sustained by means of ideology. Today, this belief has assumed the form of a self-sustaining spectacle that involves the subject in a way that does not require any particular attitude or disposition. For example, as a movie star, Bob is simultaneously a commodity sold and the vehicle selling a commodity. Inexorably, this commodity and this vehicle coincide as Bob's image, so that Bob himself is nothing but a kind of prosthesis. His subjective bearing is not in any way implicated in the process in which he is caught; hence his absolute alienation from it. The Suntory gig only brings this fact into sharper focus: as a celebrity spokesperson, his function is to embody the image of an image—a virtual mediatic universe without bottom or reference to anything outside itself.[18] Bob's image—his iconic, ubiquitous, plastic, *detached* face—is the only indexical link in this signifying chain, charged with arresting the movement of reference only because Bob "is there," an empirical person whose face the image conscripts.

Yet its indexicality marks the fact that Bob's face is itself only an effect of simulation: it is the global circulation of his (always modeled) image that retroactively posits his countenance as the referent securing its representation. Bob's burden is to be the bearer of this image, which attaches to him irrespective of his subjective relation to it. His face is not his own, and he has no consequential say in how it is inscribed within the spectacle that goes on, as it were, by means of him but without him. It is in this sense that Bob is the prototypical subject of global late capital, in which he is included *by being excluded*. This is why nostalgia is a structural feature of simulation: it is not an aftereffect to be addressed via the magic of ideological distortion, but the anachronizing engine of the image economy itself. Bob's empirical "authenticity" must be continually posited to secure the smooth functioning of the simulation, so that "Bob" is a medium of a nostalgic reference to a "lost" reality whether Bob experiences nostalgic desire or not. Even Bob's nostalgia for authenticity does not belong to him, is not a feature of his psyche as such; it is inscribed within the simulacrum as its inherent abstraction, its tediously conspicuous status as a replica or mere placeholder for the missing "real thing."

It is tempting to interpret Bob's dilemma exclusively as a familiar instance of capitalist alienation. The standard thesis is that capitalism commodifies labor itself, effectively transforming people who work into pure means to the ends of capital. As a celebrity, Bob is uniquely positioned to encounter his own commodity status as an objective reality, as well as to confront the audience with this reality. However, apart from the well-known limits of this particular critique of capital, such a reading would still have to take into account the film's explicitly critical stance toward capitalism, a stance that would be difficult to explain coherently in light of the film's own status as a commodity. After all, if capital nonchalantly and profitably produces and circulates searing indictments of its own processes, it is incoherent to claim that these are sustained by means of ideological distortion. And since they are clearly not sustained by sheer force or coercion, one is left to wonder why a system openly and universally acknowledged to be so thoroughly deleterious is permitted to remain in place—and even to turn a profit by staging attacks on itself as casual entertainment.

More to the point, however, this sort of reading begs the question of commodification itself. What, after all, is a commodity? It is worth recalling here that commodities are not exclusive to capitalism, as Marx himself points out. The problem with the commodity highlighted in the film has less to do with the reduction of people to mere means and more to do with the formulaic reduction of all social interaction and symbolic activity to mere cliché. In other words, it is not only that everything is converted into a product for profitable sale, but that in modernity everything is from the start produced according to reflexively generated protocols whose primary function is to sustain social systems without regard to the "members" of society themselves.[19] Again, the profitable circulation of commodities does not in itself constitute a capitalist order, and it certainly leaves open the possibility of uncommodified social existence. The commodity is to be understood as an exemplary case of a structural principle. Thus Bob's problem is not only that he must make himself available for sale, but also that his function as a media commodity is to sustain a fully simulated reality that includes him only by excluding him. Accordingly, the Tokyo we encounter is a replica of itself, reflexively produced for transnational consumption in accordance with marketing models, globally circulating media images, and other forms of cultural and sociological data and expertise. In addition to its implication with capitalism, this mode of self-production is typical of cybernetic late modernity, wherein the project of socializing society has, in large part but not solely by way of commodification, apparently reached its apogee.

Lost in Simulation

In sum, Bob's alienation is not fully explicable by reference to Marx's thesis regarding the commodification of labor. That is, Bob is not simply nostalgic for some sort of reunification with his authentic self, with his agentive spontaneity, or with his species-being. Exactly like his face, the nostalgia is outside, belonging to the very (im)materiality of the object-world of simulacra. Within this world, the iterability of Bob's image—and ergo that of all simulacra—posits the metaphysics of origin as a vestigial supplement, which Bob is condemned to embody. Because it is *reflexively postulated public knowledge* that the meaning of this image is an effect of an abstract code (programmed in advance according to marketing models and intertextual references to other media images), this image is able to promise escape from this code. The fantasy of authenticity, of nonalienation, of indexical reference, is the very product of simulation. This is why nostalgia is neither a misguided, retrograde *reaction* to capitalist alienation nor the misrecognized utopian repository of resistance, but a structural feature of the "postmodern" spectacle.

This insight is reflected in the film's aesthetic strategy, which differs notably from other Hollywood allegories of postmodernity. Though basically a romance or even romantic comedy, the film lacks a strong narrative drive: plotted chronologically but possessing only an amorphous, latent fabula, the narrative offers little discernible motivation to link the progression of scenes, relying largely on rhyming effects among unfolding situations, set pieces, and moods. Accordingly, each scene is meticulously composed, framed, and lit, emphasizing the moment over its place in a temporal sequence and heightening the somewhat misleading sense of disconnection among discrete events. The understated—though, in retrospect, carefully crafted—story seems to evolve by happenstance as much as by protagonist action. The leisurely, rhythmic editing pace alternates between languid, quiet takes bordering on still photographs and small bursts of faster cuts, often leaving it unclear how much time events take or how much has elapsed in between. A muted, often blue-gray color palette, matched by an ethereal soundtrack, combines with the nebulous plot and editing to produce the senses of allusiveness and latency that confer on the film its nostalgic tone. It is this ephemeral aesthetic and the elliptical quality it ascribes to the profilmic reality that take the place of the tight plotting usually associated with romance or melodrama and that become a major force driving the narrative. It is neither the protagonists' aims, nor a particular obstacle to them, but rather the very situation of pervasive, inarticulate loss itself that initially propels the story. Formally, what are "lost" are narrative motivation and sensory clarity, and thus the possibility of orienting oneself spatially or temporally within the narrative world. We are here in a permanent present extending in every direction but lacking any means of propulsion, and this lack appears as an effect of the omnivorous, confining, but nonetheless indistinct and autonomous character of hyperreality.

This artificial, reflexively produced, and thus constitutively alien world haunts Bob on his transnational adventure in a way that annihilates "home" as a habitable fantasy. A hilariously emphatic metaphor of this process is the way Bob is hounded from the moment of his arrival in the Park Hyatt by carpet swatches and faxes from his wife related to the remodeling of his study back in L.A. The study, of course, is one of those peculiarly excessive spaces inside the home supposed to denote domesticity itself. One of its key functions is to sustain the fantasy of "home" as sanctuary in the midst of a dwelling that itself never fully attains this status, insofar as it is endlessly invaded, transected, and organized by publicly circulating discourses, objects, practices, and demands. Indeed, the concerted effort to materialize an authentically personal domestic environment out of commodities scrupulously designed for this purpose is inherently self-defeating. It thus re-marks the impossibility of actually living out this domesticity, which can only be signified, and positions the home's occupant as external to the home—its generic owner *rather than* its particular dweller. The various commodities enlisted in the project of signifying domesticity as a fantasy suturing "home" as such—carpeting, paint, fabrics, books never meant to be read, decorative knickknacks, and so on—play the double, contradictory role of producing and undermining this fantasy. As reflexive production according to statistical models and technical protocols, commodification is what de-domesticates the home, transforming it into an abstract signifier of a state of being that is immediately thereby foreclosed. The study, of course, is a space without function in capitalist culture. It is for this reason that it can represent the promise of autotelic leisure that capitalism proffers in order more effectively to solicit labor and consumption as voluntary, autogenic activities.

Home, it will have turned out, named not a place or a way of life but the very imaginary procedure by means of which something like a place or way of life in their particularity could be stabilized (or "reified"). It is no coincidence, no mere plot device, that home's return is allegorized by travel abroad, to a foreign land that turns out to be not foreign at all. Alienation does not transpire, here, as a direct consequence of departing from one's own place of origin. It is, on the contrary, the destination's failure to embody adequately the model of its own foreign-ness, the nonappearance of the spatially distant as primordial and local, that functions as the mechanism of alienation. It is when the Other's home turns out to be structured by the selfsame abstract, generic logic as one's own that the bottomless contingency and artifice of tradition, locality, historicity, temporality, and agency become devastatingly obvious.

The critical difficulty lies in the fact that, insofar as it is aimed at the impasse of simulation, the critique articulated in the film is itself an instance of the reflexivity critiqued by the film. In other words, while in any given cultural text it can be argued that pleasure confines or disciplines the efficacy of critique, it must be granted that in general our active engagement in social systems—including, but not limited to, the market economy—is fully evident, so that no amount of local containment can fully explain its persistence. Reflexivity, in other words, is not enough; on the contrary, we have reason to suspect that reflexivity is itself a dimension of systems to which it is compulsively "applied." This is the impasse figured by the simulacrum.

If Bob's predicament is paradigmatic of life in the global régime of simulation—that is, at the apex of fully self-reflexive late modernity—it is the destiny of life in this predicament that Charlotte dreads. And in Tokyo, she is compelled to confront at every turn the prospect of life under simulation. Whereas Bob wearily and comically goes through the empty, mechanical motions demanded of him, Charlotte desperately seeks access to authenticity, only to be thwarted again and again by the utter artifice of her marriage, her husband, his occupation, and Japan itself.

Early in the film, as Charlotte roams the hotel, she inadvertently wanders into a room where an ikebana class is getting under way. The Japanese instructor, who does not speak English, pulls her in and installs her in front of a flower table, as if she had been expecting her all along. Unsure how to respond, Charlotte quietly takes up the task of arranging the flowers. The import of this brief scene is clear. The tourism industry includes well-established protocols for delivering "authentic" cultural practices to travelers in a way that preempts not only the need to traverse foreign spaces to engage the locals, but even the problem of translation itself. A simulacrum of Japan is already integrated directly into the experience of staying at a premium-brand hotel. It is as if the hotel thoughtfully confines its guests, its hospitality consisting in premasticating the local culture for their consumption.

It is not surprising, then, that over the first four of the narrative's nine days we repeatedly see Charlotte sitting on the windowsill of her high-floor room, hugging her knees and staring dolefully out at the expansive cityscape below, as if unable to break away from, or through, the glass that presents her with an image of Tokyo that in effect precludes her entry into it. In one of these scenes, the window frames Charlotte so as to confine her entire folded body within the shot, and a deft use of rack focus shifts from emphasizing the impenetrable sea of neon in the nighttime urban background to her isolated figure in the foreground turning to face the camera. This is one of several ways the film highlights not only the fact of her alienation but, more important, its extimate sources in the surrounding world, a world that appears as neither material or objective nor simply as a melodramatic projection of her psyche, but frustratingly effaces such distinctions.

Accordingly, things do not improve when she does manage to go out into the city. While Bob is at the Suntory shoot, Charlotte takes the subway to a Buddhist shrine, where she observes a traditional religious ritual. The film cuts to her back in her room, calling a friend Stateside. As the conversation progresses, she rapidly falls apart. Asked how she likes Tokyo, she first responds, "It's really great here, it's great." But immediately beginning to cry, she continues: "I don't know. I went to this shrine today and there were these monks and they were chanting and I didn't feel anything, you know? I don't know. I even tried ikebana, and John's using these hair products . . . I don't know, I don't even know who I married."

This long-distance run-on confession explicitly links Charlotte's overlapping forms of alienation. To make matters worse, her friend back home responds inattentively, first asking cliché questions and then, distracted, failing to hear the distress in Charlotte's voice and hurriedly telling her to "just have the best time." Clearly, if Charlotte's crisis is brought about by her journey to Tokyo, it will not be resolved by returning home. Meanwhile, when John returns, he complains that the record executives are foisting a formulaic rock 'n' roll look on the band he's shooting, whereas he would like to convey the group's authentic nerdiness. No doubt it is this ethic that attracted Charlotte to him in the first place, a mistake she's only just beginning to recognize. John, it turns out, fails to perceive the irony of his commitment to the authentic. After all, as a music industry photographer, his function is to produce simulacra of authenticity; what he is adamantly defending is not the antithesis of commercial formulas but their very product. Charlotte, of course, clearly grasps the problem; her increasing melancholy and desperation arise from the resulting sense of impotence, the impossibility of escaping the ubiquitous régime of simulation.

Her husband's growing comfort with the hollow and insipid celebrity world she detests is of a piece with her own inability to access the appropriate emotional response to traditional Japanese spiritual practice. Indeed, a key part of the problem is her very expectation that such a response should spontaneously materialize. That is, her panic is not prompted by a failure to emote—after all, she is crying on the phone—but rather by her own reflexivity regarding her emotional life. The feelings she expected to experience at the shrine belong to an established genre, part of a publicly circulating program stipulating the apposite and authentic responses. Indeed, tourists like her deliberately seek out the local opportunities to provoke these responses in themselves. Approached from any objective or subjective vantage, the entire shrine experience is a completely self-referential scenario in which cause and effect have fully merged, anticipating and mechanically soliciting each other. And Charlotte is caught in the paradox of this scenario's reflexive artifice: incoherently, she feels alienated from her authentic self because she is unable to summon a preprogrammed emotional response; yet of course she is unable to summon it precisely because it is preprogrammed. Had she been able to "feel anything," it would have been nothing but an effectively produced simulacrum.

Charlotte's error, then, consists in her effort to do what the modern protocols of autopoiesis dictate she must do: she tries to generate and manage her own singular, intimate subjectivity. She is, after all, a philosopher, or one who reflects on the best way to live life. But because hyperreflexivity is the paramount problem confronting her, the results of her efforts are more or less disastrous. For example, her unflinching critical stance toward the excesses of commodity culture alienates her from her husband, who is deeply involved in maintaining and reproducing this culture.

Not only does being a critic fail to help her, it actually exacerbates her alienation, handicapping her in social interactions. To illustrate this impasse of reflexive consciousness, the film supplies a comic foil for Charlotte in the form of a ditzy American starlet, Kelly (Anna Faris), in Tokyo to promote a formulaic action blockbuster. Charlotte and John run into her in the lobby of their hotel on the narrative's third day. It turns out that Kelly and John know each other, and Charlotte finds herself subtly excluded from some of their vaguely implied shared history. Kelly, however, is clearly a hyperkinetic and hopelessly narcissistic nitwit, and informs the couple that she is registered in the hotel under the pseudonym Evelyn Waugh. When, after they part company with Kelly, Charlotte contemptuously points out to John that Evelyn Waugh was a man, he reproaches her for being too judgmental. The cruel irony here is that success in the superficial sociability that obtains among the vapid narcissists most comfortable in global late modernity clearly demands a sort of willful naïveté, of which John is capable but Charlotte, regrettably, is not. She is incapable of it because, despite its relentless drive to commodify, the régime of simulation insistently supplies an overabundance of information, including information about its own internal processes. One may or may not be compelled to know the gender (or the work) of a given author, but the disposition to register and track the ceaseless iterability of discrete tokens of social knowledge—such as Kelly's citation of a famous name (brand)—is not simply a feature of subjectivity but is built directly into this régime. The knowing subject simulation tends to produce is from the start operating at a social disadvantage: she knows too much about the way social systems work and are thought about, and this knowledge subverts her participation in them. The clear implication here is that the only form of subjectivity appropriate to such a situation is utter vacuity—not a viable option for the film's protagonists or, by extension, its audience. Such ignorance cannot, by definition, be produced from a position of excess knowledge; one has to luck into idiocy.

After John leaves for work, Charlotte watches Kelly's promotional interview in one of the hotel's meeting rooms. The actress responds to questions with inane showbiz clichés, and when asked what it was like to work with Keanu Reeves, she explains that it was an enjoyable experience in part because "We have all these things in common—you know, we both like Mexican food, and yoga, and karate." Here is someone utterly unfazed by the incoherence of her own experience; for her, "back home" in L.A., Mexican, Indian, Japanese, and many other cultural elements blend seamlessly as so many equivalent commodities. That is, "home" is already a kind of cultural pastiche. In this regard, Kelly is a foil not only for Charlotte but also in a sense for Bob; she is a young, female, newly hot commodity blissfully unaware of her own objectification. Although, unlike Bob, she clearly "succeeds" in misrecognizing the loss of home as home, and though her stardom demonstrates that such misrecognition is valorized and rewarded, it is clear that global simulation imposes itself with such insistence that only a complete idiot could effectively get along in it. For Bob and Charlotte, another solution will have to be sought.

Despite this series of failures, Charlotte hews to the reflexivity model until becoming involved in an ambiguous relationship with Bob. Just prior to Kelly's inane press event, we see Charlotte listening to a self-help CD (*A Soul's Search*) with a poignant mixture of condescension and desperate hope. The genre that best epitomizes reflexive modernity, self-help embodies all of its contradictions, condensed within the incoherent project of producing one's most authentic self by mobilizing generic, widely circulating, commodified formulas derived from systematic observation and statistical analysis of populations and social processes.

The day after her first conversation with Bob, Charlotte walks through Shibuya in the rain, wandering into a video arcade, a veritable spectacle of simulation and its alienating effects. Hundreds of players interact individually with their machines, oblivious to the surrounding crowd. Play requires full physical involvement: kids jump around, actively gesticulating, their senses immersed in simulated interaction. The camera lingers on one teen engaged with a music machine, striking a studied Johnny Ramone pose:

clad in black, hair spiked, feet rooted to the floor, guitar slung low, cigarette dangling precariously from the side of his mouth, his wrist executing the buzz-saw strum, he is the film's counterpart to the human "batteries" famously depicted in *The Matrix*. In addition to embodying a panoply of media clichés of authenticity, his narcissistic mimetic performance is itself staged for a machine—the interface with a cybernetic system has assumed the form of sociability, or sociability the form of cybernetic interface.[20]

The irony is doubled by the fact that the simulation in which he is so fully immersed is that of mythical generic rebellion against "systems" of all kinds—that is, a fake rebellion proffered by the very reflexive processes it claims to reject. As Mark Seltzer points out, "[T]he society that makes itself from itself demands individuals who make themselves from themselves, which means that the social imperative of self-making is experienced exactly in reverse: as an unremitting war between two large abstractions, self and society."[21]

The Impasse of Autopoiesis

From this perspective, the video game pseudo-punk both embodies the fate Charlotte is desperate to avoid and the immediate self-contradiction of her effort to avoid it. The subject of simulation learns from media models how to make herself, even as these models interdict making oneself according to the clichés they themselves supply, demanding that the reflexively made self be original, authentic, and opposed to every model. Thus in the régime of simulation, every attempt at self-making not only appears preprogrammed (for example, as rebellion) and thus preempted, but directly reproduces the system of imperatives constituting the régime—that is, the system that issues the injunction to make the self and supplies the abstract, generic knowledge to facilitate the process. It is the technology of simulation that spawns the punk's rebel pose, which in turn is emblematic of the impasse of reflexivity confronting Charlotte. This impasse is what motivates her to pursue a relationship with Bob, whom she will approach, chat up, invite out, and progressively position as a kind of crypto-analyst—or *sujet suppose savoir*—in a relationship driven by the familiar logic of transference.[22]

Yet the first conversation between Bob and Charlotte also proceeds by way of clichés, whose function in the scene, the narrative, and the rhetorical project of the film is overdetermined. Though they see each other periodically in their hotel, sometimes exchanging glances, they don't meet until Bob's fourth night in Tokyo. By this point in the film, it has been clearly established that neither Bob nor Charlotte can sleep. Distressed, jetlagged, and melancholic, both repeatedly take advantage of the hotel's bar in the wee hours. In one of a series of rhyming sequences, we see Charlotte in a bath looking out the window again and listening to the *Soul's Search* CD. Unable to sleep, she clicks on the TV, and we cut to Bob channel surfing. Charlotte heads to the bar and finds Bob already there. Seeing that she is unsure what to order, Bob self-mockingly performs his Suntory bit, holding up his glass and cooing, "For relaxing times . . .".[23] Charlotte orders a vodka tonic, asking, "So what are you doing here?"

Bob: Coupla things. Taking a break from my wife, forgetting my son's birthday, and getting paid $2 million to endorse a whiskey when I could be doing a play somewhere.

Charlotte: Wow.

Bob: But the good news is the whiskey works. What are you doing here?

Charlotte: Well, my husband's a photographer, so he's here working, and, um, I wasn't doing anything, so I came along, and we have some friends that live here.

Bob, *lighting her cigarette*: How long you been married?

Charlotte: Two years.

Bob: Twenty-five long ones.

Charlotte: You're probably just, uh, having a midlife crisis. Did you buy a Porsche yet?

Bob, *looking serious*: You know I was thinking about buying a Porsche.

Charlotte: Twenty-five years. It's . . . well, it's impressive.

Bob: Well you figure, you sleep one-third of your life. . . . What do you do?

Charlotte: I'm not sure yet, actually. I just graduated last spring.

Bob: What'd you study?

Charlotte: Philosophy.

Bob: Well, there's a good buck in that racket.

Charlotte: Well, so far it's pro bono.

Bob: Well, I'm sure you'll figure out the angles.

Charlotte: Yeah. I hope your Porsche works out. Cheers to that.

Bob: Cheers to that. *Kampai.*

Charlotte: Wish I could sleep.

Bob: Me too.

The clichés with which Bob and Charlotte bombard each other serve multiple, overlapping functions. In the scene, they appear at first to be mere small talk, familiar tokens of urbane stranger sociability, and cover for a commencing flirtation. But in light of the narrative's emerging thematic concerns, the inevitable reduction of every effort to communicate to embarrassing cliché is precisely the problem: rather than facilitating social interaction, these tokens impede it.[24] One way to formulate the problem the film labors to address, then, is whether it is possible to deploy clichés—that is, simulacra—to supersede the obstacle they pose, to access or produce a world in which culture, history, temporality, sociability, and authentic intimacy somehow return.

All these implications reverberate in the dissonance of the conversation itself. For example, Bob and Charlotte get surprisingly far into their personal lives without so much as introducing themselves—a possibility secured not only by their distance from home turf, but also by their own ineluctable grasp of the prosaic predictability, the formulaic form, of their experiences. She's the recent college grad anxious about the future; he's in midlife crisis—each knows full well that these are standard moments in generic stories widely disseminated by various popular and expert discourses, the digital doxa of global late modernity. Moreover, like other modern subjects, Bob is apparently living out this scenario, so that it is rigorously impossible to say whether the cliché of midlife crisis describes the phenomenon to which it refers or programs it in advance. Bob and Charlotte are at liberty to divulge the details to strangers, because these details are a statistically projected open secret, utterly lacking in idiosyncrasy, and finally impersonal. From this perspective, even their most intimate anxieties are systematically anticipated and codified, so that they are in effect excluded from their own affective experience, unable to live even their very dissatisfaction with this exclusion.

This point is decisive: at stake is not the actual alienation that has mired Bob and Charlotte in ennui, but their paradoxical lack of access to it, its unlivability as experience or subjective orientation. Within the régime of simulation, the chief problem is not the apparent loss of authenticity but the incoherent injunction to produce it out of scripted scenarios. In Tokyo, then, Bob and Charlotte come to realize that even the nostalgia haunting them is not their own but belongs to simulation itself, as the vehicle of its reflexive self-reproduction. This fact, in turn, confronts the spectator with a performative paradox: isn't the critique of simulation the film articulates itself part of simulation's reflexive structure? Doesn't the utopian fantasy of escape from simulation simply embody reflexive modernity's injunction to autopoiesis? And doesn't the film itself belong to the régime it appears to repudiate? Doesn't this repudiation—this reflexive self-critique—effectively constitute the régime's mode of self-reproduction?[25]

What, then, are we to make of the film's narrative strategy, which seeks to leverage the generic May-December romance plot as a way of cultivating a space of intimacy where intimacy is from the start extimate, "mediated," or programmed by narrative conventions and sociological knowledge? How, in other words, can intimacy be the didactically recommended solution if media didacticism is what directly generates the problem of nostalgia for intimacy? The film attempts to circumvent this impasse by staging a passage from this vexed nascent romance to friendship. The problem, however, is that this passage itself must rely on psychoanalytic transference, the dynamics of which Bob will recognize and successfully manage in the very course of refusing to do so.[26]

The significance of this rhetorical strategy—and its inevitable, preprogrammed failure—lies in the lesson it offers to cultural critics. To the extent that politically driven analysis of culture hews to the protocols of what Fredric Jameson has called "cognitive mapping," it is prone to the same performative contradictions that bedevil *Lost in Translation*. Indeed, from this perspective, reading the film in terms of either its ideological complicity with late capitalism (for example, as affirming capital's self-serving myth of its own omnipotence) or its resolute resistance to inexorable global commodification would be equally erroneous. If the true problem is hyperreflexivity, then both ("postmodern") ideology and resistance—including "critique" itself—are themselves instances of it. If, as Baudrillard famously put it, the map has become the territory, more mapping simply extends this territory's reach.

From Romance to Friendship

As both the means to and the substance of the resulting friendship, transferential love is emblematic of the paradox of social reflexivity. The structure and stakes of this paradox become clearer as the complex pas de deux between Bob and Charlotte develops in the second half of the film.

Although it is on the fourth evening of his eight-day stay that Bob jokingly suggests they "stage a prison break," he and Charlotte finally spend their first significant time together only on the following day. Like their initial meeting, this "date" is instigated by Charlotte. That morning, when they run into each other at the entrance to the hotel pool, Charlotte invites Bob to join her and her local friend, Charlie, for a night out. That evening they meet Charlie and other young Japanese hipsters at a bar, and Bob cheerfully plays the role of clueless American tourist. At a second bar, an argument—the substance of which remains mysterious to the Americans on and in front of the screen—leads to a bizarre resolution as the group is compelled to run from a young man firing an automatic weapon that, like everything else about Tokyo, may or may not be real. Bob and Charlotte run through a noisy and disorienting pachinko palace and grab a taxi to what appears to be Charlie's apartment. After more drinking, conversation, and dancing to Phoenix's too-apt "Too Young," it's on to a karaoke bar. Following Charlie's over-the-top stab at a Sex Pistols track, Bob performs a cautiously earnest rendition of Nick Lowe's "(What's So Funny 'Bout) Peace, Love and Understanding," made famous by Elvis Costello's caustically utopian postpunk recording. Charlotte timidly follows with The Pretenders' "Brass in Pocket," and Bob concludes the singing with a wistful take on Roxy Music's "More Than This."

The scene is fairly explicitly staged as a sort of conversation conducted through pop song. Or, understood strictly within the context of the gradually developing romantic dynamic between the protagonists, the exchange is another tentative gesture in Charlotte's charmingly awkward and unsuccessful seduction of Bob—a gesture he skillfully parries. Unsure of herself but emboldened by the position of enunciation afforded her by Chrissie Hynde's lyric, Charlotte almost murmurs to Bob in a faux-coy tone:

> Gonna use my arms
> Gonna use my legs
> Gonna use my style
> Gonna use my sidestep
> Gonna use my fingers
> Gonna use my, my, my imagination
> 'Cause I'm
> Gonna make you see
> There's nobody else here
> No one like me
> I'm special, so special
> I'm gonna get some of your attention
> Give it to me.[27]

In an understated yet disarming tone, Bob delicately replies,

> It was fun for a while
> There was no way of knowing
> Like a dream in the night
> Who can say where we're going . . .
> You know there's nothing
> More than this.

It is never made clear whether Bob and Charlotte selected the songs they perform, but the selections are obviously apt, insofar as they facilitate the communication of fairly specific messages while affording the requisite degree of prophylactic deniability.

However, insofar as Charlotte's erotic interest in Bob is an instance of transference, this exchange between them directly involves the psychic—and thus social and structural—genesis of her desire: the impasse of simulation. From this vantage, the scene stages and interrogates the possibility and consequences of appropriating simulacra as means of exiting this impasse. To summarize: Charlotte is paralyzed by her confrontation with the paradoxical injunction to construct an authentic self in accordance with the models and protocols of reflexive modernity, and she intuitively sees in Bob a sujet suppose savoir—someone who has negotiated this dilemma with a mixture of success and failure from which useful lessons can be extracted, and who therefore can mediate her passage out of melancholic paralysis. In short, she is positioning Bob as the locus of knowledge about the impasse of knowledge. In the karaoke scene, this process takes the form of seduction through the mimetic performance of pop song. That is, Charlotte's effort to exit the impasse of simulation proceeds by way of appropriating the protocols of simulation to produce a genuine erotic mutuality.

As a result, the scene raises at least two important questions. The first is directly diegetic and concerns the implications of Bob's subtle refusal. The second, however, is whether Bob's refusal is a merely contingent response determined by narrative requirements or, rather, indicates a more general limit implied by Charlotte's strategy. This limit concerns the central role of reflexive appropriation in the arsenal of political gestures privileged by contemporary cultural criticism, as well as by the liberal imaginary generally. The film appears to advocate reflexivity as a solution to the putative hegemony of reflexivity itself. Since Bob, for his part, participates in this communication-by-appropriation just long enough to refuse Charlotte's advance, we are left to wonder if his very refusal confirms the viability of her strategy. Doesn't reflexive appropriation of simulacra effectively serve to mediate genuine communication between them? We are also left to wonder whether his refusal to embody the locus of metadiscursive knowledge and judgment ironically confirms him in that role. Isn't he only able to refuse because he effectively does have privileged access to a metalevel vantage on the interaction in which they are involved—access that Charlotte lacks? Moreover, won't Bob eventually find it necessary to confront Charlotte with this knowledge so as to dislodge her from her impasse? What, then, is the fate of reflexivity in the film? This is the question that begins to emerge with some urgency in the karaoke scene.

The Feedback Loop of Reflexivity

In the sung exchange between Bob and Charlotte, irony and nostalgia (the tactical and traumatic dimensions of reflexive self-distance) converge in a display of the impossibility of the personal expression both promised and demanded by the reflexive régime of simulation—but also that of the utopian persistence, underneath or alongside hollowed-out clichés, of the human subject whose "vestigial" or supplemental status within the hegemony of simulation holds out the possibility of its "return." The scene serves to demonstrate that reflexive appropriation is a myth, insofar as it presupposes and concerns already reflexive phenomena (texts, practices, modes, aesthetic forms, and so on) in a culture explicitly committed to reflexivity. Indeed, karaoke itself contains *in nuce* the possibilities and limits of social scripts; the point not to be missed is that the play of identification and dis-identification opened up in relation to these scripts is necessarily a product of social reflexivity. While there are ways of construing differences between the Japanese practice of karaoke and its North Atlantic variants, in the end these differences are immaterial for the dilemma examined by the film.

One might argue that, as an "indigenous" or contextually situated practice, karaoke serves social functions specific to its "home" culture. Along these lines, Christine Yano explains that Japanese karaoke "is a frankly mimetic activity based upon the assumption that individual expression is most effective when contained within highly developed, recognizable patterns of communication." Indeed, "the mediated quality of the performance . . . is in fact the point here. One becomes *through* patterns of form, both musical and personal." Yano notes that "although the expression may be patterned, and perhaps because it is so patterned, singing becomes one important way of knowing another . . . [because] . . . a singing voice is considered a truer index of a person than a speaking voice. . . . A person singing is less able to hide, more able to reveal."[28] The key point here is that compulsory mimesis and cliché combine to produce revelations *despite* either personal intention or aesthetic form; that is, genuine communication is the uncontrollable, incidental, and reliably surprising effect of formulaic artifice, irrespective of whether the performance is earnest, perfunctory, or ironic. There would appear, then, to exist a ruse capable of wresting authenticity from the confining framework of social scripts. This possibility, however, only begs the question of the origin of the *compulsion to produce* authenticity—the compulsion that gives rise to both the scripts and the ruse themselves.

Moreover, even if it were unambiguously the case that, as a culturally situated practice, karaoke serves social functions specific to its context, the actual functions in question presuppose a fundamental distinction between cultural scripts (the rigidly conventional genre of *enka,* the traditional mnemonic function of structured *kata*) and personal expression (the revelations of the voice, affective commitment, styled performance). Here, the scripts facilitate self-expression and a concomitant form of sociability. But this facilitation itself presupposes the value of self-disclosure *for* sociability, a presupposition that is itself socially prescribed. Karaoke therefore cannot be said to respond to an already existing subjective aspiration to community; on the contrary, it helps install such aspiration as an imperative condition of belonging. It would thus make no difference whatsoever if the practice were absolutely contextual, since this would in no way support the model of agency construed as subjective appropriation of social forms.

Of course, it is not simply the case that Japanese karaoke is culturally distinct, since it is a recent invention dependent on, among other things, sophisticated electronic technology, mass-mediated and transnational musical forms, and an array of practices associated with capitalism and urban life (such as after-office social gatherings). As Marilyn Ivy powerfully demonstrates, what Appadurai might call Japanese "primordialism" is itself an effect of the country's thorough modernization.[29] From this perspective, karaoke's invocation of an older tradition of public singing is an instance of simulation—the production according to reflexively adopted models of a "real"—and "vanishing"—referent. Thus even Japanese karaoke would already be a profoundly nostalgic and hypermodern exercise in projecting a myth of culturally authentic sentimentality.

Thus in relation to the impasse of reflexivity at stake in the film, it is immaterial whether karaoke is conceived as emblematic of reflexive modernity both in Japan and beyond it, or is imagined in terms of passage from contextually situated practice to abstract commodity on the global stage. That is because this passage is itself to be grasped as synecdochic: a ubiquitous economic technique is generalized to indicate the consequences of social reflexivization. At stake in karaoke is the play of identification and dis-identification in reflexive modernity. In general terms, identification would correspond to nostalgia for authenticity, while dis-identification would correspond to ironic distance. But the two finally belong to a unitary logic: there is no question of appropriating ironic distance against nostalgia or nostalgia against irony. Both full and tactical commitment (as well as the refusal to commit) are reflexively undertaken stances assumed from the position of metacontextual knowledge that grasps social forms *as forms.*[30] Indeed, as simulacra, these forms relentlessly and constitutively mark their own contingency, making it impossible *not* to know just what one is doing with them. After all, in simulacra, we confront not simply phenomena, but phenomena constituted as knowledge about themselves. That is, we confront them as copies, models, or other metadiscursive forms—for example, media discourses about the evils of media—and thus as placeholders or promissory notes for what can only appear as a constitutively absent or incomplete original. Simulacra are structurally nostalgic (pointing to an absent referent), even as they are structurally ironic (constitutively reflexive). No wonder all the songs Bob and Charlotte perform are not only unambiguously commodified cultural objects but are explicitly concerned with the problem of reflexive knowledge that they also instate.[31] Lowe and Costello's "(What's So Funny 'Bout) Peace, Love and Understanding" concerns the corrosive effects of ironic distance; the Pretenders' "Brass in Pocket" is about the disabling self-consciousness attendant upon the social injunction to narcissism; and Roxy Music's "More Than This" underscores the impossibility of exiting the self-reproducing circuit of pastiche culture.

So while Bob and Charlotte do succeed in communicating with each other via simulacra, this communication is itself preprogrammed; simply put, they are directly reproducing the basic protocols of the régime responsible for their ennui. Indeed, both the nostalgia and the irony to which the pop songs lend articulate form are themselves effects of this form. The multiple layers of ironic distance and attempts at authenticity (operating as thematic content and rhetorical form in song lyrics; implicit in musical form and recorded performance; characteristic of karaoke as indigenous practice, hybrid cultural form, or translocal commodity; evident in the protagonists' modes of enunciation; and operationalized in the interplay among all these levels) are strictly complementary: they are mutually constitutive dimensions of the simulation dynamic. As such, they preclude or preempt what they seem to facilitate. The reflexive attempt to compel the simulacrum to deliver on its arcadian or utopian promise by generating authentic affective mutuality is poignant in its misapprehension: Bob succeeds in conveying the sense of loss, but this sense is not the side effect but the vehicle of the pop song as commodified cultural form and endlessly repeated generic schema of intimate subjectivity and affective attachment.

One does not resist or escape its grip through mimesis; on the contrary, one is only further disabled by such "appropriation."

Seducing Simulation

And to be sure, it soon becomes clear that while communication via simulacra is certainly possible, it cannot by definition suffice to loosen the stranglehold of reflexivity. When the singing concludes, we see the couple sitting on a bench in what appears to be a hallway, with Charlotte lightly resting her pink-wigged head on Bob's shoulder as he sits uncomfortably upright. Then, as they ride in a taxi back to the hotel, Charlotte looks out the window and, when she turns around to see that Bob is asleep, smiles affectionately at him. In a shot that rhymes with that of Bob's arrival in a limo, the camera is positioned outside the car and angled to capture the reflection of neon-clad buildings on the window through which Charlotte is gazing at them. Tokyo is literally superimposed on her; finally out in the city and fully alert to it, she is a barely distinguishable face in the cacophony of its unrelenting simulation of itself. And when the film cuts to the hotel, it is Charlotte who is asleep in Bob's arms as he carries her to her room. She is hugging his neck in the trusting way a sleeping child hugs her father's, and when he puts her to bed she opens her eyes for a moment, smiles at him sweetly, and returns to sleep. Thus despite his cautious resistance, Charlotte is succeeding in positioning Bob as a paternal object of transferential love: entrusting herself to his care, she is now even able to sleep. In sum, Charlotte is doing what subjects of reflexive society are supposed to do, as Bob struggles to avoid cooperating with what he knows is a compulsory illusion on her part. The transferential relation promoted by communication via ("appropriated") simulacra can only eventuate in the sort of dead end in which Bob finds himself, since it corresponds directly to the programmatic mandate of autopoiesis.

It should be no surprise that, having put Charlotte to bed, Bob remains incapable of restful sleep and calls his wife at 4:00 a.m., only to be frustrated by her now-familiar passive-aggression. It is clear that he feels excluded from a relationship he had worked to establish and which his labor as professional simulacrum both sustains and undermines. His marriage is the "private" counterpart to the "public" régime of simulation: it is a cul-de-sac in which the effort to produce intimate domesticity directly subverts itself. No doubt Bob understands that this is the fate awaiting Charlotte if she proceeds with her own quest to produce herself through the reflexive structure of transferential knowledge.

The next day, however, Bob finds himself temporarily and comically assuming his paternal function. It turns out that Charlotte has badly stubbed her toe, and he insists on taking her to a hospital. Naturally, all their efforts at communication with hospital staff turn out to be comically ineffectual, but the humor hints at the limits of reflexivity operating in the mode of expertise, raising the question of whether it is only interlinguistic translation that produces losses. The amusing alienation they undergo at a Tokyo hospital only underscores the frustrating alienation characteristic of all discourses and institutions of expertise and thus constitutive of social reflexivity generally. The habitual availability of English only partly disguises and compensates for the incommunicability between expert systems and their human components.

That evening, Charlotte calls Bob in his room and invites him for another night out with her friends. However, when they arrive at the designated place—a bar called "Orange"—it turns out to be a bizarre strip club. They leave and head back to the hotel, where Kelly is unselfconsciously butchering a song in the lounge. They retire to their rooms but can't sleep, and shortly Charlotte finds a note from Bob under her door: "Are you awake?" Together in Bob's room, they watch *La Dolce Vita* on TV and drink sake. After a brief exchange about how they met, Charlotte says, "Let's never come here again 'cause it would never be this much fun." Later, in a meticulously composed, delightfully charged full-body bird's-eye shot of this odd couple lying clothed on the bed and staring at the ceiling, she ventures, "I'm stuck. Does it get easier?"

> Bob: No. Yes, it gets easier.
> Charlotte: Oh yeah? Look at you.

Turning to stock wisdom even he does not really believe, Bob offers: "The more you know who you are and what you want, the less you let things upset you." Articulating a complaint that impeccably captures the diabolical impasse of reflexive self-making, Charlotte explains:

> Yeah. I just don't know what I'm supposed to be. I tried being a writer, but, ah, I hate what I write. I tried taking pictures, uh, they're so mediocre—you know, like every girl goes through a photography phase, you know, like horses? Take, uh, dumb pictures of your feet?
>
> Bob: You'll figure that out. I'm not worried about you. Keep writing.

2. Film still from *Lost in Translation:* © 2003 Focus Features

Charlotte, *turning on her side toward him*: I'm so mean.
Bob, *turning to her, grinning*: Mean's okay.
Charlotte: What about marriage, does it get easier?
Bob, *hesitating, blinking rapidly, and shifting his eyes disconcertedly*: That's hard. . .

Then, as they fall asleep, he touches her foot, saying: "You're not hopeless."

As the camera looks down on the bed, we see Charlotte asleep, curled up in the fetal position and facing Bob, who is lying on his back, straight, with his face turned away from her but his hand on her foot. The image could not be more explicit in depicting the awkward status of their relationship, which is here at a pivotal stage. Charlotte is trapped by the preemptive reduction of life options to clichés, and she is unable to see that the injunction of reflexive self-production is itself the product of these clichés. Bob is trapped by his inability either to embody or to avoid the job of sujet suppose savoir. Both, in short, are trapped by the machinery of reflexive knowledge, which at once increasingly binds them to and threatens to alienate them from each other. Confined by a bed they do not exactly share, the awkward geometry of their juxtaposed bodies conveys the tension between the growing bond between them and their divergent dispositions toward the origins of this bond.

It is noteworthy that Charlotte's lament consists of reflexive acknowledgment of the predictability of such laments. The problem isn't simply that she does not know *what* to become, but that she is at once obliged ("supposed") to fashion herself and precluded from doing so by publicly circulating forms of social knowledge concerning the (mediatized) process of self-fashioning ("every girl goes through a photography phase"). Even the options she lists—writer, photographer—are rooted in romantic myths of creative genius produced by the rise of mediatic capitalism. Thus Charlotte is effectively excluded even from her own predicament, which, while it concerns the impasse of the cliché, is itself a cliché. At the same time, it is becoming increasingly clear that Charlotte is thwarted not simply by the preemptive reduction of life options to generic formulas, but also, and more immediately, by her very recognition of this reduction. Put simply, the more she identifies with the injunction to autopoiesis, the more insipid her options appear. This is because the injunction emanates from the order of simulation itself as the vehicle of this order's legitimation and reproduction.

In a lucid and instructive discussion of this problem in J. G. Ballard's *Crash,* Scott Durham sees the novel as highlighting the internal contradiction of simulation—that is, simulation presupposes yet purports not to require spectators/consumers, which are thus supplements in Derrida's sense. For Durham, the book's laudable intervention consists in exposing simulation's tacit reliance on the social bond among these excluded subjects, a bond simulation does not create but must presuppose. By contrast, I am arguing that the question is not the internal contradiction of the model as such, since both simulation and resistance are fictions. As Durham himself repeatedly points out, simulation is the fantasy of capitalism's omnipotence;[32] resistance to it is the corresponding fantasy of personal autonomy and political agency characteristic of liberal politics—and much academic cultural criticism. The putative struggle between simulation and its forlorn subjects is a rhetorical postulate of hyperreflexivization. So it is a mistake to speak of the system's internal contradiction as the pressure point for resistance; there is no system, and its antagonism with resistance is likewise a myth. This is because the quest for the real is not opposed to simulation but is its chief effect—or rather, the chief effect of reflexivization, which is experienced as the opposition between simulation and spectatorship.

Thus not only Charlotte's predicament but, more urgently, her dream of escape from it already belong to the order of simulation. If she entertains this fantasy, it is from her place as vestigial vehicle facilitating simulation. Or, in terms of reflexivity, this dream directly corresponds to the project of autopoiesis, which people undertake only because enjoined to do so and only via the protocols and media supplied by the cybernetic systems of modernity. As Seltzer reminds us, the very *opposition* between the individual (subject, citizen, consumer) and society (the symbolic order, the state or polity, the market) is factitious; cybernetic systems subsume both its poles. Not only does the machinery of representation appear as an obstacle to personal agency, genuine communication, and authentic affectivity, but it is this machinery and its sociopolitical presuppositions that will have installed these as normative ideals.

This fact has decisive conceptual and political consequences, inasmuch as it problematizes two pervasive lines of cultural analysis and models of political agency. On the one hand, the impasse of reflexivization cannot be addressed through a search for new forms of subjectivity or modes of relating to the so-called symbolic order. On the other hand, this impasse cannot be addressed by means of one or more transformations in social, political, economic, or symbolic structures. Neither politics of identity and representation nor new variants of historicism and critiques of political economy will resolve the paradox of autopoiesis, since the very notion of political agency these imply tacitly presupposes reflexive knowledge as its main lever.

To its credit, *Lost in Translation* succinctly demonstrates the mutual contingency of "the personal" and "the political." Though it does focus on the struggles of individual protagonists and never ventures to indicate possible avenues of explicitly structural transformation, it clearly locates the source of its protagonists' dilemma in social objectivity. More to the point, it meticulously reveals that the antagonism between subject and structure is itself an artifact of the project of reflexivization. If the film's undertaking is open to criticism, it is not that it fails to offer a rigorous critique of commodity capitalism, ethnocentrism, class hierarchy, and so on. If it fails or refuses to attribute causality to the global régime of capital, it does so because, within the terms of its analysis, this régime is itself nothing other than a symptomatic projection. In this regard, the film's perspective may seem to resonate with that of authors such as J. K. Gibson-Graham, who argue that, in effect, capitalism does not exist.[33] However, while Gibson-Graham and others, such as Italian autonomist Marxist Paolo Virno, go on to argue for a plurality of economic practices heterogeneous to the capitalist project, their proposals continue to rely fully on the premise of social reflexivity. Capitalism may be exposed as a myth, but the privilege of autopoiesis remains beyond question. Similarly, "radical democracy" theorists, such as Ernesto Laclau and Chantal Mouffe, correctly deny the priority of any sort of structure with respect to political antagonism while retaining and heavily relying upon an unreflectedly reflexivist notion of political agency.[34]

Simply put, even a post-structuralist politics grounded in the presumption of irreducible social antagonism and committed to hegemonic struggle as the sole horizon of political possibility elevates this commitment to a reflexively held principle and determines hegemony as fully social—if necessarily partial and incomplete—control of fully social processes. A significant merit of *Lost in Translation* is that it exposes the way this socialization of society *produces* at least some of the antagonisms Laclau and Mouffe consider irreducible and propose to manage via the production of hegemonic "empty signifiers." If, then, the film is to be criticized, it is not as a naïve or ideologically devious rendering of the crisis of agency. Nevertheless, its attempt to imagine a way out of the impasse of reflexivity is, at best, ambiguous. To see this, it is necessary to examine the trajectory of the transferential dynamic under way between Charlotte and Bob.

The Gift of Betrayal

The day after they sleep together, Charlotte takes a train to Kyoto, where she visits a temple during a wedding ceremony. The experience does not provoke another crisis, and she even attempts to participate in local tradition by tying a prayer to a prayer tree. Meanwhile, Bob, who had been desperate to leave Tokyo, now agrees to remain long enough to do a popular television talk show. The show is absurdly over the top, saturated with ironic pop pastiche; its host is an amalgamation of every cliché, hyperbolized beyond the excess of self-parody into almost sublime kitsch histrionics. But whereas he had merely tolerated or actively resisted his Suntory tasks, here Bob is much more willing to participate actively in the host's exuberant shtick. Obviously, for both Bob and Charlotte, their developing relationship is beginning to function as both a source of hope and an increasingly effective means of combating their ennui. Yet it is also becoming clear that each is experiencing a different relationship than the other is.

Back in the hotel that night, Bob takes a bath and receives a call from his wife, Lydia. The carpet they had selected for his study is not in stock, and Bob, exhausted by his struggle in their relationship, tells her, "Whatever you like. I'm completely lost." Once again, she is extremely passive-aggressive, asking, "Do I need to worry about you, Bob?" He replies, "Only if you want to." After the call, Bob takes a sauna, watches himself on the talk show, and heads back to the hotel bar. As he nurses his whiskey, the American lounge singer sidles up, turns to him, smiles, and says, "Hi."

The film cuts to the following morning, as Bob wakes up alone in bed and hears a woman singing in his shower. He is flummoxed, and there is a knock on the door. It is Charlotte, who's come to invite him to lunch. She hears the singing and, knowing she has no right to be upset with his behavior, pretends not to be. For his part, Bob is blankly unapologetic. The lunch, however, is a complete disaster. The two sit morosely in a mostly empty restaurant, neither speaking to nor looking at each other. Finally, Charlotte caustically ventures: "Well, she is closer to your age. You could talk about things you have in common, like growing up in the fifties. Maybe she liked the movies you were making in the seventies, back when you still were making movies." Quick, succinct, and devastatingly on-target, Bob replies: "Wasn't there anyone else there to lavish you with attention?" Charlotte sits up in surprise, incredulous as to the sheer brutality of this question and the escalation of the stakes it betokens. No longer a petty squabble concerning Bob's supposed betrayal of their nebulous relationship, the exchange has unexpectedly morphed into an elucidation of the nature of her investment in this relationship.

Bob's insight is what she had wanted all along; only its content is not what she had expected. Charlotte's accusation that he chose the older singer over herself indicates her perception that he must have been willing to cheat on his wife, a willingness that now amounts to a betrayal of her own nascent but inhibited romantic bond with him. But it also becomes clear that her romantic interest had been a symptom: she had been pursing her autopoietic project by means of a series of detours through supposed bearers of social knowledge—philosophy, her husband, cultural authenticity, self-help—with Bob only the most recent fount of the expertise she thought she was missing. Moreover, unlike all the others, Bob clearly grasps this fact. In this regard, he effectively does occupy the metacognitive locus she ascribes to him. From this vantage, opting for the lounge singer is hardly a betrayal. On the contrary, Bob's subsequent refusal to apologize and the insult he hurls in reply to Charlotte's sarcasm convert his act of lechery into a gift to her. In what may be a retrospective resignification of an initially impulsive act, the one-night stand becomes a selfless gesture of friendship in a double sense: it indicates their friendship at the moment of founding it, the moment when the transferential dance of reciprocal misdirection in which they'd been involved is transformed into simple elective mutuality. In response to her efforts to interpellate him as the subject-supposed-to-know, he gives her what she does not know she needs.

But the exact moment of Bob's decision must remain obscure to us. We cannot know how or when Bob's choice to sleep with the singer became a gesture of friendship toward Charlotte. We cannot even know if it became such a gesture as a consequence of a deliberate decision or through sheer happenstance. Did Bob sleep with the singer in order to help Charlotte? Did he explicitly decide to frame his act as a refusal of her transferential advances? Did he expect that such a refusal would help her, or did he simply wish to disentangle himself? Because its temporality is dispersed across a narrative sequence that confers upon it an irreducible ambiguity, Bob's gift of friendship acquires the structure of an enigma or secret. Not only does it resist a single coherent interpretation, but it may well be that Bob himself does not and cannot know if or when the decision was made. It may have surprised even him, emerging as an unanticipated side effect of his retort, uttered in extemporaneous exasperation. The narrative thus works to preempt the cybernetic logic of simulation by introducing a structural indeterminacy—a *delay* that would thwart any possible observation or multiply any single systematic account. Perhaps a decision was made; perhaps it was made in advance, or in retrospect; perhaps it was never made at all. Perhaps no form or temporality of knowledge, no logical sequence or determinable moment of decision, no model of reflexivity or autopoiesis is adequate to the structural ambiguity of this gift of friendship.

Indeed, the film concludes by staking a cautious utopian wager on the opacity of the secret. After Bob and Charlotte say good-bye in the hotel lobby and he departs for the airport, he sees her walking down the street from the back of his limousine. He has the driver stop the car and runs to catch her, kissing her gently on the forehead and whispering something into her ear. Needless to say, the audience is left out of this intimate communication: there will be no knowledge of their intersubjectivity, no way to assimilate it to the form of a genre, no way to strip it of its opacity, no way to convey its substance. Exceeding its enunciated content, the secret consists in the mode of its (non)enunciation. It denies access and refuses to circulate; it is unrecordable, unrepeatable, and thus singular; it marks and figures the limit of knowledge in its cybernetic dimension.

Referring finally only to the fact of being shared and withheld, its content is, in the end, inconsequential—a mere vehicle and proxy for the tautological enigma of friendship itself. From the nuanced, hyperreflexive perspective on the impasse of social cybernetics precariously established by the film, friendship has no content capable of being expropriated, and its self-referential form paradoxically resists reduction to that of the simulacrum. Friendship, then, becomes the matrix of sociality where the paradox of reflexivity is resignified, if not resolved. The friend can occupy the place of, and thus dissimulate, the systematic expertise and programmatic clichés that constitute modern sociality. Attuned to the specific needs of an irreplaceably singular other, the friend will be "more" than the system he instates, the codified place he occupies, the generic formulas he inexorably reproduces. The bond between friends will be intimately intersubjective, an unrepeatable haven in the heartless world of unrelenting repetition. Their mutual knowledge will exceed and thwart all external observation, statistical calculations, and counterfactual models.

Yet the friendship relation will obscure its own presupposition of a metalevel, suprarelational locus of "expert" knowledge concerning the relationship, which at least one friend must occupy at least part of the time *in order to be* a friend. Inevitably, friendship will facilitate a cybernetic model of sociality by translating its terms into those of elective affective attachment. In this way, the valorization of autopoiesis made possible by friendship as a kind of unscripted, particularistic sociality legitimates the *social value* of reflexivity. The protagonists' melancholy longing, with which audiences are invited to identify and which the transition to friendship assuages, is therefore neither a symptomatic effect nor a critical reaction; rather, it underwrites the priority of autopoiesis to which reflexive society is committed. It is the relentless reflexivity of social life that will thus be obscured or secreted, scrupulously "lost in translation."

The secret that concludes the film is supposed to resolve the impasse of reflexivity by imagining an unrepeatable singularity that exceeds the cybernetic régime of simulation. But this conclusion arrives at the end of a narrative, one that begins with an image of the impasse to be addressed. The arresting image that launches this narrative functions as a kind of promise, an hors d'oeuvre that becomes legible only in retrospect, from the vantage of the film's conclusion. Yet for this very reason, this gesture involves none of the contingency of a genuine promise, no possibility that the promise will not be fulfilled. This promise will have been redeemed from the start, even before the narrative commences. Put another way, the synoptic simulacrum that marks the impasse of simulation seems to require and produce the time of a narrative, but it also programs, and thus concludes, this narrative in advance. The film knowingly begins with an end, but it also ends where it begins.

The unrepeatable moment of the secret that concludes the film delivers on the promise implied by the film's opening image. This unprogrammable moment will thus, in effect, have been programmed. More to the point, its apparent heterogeneity with respect to the order of simulation is itself anticipated by this order, or, more accurately, by the logic of cybernetic sociality. The promise of redemption from simulation is redeemed by simulation, by its valorization of autopoiesis. What Charles Taylor once identified as "the ethic of authenticity" is, it turns out, neither a reaction to modern rationalization nor an ideological element of consumer society. Rather, it is what secures or underwrites the project of social autopoiesis. What Richard Sennett famously criticized as an essentially self-defeating narcissistic enterprise that disavows the social, public "sources of the self" is neither opposed to community (though it is in productive tension with *society,* an irreducibly counterfactual, imaginary, statistical reality) nor a contingent error to be remedied by changing perspective.[35] If individualist premises of liberal citizenship belong to the project of socializing society, then autopoiesis is a key, if not the key, *social* value. The injunction to produce one's authentic self facilitates and even compels the investment in the secret, which appears to meet the irreconcilable requirements of reflexivity and singularity. The secret would mark the blind spot of observation, the relation that remains opaque even when witnessed. But *the public sanctification of this opacity is what secures the liberal model of social cooperation required by secular, reflexive modernity.*[36]

Conclusion

The problem of organizing the plot around the evolution of Charlotte's desire is that, as the film stipulates, this desire is not hers at all but rather belongs to the order of simulation. Simply put, it is a subjective effect of the reflexivization of social life. Her quest to break out of the prison-house of simulation is itself the product of simulation. Hence the problem with the "solution" offered by Bob. The implication of his intervention in the economy of her transference is that the way forward for her means renouncing the alibi function of simulation. So while she is correct about the hollow artificiality of global simulation, this truth is but a prosthesis supporting her own willful refusal to engage in the process of self-fashioning. But this only returns us to the status quo ante: the reflexive intervention of the film stages a reflexive intervention by Bob that facilitates the achievement of full reflexive autonomy by Charlotte. In short, the diabolical, preemptively disabling social reflexivity constitutive of the liberal imaginary and identified as the chief obstacle to agency is itself advanced as the privileged solution. The film is critique; Bob is the sujet suppose savior;

Charlotte becomes master of her own life. Here, then, reflexivity is politically complicit at the very moment when it seems to offer a powerful critique of social objectivity.

What's more, it is not the case that the film first thematizes a problem that, in an additional step, it "dissolves," "manages," or otherwise attenuates; this is not a simple case of ideological containment. On the contrary, the problem is that the moment of critique and the moment of containment precisely coincide. Insofar as it instantiates the protocol of social reflexivity, the very gesture of critique is already implicated in its object. Put another way, critique is not produced and thwarted but is rather preempted by its very articulation. This is because we are in a cybernetic régime, of which critique is a key mode. In this sense, it would be erroneous to fault the film for failing rhetorically: *the very premise of critique is already an effect of that autopoietic logic whose internal limit is figured by the simulacrum.* The rigorous requirement of knowing self-production will have determined the very possibility of the film's rhetorical project, so it could hardly have been expected to disappear from this project's development.

The political problem legible in the film is that reflexive critique turns out to be self-defeating. Recall Habermas's thesis that the incomplete project of modernity consists in the salutary process of rational, secular critique. The familiar criticisms of this view have typically stressed the external limits of critique—the problem of heterogeneity, the opacity of the unconscious, the shortcomings of rationality, the irreducibility of language and representation, the implicit ethnocentrism and imperialism of modernization, and so on. In the simulacrum, we witness critique's internal limit: it is what happens *when critique effectively succeeds* and the project of modernity nears completion. To return to an older vocabulary, we unexpectedly find ourselves not in a *less* reified world but in an almost *totally* reified one. And the agent of reification—in Habermas's Weberian lexicon, the exhaustive, but for this very reason self-defeating, rationalization of the lifeworld—is not capitalism per se but rather the very logic of autopoiesis, of which global late capitalism is a paradigmatic manifestation. The failure of reflexivity coincides with its hegemony.

Put another way, the reflexivity that is central to the liberal project and renders it immune to most forms of critique is what exposes it to self-deconstructive pressure, undermining the efficiency of liberalism's basic categories and logic. Of course, it is a rigorous stipulation of deconstructive thought that every "text"—understood in the most general sense as signifying activity—is so exposed. The politically salient question, then, might be whether the rhetoric of liberalism labors to forestall or actively seeks to provoke or at least mark the inevitable deconstruction of liberal social logic. In the former case, liberalism could be castigated as arrogant, dishonest, or violent; in the latter, as modest, forthright, and ethically open to revision.

But is a discourse more commendable if it foregrounds, names, or solicits its own deconstruction? Why is *this* kind of reflexivity creditable in the first place? Whence the injunction to forthrightness that seems to impose this preference for the rhetorical humility of autodelimitation? Is not this humility actually the greatest pretense, cynically preempting the very political innovation it purports to invite? If we are disposed—if this is our ethos—to prefer, to valorize, or even to love the rhetoric of self-deprecation, is it not because we are guided by, already committed to, a suspicion of both overt and dissimulated authority? And is this not a definitively liberal commitment, ethos, or disposition? A liberal rather than simply a democratic one, if democracy names something like plain popular sovereignty or the direct rule of the demos, which is not necessarily obliged to respect individual autonomy, universal inclusion, ethnic or cultural diversity, protection for political factions or minority groups, economic fairness or efficiency, secular derivation of legitimacy, and so on? Does not this ethos constitute a demand for and inculcate sensitivity to the motivated-ness or rhetoricity of all discourse—that is, to *polemos* as the irreducible character of collective life?

At the same time, is not this sensitivity, constitutive of the liberal ethos, itself an obdurate obstacle to democratic rule, to the authoritativeness of authority and the stable integrity of a régime? Does a text that exposes the inherent failure of reflexivity at once concede its own failure as a reflexive text? And if so, does it thereby earn praise or provoke exasperation? If it marks the limit of democratic autonomy as such, does it thereby exceed the bounds of any particular democratic imaginary, or does it simply rationalize the status quo as the best of all possible worlds? Is liberalism's deconstructive disposition finally nothing but a form of narcissistic navel-gazing, the sort of Romantic self-indulgence to which Charlotte submits?

These questions are, precisely, rhetorical: they cannot and should not be answered at the level of theoretical reflection but only through analysis of rhetorical practice. In the next and final case study, I argue that, charitably understood, the self-deconstructive ethos of liberal rhetoric may turn out to be its most radically democratic feature. Through a close reading of interracial friendship in Wayne Wang and Paul Auster's film *Smoke,* I attend to the problem of race as a key site where the liberal "displacement" of politics intersects with the liberal determination of political membership as a contractual relation among normatively abstract persons. Here, all the concerns discussed in the preceding chapters coalesce within a reflexive narrative that takes as its object liberalism's account of itself in order to push liberal rhetoric to deliver on its democratic promise. Rather than simply reject as cynically ideological, futile, or self-defeating the liberal determination of citizenship as private, elective, contractual friendship, the film uncovers and mobilizes the irreducibly fictive or self-allegorizing rhetoric of this determination. The deficiencies of the liberal narrative of universal citizenship clearly exposed by the complex dynamics of race—particularly in the United States—unexpectedly transform this narrative into an allegory of its own radically democratic presuppositions. Whether this transformation properly belongs to the rhetorical logic of liberalism or subverts and dislocates this logic is a question that returns us to the problem of judgment as the irreducible risk and responsibility of making political distinctions, a risk relentlessly marked by that trajectory of the liberal rhetoric of friendship that comprehends friendship as a bond that can take place only on condition of its own impossibility—the ineluctably speculative wager on its own unmasterable future presupposed by every contract, every social bond, and every account of democracy.

5
Race, Friendship, and the Speculative Politics of Infinite Debt
Smoke

> [A] justice that would at last break with sheer equivalence, with the equivalence of right and vengeance, of justice as principle of equivalence (right) and the law of eye for eye. . . . What would an equality then be, which would no longer calculate this equivalence? Which would, quite simply, no longer calculate at all?
>
> —Jacques Derrida

> To affirm that it is necessary to dissipate a substantial portion of energy produced, *sending it up in smoke,* is to go against judgments that form the basis of a rational economy. [Emphasis added]
>
> —Georges Bataille

In *The Trouble with Friendship,* Benjamin DeMott reproaches the pervasive Hollywood narrative practice of using friendship and affect as alibis for historical and institutional racial inequality and injustice. Films and television programs depicting interracial couples or friends, DeMott explains, systematically de-emphasize differences resulting from the radically divergent social, institutional, and economic experiences of actual black and white citizens and privilege affective commonalities in order to transfer the weight of racial inequity from the contentious domain of practical politics to the placid interior space of the individual, depoliticized, private subject. Racism is thus framed as a matter of personal attitude and choice, obscuring the complex of historical struggles, relations of power, and institutional norms, practices, and effects. Insofar as such narratives are explicitly designed as a form of liberal civic pedagogy, their cumulative effect is to reassure audiences about their own moral adequacy rather than to challenge or exhort them to pursue systemic reform through the political process.

DeMott's account regards the rhetoric of friendship in narratives of race as, at worst, deviously ideological and, at best, naïvely oblivious to the harmful effects of the interracial friendship fantasy. In this regard, his critique of popular representations of racial accommodation converges with the customary critique of liberal universality, stressing the racist consequences of erasing the political specificity of racial difference. To be sure, the "ideology" of interracial friendship DeMott describes is rooted in the liberal determination of citizenship and its coimplication with race in the United States, so it is not surprising to find the effects of this determination in popular discourse on race. It is neither an accident nor a ruse that the problem of race is "depoliticized" by means of friendship narratives, since friendship encodes the liberal premises on which these narratives are based and the liberal aims toward which they are deployed. But this in turn means that, whereas critiques of liberal color blindness assert that race marks the site of a fatal flaw in the liberal scheme, in the popular narratives that pervade American public culture racial hierarchy is, on the contrary, a problem liberalism is uniquely positioned to solve. To see why, it is important to recognize the central role played by the contractual model of sociality in coordinating the relationship between race and citizenship in the emergence of American liberalism.

The liberal imaginary situates relations among individuals as taking place outside politics. This is not to say that in the liberal view political institutions do not at any given moment mediate personal relationships, but to acknowledge that the liberal project involves producing citizenship as a contractual relationship between individuals—idealized as abstract, rational agents at least notionally or analytically anterior to any given political framework—and the state. Social contract theory itself, despite the resonances of sociality, is concerned with relations among individual members of a polity only in their roles as citizens, so that it apprehends only a limited range of interactions and commitments, rendered in terms of legal status, rights, and obligations. This is clear in the way liberal discourse construes the distinction between the "public" and the "private" by orienting the former along the axis "citizen-state" and the latter along the axis "individual-individual." What is noteworthy is that between them, the two axes marginalize or underimagine the relation "citizen-citizen," and that, to the extent such a relation is imagined or theorized at all, it remains a contractual relation. At the same time, to the extent that relations among individuals in a liberal-capitalist polity are per se political, they mirror in structure the relation between the citizen and the state—that is, they are contractual in nature, representing an exchange of obligations, services, and goods. The liberal civic bond thus depends crucially upon forms of exchange.

This feature of the liberal imaginary is intimately linked to the historical development of U.S. citizenship after Reconstruction. According to Carol Horton's analysis of the relation between race and the historical development of American political culture, U.S. citizenship comes to be nationalized and centered on the principle of universal equality during Reconstruction because of the requirement to assimilate 4 million former slaves into the national economy.[1] Since the chief practical goals of Reconstruction were to safeguard the economic foundations of the young republic and to redeploy the labor of the newly freed people, this transformation of citizenship required the assumption that contractual relations among civic subjects would best ameliorate established race-based inequalities—that is, political equality was to be understood as equal participation in market relations. Maintained specifically as a principle of economic exploitation, racial hierarchy thus not only crippled black citizenship, but also discursively encoded citizenship as an economic relation.

Not coincidentally, the strains of civic republicanism, present since the founding and visible in the rhetoric and political commitments of key figures such as Jefferson and Lincoln, would be taken up during Reconstruction by black intellectual leaders—such as W. E. B. DuBois—seeking precisely to avoid the consequences of suppressing black particularity in favor of liberal-capitalist abstraction. The diminution of republican rhetoric in the white public sphere and its emergence among black civic leaders clearly signals this transition. Marked as a marginal and politically untenable position, the civic republican conception of citizenship would all but disappear from the political imaginary of the United States, leaving the latter to be organized entirely by a radicalized liberal economism that would "save" democratic citizenship by pushing its contractualism to the limit of abstraction.

Within the American context, then, race and the economistic, contractualist determination of citizenship are inextricably bound together, both conceptually and historically. On the one hand, the liberal citizen must be made to experience a civic bond that is precluded by the abstract nature of his[2] citizenship as a rights-bearing, free, equal, rational agent entering into a contractual agreement with the state. On the other hand, the black American citizen cannot even begin to enter into such a contract because of his preexisting status as rights-deficient, unfree, and unequal person whose rationality and agency are continually put in question by the existing set of political arrangements. The liberal citizen must be abstract, although this abstraction alienates him from his own citizenship; burdened by concrete history and marked by difference, the black citizen cannot be abstract, which alienates him from liberal citizenship.

From this vantage, race indeed appears to mark a fatal weakness of the liberal imaginary. On the one hand, liberalism's abstract contractualism functions to depoliticize—by privatizing—the grievances it engenders, stoking antagonisms that undermine its own legitimacy, efficacy, and stability.[3] On the other hand, insofar as abstract contractualism is constitutive of the liberal imaginary, there is no way to dispense with it in order to integrate citizens marked by racial particularity. If this is so, then popular interracial friendship narratives must function as compensatory devices, deploying the liberal figure of private citizenship to resolve imaginatively an otherwise intractable structural contradiction.

According to the familiar critical protocols, then, unmasking or otherwise troubling the friendship supplement would expose and possibly disintegrate the already vulnerable liberal edifice. But what could be the repercussions of such a gesture? And how can the place from which it is undertaken be mapped in relation to liberalism itself? Is the deconstruction of the friendship supplement produced from within liberalism? Can it, if successful, bring liberalism to an end? Such questions are infinitely complicated by the paradox of supplementarity itself. If friendship sustains a political imaginary incapable of standing on its own, is friendship integral to that imaginary—in which case the latter does, in effect, stand on its own—or not? And if not, which is the actual locus of discursive efficacy, liberal discourse or the friendship supplement that enables it? Such questions strongly imply that the peculiarly potent critical and political leverage afforded by the logic of supplementarity demands a wholesale reconsideration of the critical model that takes as its object something like a structure—however notional or incomplete—to be interrogated or subverted.

A first step in the direction of such a reconsideration is to attend to an instance of such a deconstructive gesture, one that appears to take place in the mundane milieu of liberal public culture, as part of its routine functioning. Paul Auster and Wayne Wang's 1995 film *Smoke* mounts a subtle but radical challenge to the rhetorical convention deplored by DeMott, not only by refuting it, but by reconfiguring its main components. On its surface, the film both participates in and responds to dominant practices of representation by showing how friendship, as a quintessentially particularistic mode of attachment, can supplement the abstraction of the individual inherent in the formation of liberal-capitalist political subjectivity and civic relations. But under cover of this dialectical rejoinder to the "friendship-as-alibi" convention, *Smoke* interrogates and refashions the logic of liberal contractualism, linking not only the history of racism but also the narrative strategies by means of which this logic legitimates and reproduces itself to the way in which the relation between politics and friendship operates within the liberal imaginary. The film explicitly correlates the interaction between citizenship and the figure of friendship to the speculative structure of exchange undergirding liberal contractualism, a structure that entails a specific conception of, and relation to, narrativity. As a result, *Smoke* demonstrates the way friendship, determined rhetorically as an extrapolitical relation of reciprocity integral to the racially vexed liberal model of citizenship, exceeds its own metaphorical function to facilitate an allegorical turn crucial to the resilience and efficacy of the liberal imaginary, and in the process exposes and expands the surprisingly fertile democratic possibilities latent within liberal rhetoric.

The film consists of several overlapping narratives detailing the development of friendships among characters whose paths cross at a Brooklyn tobacconist's. The shop is managed by Auggie Wren, and Paul Benjamin, a writer suffering from writer's block since the random shooting death of his pregnant wife a couple years earlier in front of the store, regularly buys Schimmelpenninks from him. Paul becomes involved with Rashid Cole when the black teenager from the nearby housing projects fortuitously saves his life. Out of gratitude, Paul invites the boy to stay with him for a few days, unaware that Rashid is on the run from a gangster whose take from an armed robbery he has inadvertently come to possess. Later, Paul persuades Auggie to give Rashid a job, and his relationship with both deepens. Meanwhile, Auggie's former girlfriend, Ruby, appears at the cigar shop to ask him for financial assistance in helping her pregnant, crack-addicted daughter, whom she claims Auggie had fathered nearly two decades earlier. The issue of paternity also concerns Rashid, who, we learn, has run away from home in part to go in search of his father, Cyrus. As the stories of these characters unfold, they intertwine in a number of ways, and friendships develop between Paul and Rashid, Auggie and Paul, and Rashid and Auggie, among others.

It may be tempting to view *Smoke*—as even some of the most perceptive critics have—as belonging to that extensive set of pop cultural narratives in which the complex political problem of racial inequality is reduced to a simpler and more easily manageable quirk of personal psychology, to be resolved by the pious modulation of affect through the trope of friendship.[4] However, we are alerted fairly early on that the film is not to be read naïvely in this way. When Rashid explains to Paul the circumstances that led to his running away from his home in the projects, Paul expresses concern that being only a mile away may not make Rashid safe. Rashid responds, "It's not that far away, but . . . it's another galaxy. Black is black, and white is white. And never the twain shall meet." "It looks like they've met in this apartment," replies Paul. "Let's not get *too* idealistic," Rashid cautions. "Fair enough," agrees Paul. This brief exchange explicitly raises—in order to dismiss—the expectation that *Smoke* will somehow resolve or attenuate the social and political dilemmas associated with race, and through this exchange the film clearly inscribes itself within the Hollywood tradition of interracial friendship films while at once reflexively distinguishing itself from that tradition's "idealistic"[5] tendency, described by DeMott, to displace the political dimensions of race relations onto the sphere of affect.

Smoke provides viewers with a number of such reflexive cues, which not only suggest how the film is to be interpreted but also mark the significance of reflexivity itself, which becomes one of the film's themes as well as a key to understanding its structure and rhetorical operation. The film is divided into seven segments. The first is labeled "Summer 1990" and it is followed by five numbered ones: "1. Paul"; "2. Rashid"; "3. Ruby"; "4. Cyrus"; and "5. Auggie." This last contains or opens onto a seventh, untitled segment which, like the first, exists both inside and outside the boundaries of the main narrative. The names of the parts do not bear an exclusive or even determinate relationship to their contents. The segments do not focus primarily on the named protagonists' actions, experiences, or points of view, as might be expected; nor does the sequence of numbers refer to a clear chronological order. Rather, the headings simply punctuate an otherwise overlapping assortment of story lines. Moreover, the five numbered parts are bookended by the two other segments, which bear a decidedly ambiguous structural relationship to the rest of the film. The first, shown after the heading "Summer 1990" but prior to the title of the film and thus marked as perhaps external to the events that follow, consists of a scene set in the tobacco shop where Paul tells Auggie and a few customers a story. Since this scene gathers up and sets going all the thematic concerns of the film, I would like to dwell on it at some length here.

The Story of the Bet

As the film begins, "an animated discussion is taking place inside the Brooklyn Cigar Company."[6] Auggie is talking with a group of customers the script describes as "OTB Men."[7] When Paul walks into the store, Auggie informs him, "The boys and I were just having a philosophical discussion about women and cigars."[8] "I suppose that all goes back to Queen Elizabeth," Paul offers.

Auggie: The queen of England?

Paul: Not Elizabeth the Second, Elizabeth the First. Did you ever hear of Sir Walter Raleigh?

Tommy [one of the OTB Men]: Sure. He's the guy who threw his cloak down over the puddle.

Jerry [another OTB Man]: I used to smoke Raleigh cigarettes. They came with a free gift coupon in every pack.

Paul: That's the man. Well, Raleigh was the person who introduced tobacco in England, and since he was a favorite of the queen's—Queen Bess, he used to call her—smoking caught on as a fashion at court. I'm sure Old Bess must have shared a stogie or two with Sir Walter. Once, he made a bet with her that he could measure the weight of smoke.

Dennis [also a customer]: You mean, weigh smoke?

Paul: Exactly. Weigh smoke.

Tommy: You can't do that. It's like weighing air.

Paul: I'll admit it's strange. Almost like weighing someone's soul. But Sir Walter was a clever guy. First, he took an unsmoked cigar and put it on a balance and weighed it. Then he lit up and smoked the cigar, carefully tapping the ashes into the balance pan. When he was finished, he put the butt into the pan along with the ashes and weighed what was there. Then he subtracted that number from the original weight of the unsmoked cigar. The difference was the weight of the smoke.

Tommy: Not bad. That's the kind of guy we need to take over the Mets.

Paul: Oh, he was smart, all right. But not so smart that he didn't wind up having his head chopped off twenty years later. But that's another story.

This scene bears a synecdochic relationship to the rest of the film, the major thematic and figural elements of which it contains in embryo, as it were.[9] In so doing, "[t]he story . . . incorporates or interiorizes the very thing of which it is a part . . . the smaller becomes, metonymically, larger than the larger."[10] The scene's location outside, or on the threshold of the "text" of the film signals that it is to be read as an allegory that encapsulates the major themes and lessons of the narration that follows. This is most clearly evident in regard to the symbolic function of smoke. But the centrality of this figure should not obscure the significance of the other elements of the story. Within this brief scene, we already have an offering or gift of a story, a story of friendship within an explicitly political context and a suggestion of the risk involved in the conjunction of the two. We do not and cannot know whether the story is true—whether Paul is "blowing smoke"—despite the fact that it is a story about the care taken and ingenuity involved in determining the truth about (the value, or valence, of) smoke. It is also a story of speculation in its relation to calculation, recounted at the site where luxurious consumption intersects with economic exchange, and proffered to and consumed by speculators—gambling men engaged in philosophical interchange. And we have the allusion to the "free gift" associated specifically with the economic circulation of tobacco and with tobacco's history. Moreover, the story's quasi-historical presentation opens the film's internal system of reference to extratextual material, which in turn suggests other links with the rest of the film.[11]

While it was almost certainly Sir John Hawkins, not Raleigh, who introduced tobacco to the English court—though it was Raleigh who made smoking fashionable—it is profitable to follow the thread of this historical allusion. Tobacco was brought to England from the New World, specifically from the colony named by Raleigh after his patron queen as a gesture of gratitude. As reciprocation for founding the colony in her name, the Virgin Queen knighted Raleigh and named him lord and governor of Virginia. In the end, however, it was in no small degree his friendship with the queen that got him beheaded in 1618, after her death. One year after his execution, representative government arrived in the American colonies with the election of the Virginia House of Burgesses. In the very same year, the first African slaves in colonial America were imported into Virginia from Africa.[12] Since tobacco formed the foundation of the fledgling colonial economy, the first economic use of slaves there consisted in exploiting their labor to produce the luxury crop.

The colony—and subsequently the state—of Virginia eventually became known as "the cradle of presidents," since eight U.S. presidents have been born there thus far—more than in any other state. One of these was Thomas Jefferson, whose relation to the history of both American democracy and American slavery—as well as to the history and valences of tobacco—is invoked later in the film when we discover that Rashid's given name is Thomas Jefferson Cole. In addition to being the author (though not a signatory[13]) of the Declaration of Independence, Jefferson was himself a highly ambivalent slaveholder who, while using slave labor to run his estate (including the farming of tobacco), worked to ban the importation of slaves into his home state, released his slaves upon his death, and appears to have fathered at least one slave's child. His name thus invokes the highly conflicted entry of African people into the colonial and national history of America and eventually into U.S. citizenship—and the relation between that history and the historically frustrated myth of American citizenship as founded on free choice.

Beginning with the story of Raleigh's bet, Jefferson's name and its connotations become indissociable from the figure of (tobacco) smoke. The preceding brief overview of the "real" history invoked by the story of the bet already links in a highly suggestive way the development of American democracy to differential forms of political allegiance,[14] (political) friendship, the conventions of naming,[15] the economics of tobacco, the political and economic institution of slavery, and the slave trade. In addition to figuring the disfigured distinction between "fact" and "fiction" through the allegorical narrativization of the history of tobacco, the smoke/tobacco trope marks the ambiguity of the opposition between a "real" and a "symbolic" economy—or the economy of the "real" and that of the "fictional."

The choice of tobacco/smoke as the central trope linking political economy to poetics is not simply fortuitous. The symbolic economy of tobacco is indissociable from its economic function, which in turn rests on its status as a luxury drug, a superfluous substance consumed exclusively for pleasure. After all, what is finally at stake here is the function of reciprocal exchange in the relation between politics and friendship. In the story of liberal citizenship, the part played by economism is undeniably pivotal. The tropology of tobacco/smoke puts in question the assumptions governing this economism by functioning as an example—the example par excellence, even—of what Derrida repeatedly calls "the madness of economic reason."[16] The allegory that comes before and opens the discourse of *Smoke* from, and to, its margins—that bridges and conflates history and fiction in a foreshadowing of the logic governing the narrative(s) to follow—this allegory says this madness in advance and haunts the unfolding and undoing of exchange-based relations throughout the film.

In this allegory, let us recall, it is a matter of a bet and of a calculation, and of equivalence secured by (a calculation of) difference. Raleigh has made a bet with his queen, a bet regarding tobacco, or, more exactly, that which is produced in the consumption of tobacco through smoking. This form of consumption gives tobacco its economic value, of course, so Raleigh's bet concerns the product generated in the fulfillment of tobacco's economic function. (It is a safe bet that we will return to the excessiveness of this function soon.) It is a bet concerning the precise value of the economic essence of tobacco. (This is why the comparison to weighing the human soul is appropriate on its face and can be passed over as "natural" by the viewer; the simile's poetic function rests on this apparent appropriateness.) But why should this value be the subject of speculation at all? Shouldn't the tobacco trade—and with it, the future of justice-through-equality, democratic citizenship, and the exchange of goods for people—depend on exact knowledge of this value? Of course, tobacco is bought and sold by weight despite the fact that the quantity of plant matter is only an approximate index of the potential yield of smoke and a still less precise measure of the pleasure it might produce or of the social bonds it might secure. Both the smoke and the pleasure can only be extracted as they are produced; they are produced and consumed at one stroke and cannot be stored, measured, or exchanged. Since the production/consumption of tobacco is a necessary condition of this extraction, the idea that Raleigh's cigar contained any quantity of smoke in advance of the mediating act of smoking is fallacious. Therefore, the calculation that would secure the value of the cigar's smoke is based on, at best, a speculative assumption of the existence or presence of this value. Thus a very "real" economic complex—one that produces a range of significant economic, social, and political consequences—is constituted on the basis of a product that *by nature* resists full quantification, a product that can only engender speculation in the determination of its "real" value.[17] Speculative in advance in both its history and symbolic function, smoke is only "naturally" both the subject and the vehicle of speculation in the story of the bet. Given its complex signifying structure in the story and in the film, then, tobacco/smoke comes to figure the general economy of signification itself: as it allegorizes the ambiguity it also marks historically, it comes to stand for the instability of the opposition between ("historical") fact and ("fictional") sign.[18]

In sum, Paul's story, both by its tropology and mode of inscription within the textual economy of the filmic narrative, explicitly links the ambiguous narrational relation between history and fiction to challenges posed by the concrete history of African Americans to speculative fictions that organize the liberal-capitalist political imaginary; while at the same time and by the same token—the figure of smoke—highlighting within this problematic the complex operation of always-already speculative and excessive reciprocal exchange. The story articulates a conceptual and tropological chain that the rest of the film proceeds to deconstruct.

Speculations—On the Law of Friendship

Speculation plays a key role in organizing all the friendships that together form the subject of the film. Each relationship develops as a form of exchange when characters attempt to reciprocate favors or gifts, yet each attempt to follow the rules of reciprocity is frustrated by ambiguity, chance, and excess, so that the final settling of accounts is indefinitely deferred—and this infinitely excessive deferral is finally what binds characters to one another in friendship. What marks the irreducible, excessive speculation at the heart of the contract, and thus at the heart of the bond—which is both the bond of friendship and the political bond—is the gift.[19] The exchange that would secure all economic and political relations is haunted by the problem of the gift in advance; thus it is not surprising that, immediately following the hors d'oeuvre that is Paul's story of a friendship organized around the political economy of superfluous consumption and haunted by the conflation of ambiguity and exactitude in speculative exchange, Paul himself receives a gift he feels obliged to repay.

Distracted, Paul walks out of Auggie's cigar shop and is about to step out into moving traffic when he is pulled out of the way of an oncoming tow truck by a black teenager, who happens to be walking by, and they both fall on the sidewalk. As they disentangle from each other, the young man says, "You better watch out, man! You'll get yourself killed that way." Paul looks at him, then back toward the place where he was almost killed. The screen turns black and the heading "1. Paul" appears briefly on it. While it is still on-screen and a second before we return to the interrupted scene, we hear Paul's voice say, "It's a law of the universe. . . . You have to let me do something for you to put the scales in balance." "It's okay. If I think of something, I'll send my butler over to tell you." "Please! Let me at least buy you a cup of coffee," begs Paul. "I don't drink coffee," scoffs the boy. Paul slaps his hands on his thighs in exasperation and looks at his benefactor in search of cooperation. The young man obliges: "Look—since you insist—if you offered me a cold lemonade, I wouldn't say no." With palpable satisfaction, and stretching out his hand, Paul says, "Good. My name's Paul." "I'm Rashid, Rashid Cole."

The first scene that clearly belongs to the main body of the filmic text, this encounter sets the multiple stories of *Smoke* going. In this simple incident, all the main themes relating to exchange at once come into play. In an episode that takes its departure from the scene of smoke, Rashid has *given* Paul his life back, and he has done so by chance. Now, in accordance with "a law of the universe," Paul feels obliged to give Rashid something in return, to balance the scales. What is the source of this obligation? Why doesn't the random, unintended nature of Rashid's "gift" remove this obligation? What law of the universe is this and what scales must be balanced—and how, according to what calculation and principle of accounting? In any case, can one ever fully repay the gift of life? But by the same token, under what circumstances can one be given that which one already has?

In *Given Time,* Derrida takes up these questions among others relating to the paradox of gift exchange. In order to elucidate more fully the multiple implications of this scene of originary gift and exchange in *Smoke,* I would like to turn briefly to Derrida's discussion of these matters. For it turns out that not only the exchange of gifts but the gift itself is impossible, and it is this impossibility that in truth organizes not only the first encounter between Paul and Rashid, but also the remainder of the film—and the remainders (say, smoke) in the film.[20]

In brief, the paradox of the gift consists in the fact that if the gift is recognized as a gift, it cannot be a gift:

> For there to be a gift, there must be no reciprocity, return, exchange, countergift or debt. . . . For there to be a gift, *it is necessary* that the donee not give back, amortize, reimburse, acquit himself, enter into a contract, and that he never have contracted a debt. (This "it is necessary" is already the mark of a duty, a debt owed, of the duty-not-to: The donee owes it *to himself* even not to give back, he *ought* not owe and the donor ought not count on restitution.) It is thus necessary, at the limit, that he not *recognize* the gift as gift. If he recognizes it *as* gift, if the gift *appears to him as such,* if the present is present to him *as present,* this simple recognition suffices to annul the gift. Why? Because it gives back, in the place, let us say, of the thing itself, a symbolic equivalent.[21]

In order that it not be annulled, the gift must not be reciprocated in any way; it must be an expenditure without return. Because it must not yield a profit, it is in no sense an investment of capital but an essentially luxurious expenditure. And since, in order to preempt any possible reciprocation, there must at no point be any intentionality or consciousness of donation, "*[t]he gift must be given by chance:*"[22]

> *At the limit, the gift as gift* ought *not appear as gift: either to the donee or to the donor.* It cannot be gift as gift except by not being present as gift. Neither to the "one" nor to the "other." If the other perceives or receives it, if he or she keeps it as gift, the gift is annulled. But the one who gives must not see it or know it either; otherwise he begins, at the threshold, as soon as he intends to give, to pay himself with a symbolic recognition, to praise himself, to approve of himself, to

> gratify himself, to congratulate himself, to give back to himself symbolically the value of what he thinks he has given or what he is preparing to give. The temporalization of time (memory, present, anticipation; retention, protention, imminence of the future; "ecstases," and so forth) always sets in motion the process of a destruction of the gift: through keeping, restitution, reproduction, the anticipatory expectation or apprehension that grasps or comprehends in advance.[23]

At the same time, the bond of mutual obligation that the exchange of gifts would constitute is a condition of the gift as such:

> For the gift to be possible, for there to be gift event, according to our common language and logic . . . [there must be] an unsigned but effective contract between us. . . . This whole presupposition will remain indispensable at least for the *credit* that we accord each other, the faith or good faith that we lend each other, even if in a little while we were to argue and disagree about everything. It is by making this precomprehension (credit or faith) explicit that one can authorize oneself to state the following axiom: In order for there to be gift, gift event, some "one" has to give some "thing" to someone other, without which "giving" would be meaningless."[24]

We are thus always already *obliged to give credit* to the other. This paradoxical formulation is the "law of the universe" to which Paul is finally referring, and it gives the reason for the irreducible ambiguity and infinite excessiveness of gift exchange: what appears as a *cycle* of exchange turns out to be a spiral along which the debt owed the other is forever deferred. When Paul tells Rashid, "I owe you something," he is acknowledging an obligation that cannot be expunged by the simple fact that Rashid has not given him anything. After all, since he was acting on reflex and instinct, Rashid could not have formed an intention to give—if he gave, it was *by chance.* Moreover, it is plainly the case that he could not have given Paul Paul's own life, since it is impossible to give what one does not possess. The only sense in which it can be claimed that Rashid gave Paul his life *back* requires the *speculative* assumption that Paul *would have been* killed by the tow truck had Rashid not intervened. This "would have been" marks the basic structure of all speculation, which is defined by the strict impossibility of ascertaining its truth-value, except in retrospect. It is the organizing principle of judgment: an evaluation made in the present (assuming we know what this would mean) is made in accordance with an imagined future moment from which the present would retrospectively achieve full transparency. Such a transparency would depend essentially upon a speculative leap forward and a speculative look back. The present is thus *haunted* by the future in advance, since it derives its present value, or its value *as* present, not from some determinate assessment in or of "the now," but from that which has yet to occur, may never occur, and—most important—could only occur as a consequence of the given present itself. This is why, in Paul's story about Raleigh, the calculation of "true" value is linked to the speculative movement of the bet—and to the "free gift." It is also why Rashid, had he given, could only have given *back*. Because of this temporal distension, truth-value is always haunted by speculation—what is true at any *given* moment depends upon the speculative movement of expectation and remembrance. In other words, *the present is given on credit.*

Because it cannot be known if Paul would have been killed, and because (his) life itself is (a) given, Paul's speculative debt to Rashid is infinite—that is, since the determination of the value of Rashid's gift is forever forestalled and thus impossible, this value has no limit. Repaying this gift would require the speculative calculation of an ungraspable difference—"like weighing a human soul"—in order "to put the scales in balance." Moreover, it is important to keep in mind that it is Rashid's own interruption of events that forestalls this determination (an act that itself would have been senseless or impossible had this determination been possible—that is, had Paul died). It is as if Rashid has given Paul's obligation to himself by giving Paul something Paul had not lost and he, Rashid, could not have had, even—*especially*—had Paul lost it. Strictly speaking, *nothing* has been lost, taken, given, or given back. No intention has been formed, no determinable "thing" has changed hands, no contract has been entered into. In retrospect, it will have been unclear whether any giving or receiving subjects were even involved in this (non)transaction, since Rashid is not who he claims to be and Paul, a writer who cannot write, is not himself—so much so, that Rashid will take Paul's name and the two will invent and exchange identities later in the film.

Thus it seems all the impossible conditions of the gift have been fulfilled. This is the other reason why Paul's acknowledgement of debt to Rashid does not annul it (although, even if it did, the speculative nature of this debt renders it spectral—since its "reality" cannot be determined once and for all, it would haunt and govern the relationship forever). Indeed, Paul is clearly distraught by the possibility that he won't be permitted to make restitution, and it seems Rashid is doing him yet another favor by acquiescing. This suggests that even if there *would have been* a given debt, Paul could, in principle, repay, and if he were to repay it, he would still "owe" Rashid for being *given* leave to do so. Like a kind of black hole, the obligation imposed by the—real or imagined—gift exerts an infinite force: if you owe me something and I refuse restitution, I do not thereby remove the obligation but, on the contrary, "hold it over your head," as it were; however, if I accept restitution, you are now obligated to me for the removal of the original obligation. Thus the "symbolic" dimension of exchange overwhelms and overdetermines it from the start in a way that forever precludes a final balancing of scales. What we are given to witness in this scene, finally, is the centripetal force of the spiral of speculation and excess that will have governed all the friendships in the film. In the absence of the gift, there is still obligation to give and obligation to give credit, obligation whose origin is indeterminate and whose limit will never be reached—obligation that binds the one to the other in a relation they cannot choose to enter or exit, governed by "a law of the universe."

We are here already in the realm of a legible universe, a "book of nature" that can be interpreted and *ought* to be interpreted as law, as demand, requirement, or duty.[25] This "natural" law would have to be something like a natural *force,* such as gravity. But even this requires an act of reading: it must be possible to interpret nature as being *organized* through a set of "laws" and to *read* the *signs* of their operation inscribed in it. Nature (assuming for the moment that we know what this would be) must be *read,* its laws derived through a process of interpretation. Nature itself must therefore be a text. Moreover, it cannot be *like* a text; it cannot be a matter of applying to it conventions of legibility derived independently of it. The very possibility of the phrase "natural law" indicates the a priori indissociability of nature and legibility. Legibility, then, cannot be exclusively conventional; nor can it be a purely natural phenomenon. The "precomprehension" of legibility itself is the law of (natural) law, the condition of possibility of both "law" and "nature."[26] The necessity of this precomprehension renders natural law radically speculative and spectral, based on the very same "will have been" structure as the obligation of the gift. Apart from the ordinary sense in which Locke's story of man before the law of the state is an intentionally speculative fiction—or allegory—used to legitimate liberal political order, by way of an "as if," through an imagined moment of choice, the law of (natural) law dictates that such a choice could *only* be imagined. Far from rendering this moment effete, on the contrary, the radical indeterminacy of the reality of its origin renders it infinitely powerful as a generative force.

The obligation to give and the obligation to reciprocate are at full force from (before) the start. As Derrida explains, from Marcel Mauss we learn that exchange is principally a symbolic social operation that fundamentally engages and determines the legal and social status of the parties involved. It is therefore a political or *civic* phenomenon that is only incidentally economic, a fact underscored by the *superfluousness* of the objects given/exchanged.[27] Moreover, as a condition of its function in generating the civic bond, exchange commingles friendship and politics because it is friendship that serves as the "protopolitical" mode of attachment in the "archaic" societies Mauss explicitly describes as prototypes for contemporary Western civilization. As the opening gesture of his essay, Mauss offers an ancient Scandinavian poem to "plunge the reader into the immediate atmosphere of ideas and facts in which our exposition will unfold." While Mauss himself does not make much of the fact at this juncture, one of the central concerns of this poem, which he describes in a note as "a very ancient form of law," is, it turns out, friendship:

> With weapons and clothes,
> *Friends* must give pleasure to one another;
> Everyone knows that for himself.
> Those who exchange presents with one another
> Remain *friends* the longest
> If things turn out successfully.
> One must be a *friend*
> To one's *friend,*
> And give present for present;
> One must have
> Laughter for laughter
> And sorrow for lies.[28]

The stanzas quoted by Mauss are as much a primer on friendship as they are on the practice of gift exchange; the two are indissociable parts of the same phenomenon, "the law of friendship and contracts" Mauss describes.[29]

We can speculate as to the features of friendship that might make it a particularly suitable model for what we today imagine as properly political relations. Friendship is conventionally distinguished from the familial bond as being voluntary and subject to transformation or discontinuation. It is distinguished from purely economic ties as involving an inherent and unconditional element of confidence or trust. And it is distinguished from romantic love, which is understood as involving a diminished capacity for choice and, at least in the West, to be possible exclusively between two people, whereas friendships can involve multiple participants. While it is understood that all of these distinctions are socially constrained and arbitrary, within our own social matrix, where they obtain, friendship clearly appears to have the closest affinity to civic relations, which are likewise understood to depend upon choice, loyalty, and trust, as well as a more explicit dynamic of reciprocity than is found in familial or romantic modes. In the end, however, it is less a question of any "natural" similarity between friendship and citizenship than one of their mutual codetermination. Citizenship does not simply rely on friendship as a privileged foundational metaphor (although it often does so within delimited contexts). Rather, Mauss's account of the gift implies that the two modes of attachment share historical and conceptual origins and governing logics. This is why Mary Douglas observes, "The theory of the gift is a theory of human solidarity."[30] If, then, it is by way of the logic of exchange that politics and friendship are intimately related, it is vital to understand the main features of this logic. This is what Mauss sets out to do in his essay on the gift.

As Derrida reminds us, "Mauss's discourse is oriented by an ethics and a politics that . . . oppose a liberal socialism to the inhuman coldness of economism . . . capitalist mercantilism *and* Marxist communism" by showing that economic relations themselves are founded on generosity—the giving of gifts: for Mauss, "it is a matter of thinking the economic rationality of credit on the basis of the gift and not the reverse. The gift would be originary."[31] In responding to the ideological program of utilitarianism, Mauss challenges the idea that gifts are ever free. All gifts, he argues, are caught up in a system of reciprocity. He attempts to account for this reciprocity while retaining the idea of gift by supposing that the gift itself—the thing given, in virtue of being given—generates some demand or obligation to reciprocate. Recognizing that "it is not individuals but collectivities that impose the obligations of exchange and contract upon each other," Mauss concludes that the thing given is the repository of social expectations. This is why gifts are not free but are exchanged under obligation. This obligation Mauss considers superior to the purely economic obligations governing contemporary Western culture, because the exchange of gifts engages the honor and virtue of specific individuals and social groups, rendering the stakes of the relation thus constituted much more concrete than the abstract tokenism of money: "this whole economy of the exchange-through-gift lay outside the bounds of the so-called natural economy, that of utilitarianism. . . . the notion of value functions in all . . .

societies. Very large surpluses . . . are often expended . . . with comparatively enormous luxury, which is in no way commercial. These are the signs of wealth. . . . It is indeed something other than utility that circulates."[32]

The "natural" economy of utilitarianism that has come to rule Western political systems, is, for Mauss, debased, because exchange is supposed to be a principle of sociality, not atomism and alienation. This is why he is impelled to continue using the word *gift* even as his own discourse makes it clear that the system of exchange renders this term meaningless; and it is also why his account absolutely requires the *hau,* that extra "something," a supplemental quantity beyond purely economic value that, as we shall see, haunts all exchange in advance.

Mauss even refers to an aspect of this haunting when he says that "our lives themselves are still permeated with this same atmosphere of the gift, where obligation and liberty intermingle." This "atmosphere of the gift" is linked to two excessive obligations: the obligation to give and the obligation to give back with interest. Even prior to the obligation to reciprocate, "[t]o refuse to give . . . just as to refuse to accept, is tantamount to declaring war; it is to reject the bond of alliance and commonality." An obvious question immediately arises: What "bond of alliance and commonality" is being rejected *before* the parties have chosen to enter the exchange relation? If there is an obligation to give *in the first place,* then the system of exchange must presuppose such a bond and constitutes a response to its demand. The attempt to "balance the scales" is thus doomed from the start, since the obligation to give exceeds the limits of the system of exchange. This, in turn, is why "[w]e must give back more than we have received."[33] In sum, when Mauss introduces the supplemental hau into his account of the system of gift exchange, he is responding to the irrepressible intuition to represent within the system the force that drives it from its margins, a force the system can never assimilate.

Proceeding from Mauss's insight that exchange is the organizing principle of all social life, Lévi-Strauss concludes that, not only are gifts not free, but, in effect, there are no gifts. He chides Mauss for believing that the demand of repayment springs from "a virtue of the thing itself" (the hau), arguing that since, as Mauss himself points out, the gift is a "total social fact," the demand for repayment is a manifestation of the general principle that constitutes the social group itself. In other words, societies do not simply *engage* in (gift) exchange; exchange constitutes them as societies—it is the principle of sociality itself. For Lévi-Strauss, Mauss's mistake—despite the evidence of his own insights—is to privilege the specificity of the social bond itself over the abstract principle of its operation. In other words, Mauss is misguided in mistaking the universal law of economic exchange for the concrete bond of friendship, a false step marked by his insistence on retaining the term *gift* and annexing the term *hau.*[34]

However, as Derrida explains, Lévi-Strauss's formulation is no less troubled, as he in turn fails to see that the excessiveness of the gift haunts all exchange. In order to function as the *arché* of social organization, exchange must be orderly and reciprocal—it must obey a *logos,* that is, remain at all times accountable. Lévi-Strauss himself senses the difficulty right from the start and claims, counterintuitively, that as a symbolic function, exchange is "anti-economic" because it involves no profit but only an increase in prestige. It should be clear that, on this very level of the symbolic, prestige constitutes profit. But the concept of "profit" threatens Lévi-Strauss's determination of exchange as the principle of sociality by introducing into it a form of unaccountable excess or superfluousness that he immediately tries to obliterate by changing its name.

Moreover, as Mauss demonstrates, the potlatch form of gift exchange clearly underscores the central function of *interest* in maintaining the system of reciprocity. Mauss also claims that the excesses of the potlatch form the antecedent of contemporary systems of credit. The system of exchange, in other words, is not purely reciprocal. As Derrida points out, what keeps exchange going are various forms of excess inextricably bound to temporal deferral, since interest represents an arbitrary value attached to a period of time. Likewise, the demand of reciprocation (the hau) given in the gift also implies a period of time, or term. Thus what makes the system appear as a system is this temporal deferral: there would be no reason (logos) to engage in the *cycle* of exchange if the entire process were simultaneous; its value, or raison d'être, derives entirely from the deferral which, in turn, enables it to produce surpluses. If, on the other hand, the excess of deferral were removed from the system and its scales balanced at the same time, the system would come to a halt and, in equilibrium, cease to function as a principle of sociality. In other words, to the degree that this "total social fact" is a social, political, and ethical as well as economic force, the relations it generates and sustains would likewise lose their pertinence. Without the excess of the gift/exchange process, there is no socius, no law, no politics, and no friendship. It turns out, however, that the excessiveness of exchange—its unexpected but constitutive generosity—can never be fully controlled, because it is not a system governed by the forms of rationality it presupposes and proliferates, but is subject to an altogether different principle of accounting, that of speculation.

Since the obligation to give is an obligation to superfluous expenditure, it becomes clear why luxury goods—things that answer no basic need—

should be so highly prized within all economic systems: their value is determined not in terms of usefulness, but in accordance with their symbolic function. In the history of the American continent, tobacco has played a key role in sustaining the symbolic economies that have governed the nexus of intertwining histories that has issued in the contemporary United States. In addition to functioning as a privileged object of luxurious expenditure, tobacco/smoke both represents such expenditure symbolically (it is thus a self-allegorizing symbol) and functions explicitly to mark the formation of contractual ties that such consumption is typically deployed to produce.

In tobacco, then, the multiple overlapping significations of luxurious expenditure are condensed and explicitly thematized. As that which is expended without return, smoke is indissociable from the gift. At the same time, tobacco—and luxurious expenditure generally—is indissociable from the logic of exchange that governs all economic activity and sociality. Indeed, Mauss himself focuses on tobacco at the end of his "Moral Conclusions," offering the example of the Winnebago as a way of underscoring the fact that "the principle of our life has always been a principle of action and will always be so: to give, freely and obligatorily."[35] To the degree that it is consonant with Derrida's analysis, *Smoke* would appear to obey a certain necessity in linking the irreducible ambiguity of gift exchange to tobacco/smoke: "thought of the gift should accord with a certain experience of the *trace* as *cinder* or *ashes*."[36] Produced and consumed at one stroke, smoke is both the essence and the remainder, the supplemental quantity that *gives* tobacco its value. It therefore figures the ambivalence of the supplement, which is both superfluous and essential to that which it supplements. Produced and consumed at one stroke, "smoke signals . . . smoke screens"—symbolizing the symbolic, it communicates and dissimulates its own communicative function.[37] As the "thing" exchanged, it is *nothing* but the sign of exchange, nothing *as* the sign of exchange, pure luxury, uselessness or superfluousness consumed in its production and produced in its consumption. As Paul, Auggie, and Rashid tell each other stories, they are "blowing smoke" whether they tell "the truth" or not; smoke is what they give each other. They give the demand and the obligation to give; they give the bond of friendship that obligates them to give. Telling stories, "blowing smoke" at each other the way Auggie does at Paul at the end of the film, is their form of participation in and (speculative) accounting for the process of (speculative) exchange that binds and obligates them.

That is, the tropology of *Smoke* is not simply an arbitrary set of terms and relations produced and countersigned by an authorial figure, but conforms to a far more thoroughgoing logic, one whose traces could, in principle, be read in the film notwithstanding its thematic orientation. "The symbolic opens and constitutes the order of exchange and of debt, the law or the order of circulation in which the gift gets annulled."[38] That the operation of exchange is an essentially and primarily symbolic process necessarily means that what are exchanged are always signs, discourses, not the least of which is the demand for repayment itself: that is, when I give, what I give is a demand. This would be the substance of the social bond governed by exchange: signs proliferating demands. "It is a law of the universe," says Paul, that favors given must be repaid. That is, we are already bound by a conceptual chain that links the gift to law—thus to ethics and politics—and to sign, discourse, and account—in short, to narrative. This conceptual chain is itself given (this is why it amounts to a demand); it comes to us from beyond the opposition between nature and culture. Moreover, since what is given is always a demand, the logic of the potlatch governs the process in all its forms.

Reciprocation is impossible, since countergift always also implies a demand and an obligation. This demand is never satisfied but is simply always deferred, moved down the chain of giving and payment. This demand thus always exceeds the circle of the gift/exchange and is for this reason this circle's driving force, the hau that haunts the process, never to be exorcised or consumed. It is this excess that is figured by smoke in the story that opens and sets going the proliferating narratives of gift, debt, and friendship in the film *Smoke.* With the help of Derrida's analysis, it becomes clear how this aporetic structure continues to haunt the symbolic economy of liberal capitalism throughout, so that the logos (logic and story/account) of exchange depends, finally, on the faith/credit that friendship renders representable. Friendship serves as the supplement to the aporetic structure of exchange by figuring and domesticating the excessive "as if," the speculative logic of credit that Mauss shows to be the impossible origin, rather than an achievement or side effect, of economism. Beyond its idiosyncratic inflection of the Hollywood tradition of racial pedagogy and beyond its response to the rhetorical function of intimacy in neoconservative political discourse of popular culture, it is above all the operation of this supplementarity that is finally the theme of the film.

Names and the "Law of the Universe": Denaturalizing (the Bond of) Citizenship

While citizenship is imagined by liberal capitalism as a contract based on universal natural law, it is in practice a birthright conferred not by an act of consent but by genealogy. The necessity of this fact is underscored by the irony that foreign-born U.S. citizens—the only ones who do formally consent to enter the social contract—are said to be "naturalized." That is, their citizenship *only* thereafter is as much derived from "nature" as that of all those born into the nation. But not everyone born in the United States has been granted citizenship, despite this affinity between "natural" law and genealogy. On the contrary, people of African descent who were denied political membership for generations were denied it precisely on the pretext of "nature." Moreover, while "[l]iberalism has always condemned, in principle if not in practice, the norms of social hierarchy and political subordination based on inherited or ascribed status, . . . liberals have historically applied this tenet only to the public realm of civic relations."[39] "Nature" served to make liberal citizenship appear coherent by excluding blacks from this realm because this universal law turned out not to be so universal or so natural after all.

Transfiguring the import of "natural" law for all forms of the social bond has consequences for possible accounts of entry into citizenship. While the story of liberal citizenship depends upon an imagined moment of choice that implies a history prior to the social contract and politics (the story starts from nature, not previous forms of government), this history is, as it were, dehistoricized—it is left untold, untellable, and abstract. At the same time, while for liberalism it is a purely fictive formal subject who, with others like him, founds the order of the political, the history of American democracy is inextricably bound to a highly determinate genealogy. For certain members of the American polity, nothing could be less abstract than this membership and its history. Thus when Paul and Rashid discuss the possible meeting of white and black at a determinate place (Paul's Brooklyn apartment) and time (summer 1990), the exchange takes place between a still-abstracted, self-alienated Paul—a white writer literally unable to tell his own stories, estranged from his sense of himself by the interruption of historical, narrative time[40] that was the random, chance killing of his wife and future child[41]—and an all-too-storied Rashid, a black youth whose strong apprehension of the significance of genealogy has led him in search of his father, caused him to change his name, and impels him to tell one "fiction" after another. These fictions mainly concern the young man's ambiguous identity and social status, and they are irreducibly connected to his name.

When Rashid saves Paul's life and the two drink lemonade at a local diner, Paul, still feeling indebted and apparently assuming that the boy has no place to stay, offers to put him up for a few days. Rashid declines, but an indeterminately short time later appears at Paul's place. He stays with the writer for two days, an arrangement Paul finds intolerable because Rashid interrupts his obviously tortured attempts to write. Two days after asking the young man to leave, Paul receives a visit from Rashid's aunt, who is looking for her nephew, Thomas. Through their conversation, we find out that Rashid's real name is Thomas Jefferson Cole, and the two adults speculate that he has gone in search of a man who may be his father, whom he has not seen in the twelve years since the death of his mother.

Thomas Jefferson Cole is named for one of the "founding fathers,"[42] a slaveholder[43] who helped ban the importation of slaves, the "author" of the Declaration of Independence,[44] likely father of at least one slave's child, U.S. president, progeny of Raleigh's Virginia,[45] and political philosopher of minimal government and agrarian civic virtue who owned a plantation that produced tobacco among its crops. Thomas, we must speculate, was named by his parents, both presumably descendants of slaves whose English family name, if derived in the usual patrilineal way, would have been imposed by a white slaveholder. We later find out that his father, through irresponsibility and "stupidity" (basically, a lack of self-*possession*) accidentally killed Thomas's mother while driving under the influence of "spirits" (ghosts and/or alcohol), an event that haunts both father and son.[46]

Thomas is thus a child of chance and simultaneously the progeny of a history that is both irrevocably his and utterly alien to him, both particular or determinate and generic or abstract. (This doubly double genealogical structure is homologous with what DuBois described as "double consciousness," in which public visibility does violence to private legibility, the impersonality of citizenship invades the intimacy of the body, and the weight of history clashes with the promise of the future.[47]) In order to entitle himself to authority over his own life, to *give* himself a voice[48]—in a sense, to become his own father—Thomas re-names himself.[49] He chooses the name Rashid, a name linked to an alternate African American history, one imagined as more autonomous and authentic, yet one which remains abstract, speculatively chosen (an "authentic" history must be *given* and *given by chance*) and, on the whole, alien (Islam is no more "native" or proper to Africans than to African Americans) both to Thomas and to his race.

Thomas/Rashid plays with his identity—or, more accurately, with the necessity and possibility of having a determinate identity as a condition of entry into social space. In short, he lies. But the lies vary in kind and inner logic, and, taken together, open the question of the relation between abstract citizenship and racial particularity. When Paul first attempts to reciprocate his favor, Rashid's offhand remark is "If I think of something, I'll send my butler over to tell you." He then lies about his name. Subsequently, when he comes to stay with Paul, he lies about his family situation and class position. When Thomas first introduces himself to Cyrus, he lies about his name again, this time claiming to be Paul Benjamin. Later, when he and Paul encounter a female fan of Paul's, he lies—in obvious jest—to her that he is Paul's father, a lie that Paul pretends to support. This last "lie" comes soon after Paul tells Rashid a story about a skier who, by nearly miraculous coincidence, finds the frozen corpse of his own father, whom he recognizes because of the uncanny similarity of appearance the two share and who is paradoxically younger in death than the son is in life. Finally, Thomas/Rashid attempts abortively to fabricate yet another identity when prodded by Paul and Auggie to reveal his given name to Cyrus.

This series of fictions concerning his genealogy, name, identity, class, and history indicates that Thomas/Rashid's subject position should be inferred as something like: "'I' am not what 'I' will have seemed," where both the "I" and the "seemed" are fully unstable from the start, the elements of identity structure being put speculatively into play. When Rashid makes the comment about having a butler, it is clear that he is speaking facetiously. This facetiousness, however, implies that he is at once abstracting himself from his given history/status and reappropriating this history/status. This counterfeit lie—this lie that, in being offered, also offers the acknowledgment that it is a lie—thematizes the youth's particularity as it thematizes his reflexivity about this particularity; it represents an ironic stance that articulates the conundrum inherent in DuBois's "double consciousness." Given the double crisis of black liberal citizenship—that is, the paradox whereby only abstract subjects can be citizens and black citizens cannot be abstract—this double gesture of abstracting oneself from particularity by reappropriating this particularity is the only "rational" attitude available. On the other hand, when Thomas lies to Paul about his name and living situation, he seems to be eager to disown his particularity—or, more accurately, exchange it for one more amenable to being read as nonparticularity. That is, by fictively elevating his class position, he appears to be trying to minimize the impact of racial marking on his own legibility.

When he lies to Cyrus, it is apparently for strictly strategic reasons. Still, as a young man whose sense of self can "naturally" be expected to be in flux and who has been denied access to the conventional structure of filiation, the fact that he lies to his biological father about their relationship gives him some control over the nature of this relationship and the conditions of its emergence. He thus becomes—at least to some degree—the "father" of his relationship to his father (it is because he loses this advantage that he is upset when forced to reveal his name); and this lie permits him to enter into a more or less equal and abstract economic relation with Cyrus.

When he lies about being Paul's father, he is assimilating Paul's lesson concerning the uses of fiction—of "blowing smoke." Rashid has learned something about the critical distance afforded by fiction and, more important, by the productive instability of the opposition between "truth" and fiction. In deploying the story concerning the paradox of filiation as a gesture of sociality or "small talk," he puts this distinction into play at the exact moment when his and Paul's relationship with the young woman begins to take form. He thus enters into relation with her not simply as Thomas, nor as Paul's father, but as the kind of subject whose subjectivity consists, in part, in negotiating the difference between being a subject and not being one—and between being particular and being abstract. The condition set up for the young woman's entry into a relationship with him is that she accept him as a radically unsettled subject. This, in turn, requires that she accept a different kind of particularity—not simply a black youth named Thomas and his "real" history, but his ambivalent and critical relation to this history. In this gesture, Thomas comes to particularize his abstractedness and to abstract his particularity.

This dynamic, however, is not entirely subject to his influence. In addition to playing with his identity, Thomas is the subject of this play. He is never able fully to control these representations of himself or the fictions he disseminates. Indeed, a tacit acknowledgement of this impotence is one of the sources of his sometime ironic detachment. Thus a productive tension is established in *Smoke* between the influence of history and the autonomy of invention, a tension that not only mimics the thematic trajectory of the mythic history of the United States, but is closely linked to the problematization, if not the effacement, of the opposition between "truth" and "fiction" throughout the film. Given the complex negotiation between abstraction and particularity Thomas/Rashid embodies, to argue that *Smoke* shows how black people can enter the abstract public world with their particularity intact would be as careless as to claim that the film disingenuously displaces the dilemma of race onto the sphere of affect. Since the problem of particularity is irreducibly linked to an unstable configuration of the public/private distinction, it should be clear that it is this distinction itself that *Smoke* works to put in question.

Thomas's "real" name, family history, and social status are revealed to Paul by his aunt; he eventually reveals it to his father (when prodded by Paul and Auggie).[50] But in what sense is any name "real"? There is no necessary link between the word and its referent, but rather—we are given to see—the name names a set of *relations,* namely, those of the citizen to the nation (in this case already double, dissonant, and incoherent) and—not coincidentally—the son to the father (which, it is clear, is no more "natural" and just as unstable). But in so naming them, the name's iterability or arbitrariness—its fortuitous, chance dissemination, as well as its presumption to self-authorization—put in question and trouble those very relations. The undecidability of paternity, relayed through the aporias of the name, disturbs and ambiguates the "natural" order of filiation. Thomas/Rashid, the progeny of a system of slavery, has—literally as well as figuratively—no "real" father. His "real" father would be the one who names him in the name of names past, names that produce and haunt the conflicted history of the nation. But his name bears the traces of his family history only obliquely; it is the institutionally produced and legally sanctioned amalgam of the name of a "founding father" and that of a slaveholder, yet one that comes to him by way of his biological father.[51] This "real" father (in the sense that nature is privileged as the mark of authenticity/reality) is missing or missing *as a father.* Similar ambiguation of filiation is repeated throughout the film: Rashid, it is claimed, is Paul's father; in Paul's story of the skier, the son is the "mirror"—the twin, double, or *replacement*—of the father who is paradoxically younger than—temporally or historically posterior to—the son; Ruby's daughter may or may not be Auggie's. By ambiguating filiation, which is indissociable from racism, *Smoke* denaturalizes and re(con)figures citizenship itself by dislocating ascriptive genealogy as condition for civic membership. Raising the double *specter* of slavery and racial hierarchy as a condition of im/possibility for African American citizenship, the film does not simply supplant "nature" with "friendship." Rather, friendship is itself subjected to the critique of liberal capitalist modes of attachment.

The Family Contract

When he locates him, Thomas/Rashid creates, ex nihilo, a relationship with Cyrus by entering into a set of would-be economic transactions with him, a reciprocal relation he soon interrupts by offering Cyrus a gift (a gift of a drawing, of a superfluous creativity and productivity).[52] The young man sits across from Cyrus's garage and makes himself conspicuous. Cyrus comes over to inform Thomas/Rashid that there is nothing on the premises worth stealing—thus initiating a hostile exchange between them based on a lack of trust, faith, or credit and rendered in specifically economistic terms. The young man dismisses the accusation, and when Cyrus realizes that Thomas/Rashid has been drawing a picture and asks to see it, the boy refuses, replying that he can't show Cyrus the picture because if he does, Cyrus will want to buy it because he will become emotionally overwrought by its beauty. Once again, then, in this scene the logic of economic exchange is suffused with speculation and excess, which in this case is an excess of affect linked to the expenditure-without-return of art.

Since Cyrus is unwilling to enter into commerce with him through art, Thomas/Rashid suggests that Cyrus hire him. Cyrus balks, explaining in a condescending manner born of frustration that he "can't even afford to pay my own wages." Nonetheless, a short while later he does hire the youth to clean out the attic of his newly purchased but run-down garage for $5 an hour. It is at this point that the two introduce themselves to each other and Thomas/Rashid gives his name as Paul Benjamin. As Thomas/Paul removes the remnants of someone else's past from the site of Cyrus's economic future, he works very quickly—so quickly that Cyrus tells him, "Relax, kid." It is as if he is trying, despite what appears to be a considerable debt already owed him by Cyrus, to minimize his own compensation—to reduce any future debt.

As they take a lunch break together, Cyrus lights a cigar and pats Thomas/Paul on the back. The young man inquires, "I don't mean to be nosy, but I was wondering what happened to your arm." Cyrus smiles, takes a puff of his cigar, and begins:

> See this, ugh, ugly piece of hardware here, you know. Look at it. Tell you what happened to my arm. Tell you what happened. Uhm, twelve years ago, God looked down on me and said, "Cyrus, you're a bad, stupid, selfish man. First, I'm gonna fill your body with spirits. Then I'm gonna put you behind the wheel of a car. Then I'm gonna have you crash that car, kill the woman that loves you. But you, Cyrus—I'm gonna let you live." 'Cause livin's a lot worse than dyin', kid. "But just to make sure that you don't *forget* what you did to that poor girl, I'm gonna rip off your arm, I'm gonna replace it with a hook." Now he could have ripped off both my arms, both my legs. But, uh, nope, mm. He was gonna be merciful and just rip off my left arm. So every time I look at this hook, I can remember what a bad, stupid, selfish man I am. "Let that be a lesson to you Cyrus! A lesson so you can mend your ways." A warning.

Now, accompanied by tobacco smoke, the story Cyrus tells is true . . . or is it? Certainly, we are given no reason to doubt that the basic facts, as it were, are true: Cyrus got drunk and crashed the car, inadvertently killing the mother of the son before whom he does not realize he is accounting for it. But Cyrus does not simply give these facts; along with Thomas/Paul, we must perform an act of interpretation to receive them from his account. It is not difficult; after all, we know—don't we?—that God had nothing to do with Cyrus's tragedy. Still, we must speculatively read between the allegorical lines of his story. At the same time, Cyrus himself seems to understand the "truth" of his story differently than we, as an interpreting audience, might. This, in turn, means that we are given two stories: on the one hand, the factual story of the events that led to Cyrus's crippling injury, and, on the other hand, the story of the lesson Cyrus learns from these events.

Still, this lesson does not depend directly on those facts, but on a speculative reading of those facts as being the work, or the gift, of God. Cyrus could have understood those events—as we almost certainly do, and he himself perhaps actually does—as the direct consequences of his "stupidity" or "selfishness." But Cyrus describes them as the tools God used to make him conscious of these qualities in himself. Through this one gesture or figure, Cyrus accepts responsibility for being "bad, stupid, and selfish" and displaces or defers responsibility for the accident itself: he is still guilty, but now not of causing the accident but of causing God to cause the accident. The truth of the facts and of responsibility is here irreducibly intermingled with the speculative deferral of Cyrus's narrative. Through this deferral—this detour through narrative or the smoky conflation of fact and fiction—Cyrus both gives and becomes the subject of God's gift.

This detour of speculation is simultaneously linked to the structure of haunting. Not only is Cyrus filled with spirits prior to and during the accident, but he is haunted to this very day through the prosthesis of his artificial limb. Indeed, his life and his identity are constituted on the basis of this prosthesis: after all, God *could have* killed or decimated him, and the lesson he learns is inferred from this past possibility read as a sign of supernatural intentionality. This speculation is what haunts him, and this haunting constitutes his self—the self that is continually trying to overcome its selfishness. It is this dynamic that his cigar smoke marks as he shares a meal with Thomas/Paul, the young man to whom he has given a job after making it absolutely clear that he cannot afford to do so and to whom he is giving an account of himself. Soon after hearing the story, Thomas/Paul slips his drawing of Cyrus's garage under his door.

Cyrus's story is located at the center of a dynamic of exchange that is, like Cyrus himself, haunted and crippled by the spectral movement of debt, obligation, superfluity, and gift that never permits any "true" reciprocity, any balancing of scales. Thomas/Paul enters into exchange with Cyrus by offering to sell him a picture, but the sale is replaced by a gift—a fact that does not prevent the nontransaction from giving rise to an economic relation. Cyrus hires Thomas/Paul, but this otherwise purely economic act is, perhaps, a gift—indeed, a gift Cyrus can hardly afford, even a kind of luxury. In light of this, Thomas/Paul's gift of the picture might be reciprocation, but if so, it is in excess of the money Cyrus would pay him—unless Rashid owed Cyrus for the *fact* of the gift of work. Then again, at least from the boy's point of view, Cyrus already owes him more than he could ever repay—unless, again, Thomas/Paul thinks Cyrus's loss has been payment enough, even if it has not been rendered to him except in the form of a story. The system of obligation is here utterly intractable; its accounts can be squared only through ceaseless speculation. Getting exchange to function properly here would be, in short, like trying to weigh smoke.

Up until the conclusion of the film (and perhaps even then), when Thomas is forced to reveal to Cyrus his actual full name, the relation between the two is not that of father and son. Neither is it quite a relation between an employer and employee; nor is it a friendship. It is, rather, an indeterminate mixture of all three types of relation, so that the logic of exchange—which works by failing to work as promised—is to be understood in the context of the film to correspond to a general economy of sociality. And just as genealogy, economy, and friendship commingle to structure the account of liberal-capitalist citizenship, the reconstitution of the relation between Cyrus and Thomas Jefferson Cole takes place through speculative narrative under the sign of tobacco smoke. The general economy of ambiguity and excess "[p]erhaps . . . reminds us of the institutionality of this institution, but of an institution that can only consist in passing itself off as natural. [It] invites us perhaps to suspend, at the end of a question, the old opposition between nature and institution, *phusis* and *thesis, phusis* and *nomos,* nature and convention, knowledge and credit (faith), nature and all its others." In other words, "[t]here is no nature, only effects of nature: denaturation or naturalization. Nature, the meaning of nature, is reconstituted after the fact on the basis of a simulacrum (for example, literature) that it is thought to cause."[53]

It is this structure that governs the social contract, and despite liberalism's reflexivity concerning its fictive derivation and legitimation, the configuration of liberal-capitalist citizenship rests on an obliviousness to the full implications of this fact.

Tobacco and the Law

Immediately after Paul, in his effort to "put the scales in balance," offers Rashid a place to stay and gives him his address, we return to the cigar shop, where Auggie is talking to the store's owner, Vinnie.

> Vinnie (*laughing and lighting a cigar*): You never take anything too serious, do you?
>
> Auggie (*laughing and smoking a cigarette*): I try not to, anyway. It's better for your health. I mean, look at you, Vincent. You're the guy with the wife and the three kids and the ranch house on Long Island. You're the guy with the white shoes and the white Caddy and the white shag carpet. But you've had two heart attacks, and I'm still waiting for my first.
>
> Vinnie: I should stop smoking these, is what I should do. Fuckers are gonna kill me one day.
>
> Auggie: Enjoy yourself while you can, Vin. They're gonna legislate us out of business pretty soon anyway.
>
> Vinnie: Yeah. Pretty soon they catch you smoking tobacco they're gonna line you up against a wall and shoot you.
>
> Auggie: Tobacco today, sex tomorrow. In three or four years, it'll probably be against the law to smile at strangers.
>
> Vinnie: Speaking of which, you still going ahead on that deal with the Montecristos?
>
> Auggie: It's all set. My guy in Miami said he'd have them within the next few weeks. Are you sure you don't want to go in with me? $5,000 outlay, guaranteed $10,000 return. A consortium of Court Street lawyers and judges. They're just drooling to get their lips around some Cuban cigars.
>
> Vinnie: Look, I don't care what you do—just don't get caught, huh? Last thing I heard, it's still illegal to sell Cuban cigars in this country.
>
> Auggie: It's the law that's buying! That's the beautiful thing about it. I mean, when's the last time you heard of a judge sending himself to jail?

Once the seal of the social contract, tobacco is now among the luxuries disciplined by the law, which, not surprisingly, stands in a contradictory relation to its pleasures. That these pleasures—and, specifically, their legal status—are aligned with those of sex is to be expected, but it is telling that they are also likened to "smiling at strangers." In a perverse development, it would appear that under existing political conditions the sign of sociality that marks the endorsement of law and the law of law is threatened with legal suppression—with being outside the law. And the "consortium"—an informal and illegal association—is defined by, on the one hand, a common economic purpose and, on the other, the illegality of that purpose, both of which factors stem directly from the uncontrollable ambivalence of the sign of tobacco/smoke.[54]

Moreover, both tobacco and the law are here the subjects of economic speculation and excess. The "guaranteed" profit is ironically assured by the social and legal standing of the criminals involved; but the guarantee is, for that very reason, without guarantee, and the possibility and size of profit depends on the legal risks involved. While the law has been alienated from its own social foundations, it is the illicit mutual promise among lawyers beyond the law that must suffice for the surreptitious reappropriation of (the pleasures of) sociality. In accordance with the law of law, social obligation comes from beyond the contracts it would guarantee, coded in this case as irreducibly foreign tobacco.[55] And it is the unsignability of their economic contract that would yield its profit. Alien and illegal, their contract is null on its face and thus cannot supply the surface necessary for a signature. It binds like the honor among thieves, from the start in excess of legal guarantees. In sum, the tobacco/smoke trope marks the irreducible ambiguity of the social contract, the speculative and excessive nature of which is dissimulated by the self-authorizing fictions generated by the liberal-capitalist political economy it founds.

Auggie's Photo Album

Inadvertent, accidental gifts pervade the film, invariably leading characters and relationships in unanticipated directions. One example follows Auggie and Vinnie's conversation about Cuban cigars. As Auggie is closing the store, Paul runs up, asking if it's too late to buy more Schimmelpenninks. Auggie opens the store for him, and as the purchase takes place, Auggie realizes he'd left his camera on the counter. It turns out he's been working on a personal project for four thousand days straight, taking black-and-white photographs of the store from across the street every morning at 8:00. The minor favor he does for his friend Paul by reopening the store is more than repaid when what he calls his "life's work" is (perhaps) saved from interruption, an interruption that, given the nature of the undertaking, would have destroyed it at one stroke.[56]

Auggie has collected all these photographs, and he now takes Paul to his apartment to show them to him. As Paul leafs through album after album, Auggie tells him, "You'll never get it if you don't slow down, my friend." "What do you mean?" asks Paul, tapping his cigar into an ashtray. "I mean you're going too fast. You're not even looking at the pictures," explains Auggie. "But they're all the same," Paul chuckles politely. Answers Auggie: "They're all the same, but each one is different from every other one. You got your bright mornings and your dark mornings; you got your summer light and your autumn light; you got your weekdays and your weekends; you got your people in overcoats and galoshes and you got your people in T-shirts and shorts. Sometimes the same people, sometimes different ones. Sometimes the different ones become the same and the same ones disappear. The earth revolves around the sun and every day the light from the sun hits the earth at a different angle."

As he is speaking, the screen is filled with his snapshots, one dissolving into the next. When he finishes, he takes a drag of his cigarette. Paul, saying, "Slow down, huh?" takes a drag on his cigar. "That's what I'd recommend. You know how it is. 'Tomorrow and tomorrow and tomorrow, time creeps in its petty pace'," Auggie says. Paul nods and begins looking at the photos again, and again, one after another, the photos take up the screen. After a few are shown this way, we return to Paul who, paging a bit more, comes upon a certain photo and says, "Oh, Jesus. Look. It's Ellen."

In this scene of bonding over tobacco and photographs, a blocked storyteller learns an important lesson about narrativity from a cigar store manager—that is, a master of blowing smoke. Issuing from a prior scene of simple exchange transformed into the chance gift of a "life's work," this conversation is an accounting. Auggie is explaining himself, giving an account of himself, to his friend the writer. He is giving an account of his "life's work," which is itself a kind of account, "the record of my little spot." Auggie is an author endorsing his narrative in order to deliver its lesson over to his author friend Paul. Derrida observes that

> there is problematic of the gift only on the basis of a consistent problematic of the trace and the text. . . . This is why we always set out from texts for the elaboration of this problematic. . . . And we are unable to *take our departure in texts insofar as they depart* (they separate themselves and their origin, from us) *at the departure.* . . . The most apparently direct writing, the most directly concrete, personal writing which is supposedly in direct contact with "the thing itself," this

> writing is "on credit:" subjected to the authority of a commentary or a re-editing that it is not even capable of reading.[57]

What Auggie has realized is that the merest, most arbitrary and inconsequential act of intervention in the purely random flux of "things in themselves" results in the imposition of a textual order. Without the least authorial intention, he produces a text. He records the endurance of a place through time, but in so doing he records the trace of the operation of différance. "They're all the same, but each one is different from every other one": that sameness depends on this difference, and this difference—articulated by way of a deferral—marks itself in that sameness. The systematicity of Auggie's project depends upon the gift of random chance, and its legibility depends upon an infinitely deferred closure or elimination of this chance. Thus what Paul will never get if he does not slow down is not the meaning recorded in the story, but the meaning of narrativity as such. In his rush to the conclusion, Paul expects to find the photo narrative vindicated, resolved. It will have become legible, accountable, in retrospect. But because no such conclusion is ever forthcoming, Auggie teaches him to attend to the temporalizing articulations of the trace. Stories, Paul is given to learn, can never be fully redeemed by the future because the future never arrives. Instead, there is no choice but to "give credit" to them, and to give it provisionally, pending a "reediting." Auggie's photo story is such a "reediting"—and it implies that the story of the promise that legitimates liberal citizenship is subject to such a reediting as well. The power of that story derives from the infinite deferral of this promise's fulfillment, and while this fact makes it possible to excuse or overlook, at any given time, the shortcomings of actually existing political conditions, the selfsame fact renders the story forever subject to reediting—a life's work for masters of blowing smoke.

It may seem capricious to read this scene politically in this way. But this speculative reading will have been vindicated. Auggie will end up telling Paul another story assembled out of the random detritus of everyday life, and that story will specifically concern the operation of exchange, law, and filiation in interracial friendship. Neither determinately true nor false, that story will also have been a "reediting" given "on credit." This bricolage will not have assembled a fable out of, or about (a given) reality or its fragments, but will have produced reality *as* a fable, *as* allegory. In a scene of gift and exchange, Auggie will both literally and figuratively "blow smoke" at Paul in a transaction acknowledged as an act definitive of friendship: "If you can't share your secrets with your friends," Auggie will say, "then what kinda friend are you?"

"The Creeper" and the Fortuitous Circulation of Illegitimate Money

The concept/trope that animates and orients Derrida's reading of Baudelaire's story is given in that story's title, counterfeit money: "We can no longer avoid the question of what money is: true money or counterfeit money, which can only be what it is, false or counterfeit, to the extent to which no one knows it is false, that is, to the extent to which it circulates, appears, functions *as good and true money.* The enigma of this simulacrum should begin to orient us toward the triple and indissociable question of the *gift,* of *forgiveness,* and of the *excuse.* And to the question of whether a gift can or *ought* to *secure itself* against counterfeit money."[58]

This paradoxical opposition between "true" and "counterfeit" signs is the one thematized in the film by way of the proliferation of narratives, the "truth-value" of which is constantly in question. And just as it happens in Baudelaire's story and Derrida's reading of it, the film links this paradox to that of gift exchange by way of the circulation of money.

Thomas's gift/compensation to Cyrus is followed directly by another. Immediately after we see Rashid's drawing of Cyrus's garage slipped underneath a door, the film cuts to Paul's apartment. The doorbell rings, and when Paul opens the door, Rashid walks in with the TV set he "found" among the bric-a-brac upstairs at Cyrus's:

> Paul: Oh, it's you.
>
> Rashid: Look, I just wanted to give you this as a token of my appreciation.
>
> Paul (*laughing softly*): Appreciation for what?
>
> Rashid (*shrugging*): I don't know—for helping me out. You want it?
>
> *Groaning, Paul gestures toward the dresser. Rashid places the TV on top of it.*
>
> Paul: Where did you get that thing?
>
> Rashid: Bought it. $29.95, on sale. Goldbaum's TV and Radio. Well, I guess that just about does it. Now you'll be able to watch the game, take a break from your work.
>
> *Rashid walks out the door.*
>
> Paul (*feigning annoyance*): Where do you think you're going?

Rashid: Business meeting. Meeting my accountant at 3:00.

Paul (*in an annoyed voice*): Cut it *out.* Cut it out. Come back here.

Rashid: I don't have time.

Paul: Close the door.

Rashid walks back in and shuts the door.

Paul: Sit. In this chair.

Rashid removes his backpack and sits.

Paul: Now listen carefully. Your aunt Em came by a couple of days ago. She was . . . sick with worry. She was out of her mind. We had an interesting talk about you. *Thomas.* You understand what I'm saying? Your aunt Em thinks you're in trouble. And so do I. Tell me about it, kid. I want to hear all about it right now.

Thomas: You don't really want to know.

Paul (*now genuinely annoyed*): I don't, huh? What is it that makes you such an authority on what I want and don't want?

Thomas: Okay, okay.

Paul: Well? Jesus.

Thomas: Okay! It's all so stupid. There's this guy, see? Charles Clem, the Creeper—that's what people call him. The kinda guy you don't wanna cross paths with. And I crossed paths with him. That's why I'm trying to stay clear of my neighborhood, to make sure I don't run into him again.

Paul: Does this have something to do with whatever it was that you weren't supposed to see?

Thomas: Yeah. Look, I just happened to be walking by. All of a sudden, the Creeper and this other guy happen to run out of the check-cashing place with masks on their faces and guns in their hands. They just about run smack into me. And the Creeper recognizes me. And I know he knows that I recognize him. If the guy from the check-cashing place hadn't run out screaming bloody murder, he woulda shot me. I'm telling you, the Creeper woulda shot me right there on the sidewalk! But the noise distracted him, and when he turned around to see what was going on, I took off. One more second, and I would've been dead.

Paul (*shaking his head*): Why didn't you go to the police?

Thomas: The man has friends. And I don't think they're likely to forgive me if I testify against him.

Paul: What makes you think you'll be any safer around here? You're only about a mile from where you live.

Thomas: It's not that far away, but . . . it's another galaxy. Black is black, and white is white. And never the twain shall meet.

Paul: Well, it looks like they've met in this apartment.

Thomas: Let's not get *too* idealistic.

Paul (*offscreen, giggling*): Fair enough. We wouldn't want to get carried away, would we?

Thomas (*inaudibly, shaking his head*): No.

Paul walks over to Thomas.

Thomas (*looking disconcerted*): What?

Paul takes Thomas by the scruff of his T-shirt and makes him stand up.

Paul: Call your aunt Em and tell her you're still alive.

In the next shot, it is evening and Paul and Thomas are watching a baseball game on the TV Thomas brought over earlier. Both are smoking cigars. They are silent. Thomas takes a puff and chokes on the smoke, coughing to clear his throat. He takes another, and this time blows the smoke gently and self-consciously in Paul's direction.

This scene, which indicates the moment at which the relationship between Paul and Thomas develops from a simple exchange of favors into a bond marked by a long-term commitment to each other's welfare, begins with an act of reciprocation through countergift. Rashid, having just given Cyrus a contradictory gift in compensation for goodwill, takes (and here we can only speculate as to whether this is a theft: does Cyrus know of the existence of this TV? Given that it is the surplus left him along with the garage, would he consider it his property? And if so, would he care that Thomas/Paul took it? Is theft—and therefore property itself—a purely legal matter, or does it depend on the knowledge and attitude of the owner? Can the owner of property be an owner if he has no reason to consider himself one? Is property an attribute of persons, as liberal legal theory presumes, or is it a function of knowledge and thus subject to the vagaries of communication?) a TV and gives it to Paul as "a token of my appreciation." He then indicates that the transaction between them is, perhaps, completed: "Well, I guess that just about does it." Again, we can only speculate whether this gift is just compensation or is in excess of it. After all, Paul wanted to "put the scales in balance " for the gift of life, and it is an open question whether this is ever possible. But if it were possible, then perhaps he has done so by hosting Rashid for a couple of days. If so, then Thomas's gift of the TV is excessive, unless, once again, we view it as compensation for Paul's goodwill, which would itself be in excess of the act of letting Rashid stay with him. All that can be clear at this point is that both Paul and Thomas continue to experience and be governed by the obligation to reciprocate, and that they are unable to calculate the moment when the scales of gift/countergift are balanced. The gift keeps on giving, as it were, and they are powerless to stop it or to resist its power. This excess of the gift moves their relationship forward and constitutes the bond of their friendship for the remainder of the film.

Thomas's story of his encounter with the Creeper links the exchange of gifts to the circulation of money in a number of ways. First, this story is contiguous with Thomas's gift transactions with Cyrus and Paul. Second, the robbery Thomas witnessed is juxtaposed with what may or may not be his larceny of the TV set when we find out that he has ended up in possession of—that he has, perhaps, stolen—the stolen cash. Third, when Thomas witnessed the robbery and—he speculates—was perhaps nearly killed, he was in the wrong place at the wrong time, just as he had been in the right place at the right time to—perhaps—save Paul's life and thereby enter into the spiral of gift exchange with him.[59] Finally, the money stolen by the Creeper enters the dynamic of gift exchange through Thomas's encounter with Paul and comes to reproduce this dynamic by involving Auggie, and then Ruby, in it.

When Thomas (then still Rashid) comes to stay with Paul, he leaves a brown paper bag containing the stolen money behind some books in Paul's bookcase. (Given this, we are forced to speculate whether Thomas takes Paul up on his offer in order to hide the money in the first place, as well as whether he returns with a gift in order to regain access to this money.) Later, Paul asks Auggie to give Thomas a job at the tobacco shop. Auggie does, and Thomas inadvertently destroys Auggie's stash of illegal Cuban cigars, a stash that represents the investment of all of Auggie's life savings, plus profits. To compensate Auggie, Thomas gives him the stolen money, which Auggie then gives to Ruby—something he had been unwilling to do earlier, using the excuse that all his cash was tied up in a business venture—despite the fact that there is only "a fifty-fifty chance" that he is the father of her daughter. Just after Thomas repays Auggie, the Creeper shows up at Paul's apartment, and he and his accomplice beat Paul up in an effort to find out where Thomas and the money are. Paul does not crack, keeping Thomas's secret and risking his own life to save—perhaps—that of the young man, thus—again, perhaps—repaying the gift of life that set the spiral going in the first place.

The money that, in its sheer circulation, generates exchange and transforms relationships among the main characters in *Smoke* is of dubious legitimacy or value. Representing, perhaps, the usurious profit produced by the "check-cashing place," it is the surplus generated through the temporal deferral that is interest, the excess that springs forth, as if miraculously, from the exchange of one form of money (a check) for another (cash). Money exchanged for money somehow yields a surplus through the detour of time. In any case, this money is stolen by armed robbers, becoming at that point evidence in a crime. Possessed by the robbers, it would no longer be property, or, at least, its value as property and as currency would be, at least in principle, suspended for the period of time required for the legal process to make use of it in a criminal proceeding, if there were one. If not, however, the money could be used as money by the robbers themselves, but not rightfully. Thomas (or Rashid, "the righteous one") picks up the bag the Creeper drops, but in so doing he is not exactly stealing the money, since, as already stolen, it does not "really" belong to the one who drops it. Thomas is in possession of evidence, and therefore is not legally entitled to keep the cash. Still, it is unclear whether he has stolen from the thief. This highly ambiguous money, from the first representing the speculative excesses of capital, Thomas calls "my future" before he uses it to pay Auggie for the loss of capital Thomas caused. In its circulation, money is a free-floating signifier, marking not *value* but *difference* in value—like the difference at stake in Raleigh's bet—and thus appropriately comes from nowhere determinate into Rashid's hands, by luck, fortune, or chance, like a gift of nature.

When Paul brings Thomas to talk to Auggie, he first offers an apology: "The kid's sorry, Auggie." "Yeah?" asks Auggie, "Well, I'm sorry too. Took me three years to save up those 5,000 bucks, and now I'm broke. I can't hardly pay for this beer. Not to speak of having my credibility destroyed. Do you understand what I'm sayin'? My credibility. So yeah, I'm sorry too. I'm about as sorry as I've ever been in my whole fuckin' life." At this moment, just before Thomas gives Auggie the bag of money, it is clear that while the financial debt will perhaps have been repaid, Auggie's "credibility" will not have been restored so easily. The faith and credit extended him will have become suspect, and for a master of "blowing smoke," this would be an intolerable loss. Indeed, credibility is what is at stake in this scene of compensation and forgiveness. Auggie does not trust Thomas's gift, asking, "What is this, some kind of a joke?" and initially refuses to accept it, speculating, "It's probably stolen anyway." When he asks Thomas why he wants to "give" him money, Thomas replies, "To get my job back." In other words, the money that would have been Thomas's future is being offered to restore the previously established relation of exchange, which, of course, it cannot do in principle because the credibility risked in any such relation is always already in excess of the goods exchanged. But it would seem Thomas has also lost credibility. Even if he settles his financial debt, the return of his job would constitute a gift—indeed, since the job remains a simple matter of contract, its return in the wake of the loss of credibility would be possible only on the condition of trust. It would be the gift of trust, unsecured by anything at all. In addition to—perhaps—losing the credit owed him, Auggie is being asked to extend further credit to Thomas. It is no wonder he calls the kid "crazy." But at this point, Paul says to Auggie, "No, he's not. You are," to which Auggie responds, "You're right. I just didn't think you knew." Given that the goods, gifts, and forgiveness involved here are heterogeneous and incommensurable—given that they cannot function as objects of exchange in a system that would yield balanced scales—it would not be unreasonable to read this admission as an acknowledgment of the "madness of economic reason" described by Derrida. Indeed, an appreciation of this madness is just what Auggie acquires in this exchange, which is why he decides to give the money to Ruby despite the clear uncertainty concerning both his paternity and the likelihood that it would rescue Felicity and her unborn baby from drug addiction.

When Auggie offers his forgiveness to Thomas by saying, "Fuck you, kid" and Thomas reciprocates with "Fuck you too, you white son of a bitch," it remains unclear whether gift or exchange has taken place between these two men.[60] The exchange of expletives, delivered with irony born of obvious affection, underwrites their newfound incommensurable equality. Previously employee and employer, the kid and the son of a bitch have been reborn, as it were, into a relation of equality clearly marked by (racial, class, and generational) difference. Through the mad, chance circulation of illegitimate, speculative capital, they have risked, lost, given, and returned credit, thereby becoming subject to the paradoxical obligation to give, an obligation that, in virtue of being incalculable, comes to serve as the unsecured guarantee of equality without imposing the law of abstraction-through-calculation. What circulates in this scene—what, in the end, money, legitimate or not, represents—is trust, faith, or credit itself.[61] Certainly the significance of the money has been transformed. As pure abstraction, dependent wholly on its social context for both use- and exchange-value, the infinite iterability of the ultimate floating signifier finally stands for the credit extended as a condition of communication and sociality, the very same credit that is both the precondition and the speculatively generated product of friendship and the principle of speculative accounting that generates narrative—for example, Auggie's Christmas story.

Auggie's Christmas Story

Near the end of the film, once all the relationships have gone through their various transformations, Paul comes into Auggie's shop and tells him that he's been invited by the *New York Times* to publish a Christmas story, but that he has been unable to come up with anything good. He asks Auggie if he knows any Christmas stories, and Auggie says, "Christmas stories. Sure. I know a ton of 'em." "You know any good ones?" Paul asks. "Good ones? Of course! You kiddin'? I'll tell you what—buy me lunch, my friend, and I'll tell you the best Christmas story you ever heard. And I guarantee every word of it is true," boasts Auggie.[62] In the next shot, Auggie is sitting at a diner waiting for Paul to join him at the table. In his hands is a newspaper, the front page of which shows the mug shots of the Creeper and his accomplice, Roger Goodwin. Paul sits across from Auggie, and the master of blowing smoke begins his narrative, which begins during "the summer of the Bicentennial" and will concern the first and only camera Auggie ever had.[63] He tells of how he chased a shoplifter from his store, and while he did not catch him, he found his wallet on the sidewalk a block from the store. The young man's name was Roger Goodwin, and his address was in Boerum Hill. An attentive viewer will by now have noticed that the elements of the story are gathered from events depicted in the film: earlier, Auggie does chase away a kid shoplifting in his store; Boerum Hill is the housing project where Thomas Cole lives; and there is Roger Goodwin's name. But Paul is apparently not sufficiently attentive, because he does not suspect that the story may not be true until Auggie is finished describing how he spent Christmas with the blind old grandmother of Roger Goodwin under the pretense, supplied by her, of being Roger himself; how he lied to her about the events in his/Roger's life; and how he inexplicably and spontaneously decided to steal a camera from an unexpected stash in her bathroom.

When Auggie is finished, Paul asks, "Did you ever go back to see her?"

> Auggie: Once, about three or four months later. I felt so bad about stealing the camera, I hadn't even used it yet. I finally made up my mind to return it, but Granny Ethel wasn't there anymore. Someone else had moved into the apartment, and he couldn't tell me where she was.
>
> Paul: She probably died.
>
> Auggie: Yeah, probably.
>
> Paul: Which means she spent her last Christmas with you.

Auggie: I guess so. I never thought of it that way.

Paul: It was a good deed, Auggie. It was a nice thing you did for her.

Auggie: I lied to her, and then I stole from her. I don't see how you can call that a good deed.

Paul: You made her happy. That camera was probably stolen anyway. It's not as if the person you took it from really owned it.

Auggie: Anything for art, eh, Paul?

Paul: I wouldn't say that. But at least you've put the camera to good use.

Auggie: And now you've got your Christmas story, don't you?

Paul: Yes, I suppose I do.

As Auggie begins to grin coyly, a look of suspicion comes over Paul's face.

Paul: Bullshit is a real talent, Auggie. To make up a good story, you have to push all the right buttons. I'd say you were there among the masters.

Auggie: What do you mean?

Paul: I mean, it's a good story.

Auggie: Shit. If you can't share your secrets with your friends, then what kinda friend are you?

Paul: Exactly. Life just wouldn't be worth living, would it?

The two men sit quietly across from each other, lovingly blowing smoke in each other's direction. As the blue credits begin to roll, a silent, black-and-white mini-film of Auggie's story rolls on the screen as Tom Waits's "You're Innocent When You Dream" supplies the suggestive soundtrack. In the film-within-the-film, it becomes clear that conspicuously absent from Auggie's account is the fact that Granny Ethel is black. The audience should have been able to surmise as much from the mug shot of Roger Goodwin, but Paul would have no way of knowing either Roger's or his grandmother's race from Auggie's story. At most, he might make an assumption based on the information that they lived in Boerum Hill. Because the film version of Auggie's story is in black and white, the racial difference that Auggie elides in his account and to which Granny Ethel is literally blind is partly effaced. This is especially true in one scene, where Granny Ethel hugs Auggie/Roger and their faces are pressed together cheek to cheek in a close-up shot. Their features are remarkably similar, and the absence of color leaves only a negligible difference in their skin tones. Viewed in black and white, black and white begin to disappear as markers of race.

3. Film still from *Smoke:* © 1995 Miramax Films

It is moments such as this one that appear to inscribe *Smoke* in the Hollywood tradition of interracial friendship derogated by DeMott, and while the film does participate in that tradition in its own idiosyncratic way, the effacement of racial difference in this scene should not be viewed as a manifestation of the abstract, universalistic logic of liberal social theory. This is because both Auggie and Granny Ethel are faking it: as Auggie puts it, "It was like a game we both decided to play—without having to discuss the rules. I mean, that woman knew I wasn't her grandson. She was old and dotty, but she wasn't so far gone that she couldn't tell the difference between a stranger and her own flesh and blood. But it made her happy to pretend, and since I had nothing better to do anyway, I was happy to go along with her." Granny Ethel would seem to understand as well as Paul and Auggie do that it is more important that a story be good than that it be true. And she should: the game—the exchange—between her and Auggie depends on the "precomprehension" of this "law of the universe" described by Derrida. And what makes this particular story good, for Granny Ethel as well as for Paul, both of whom receive it as a gift from Auggie, is the effacement of "the difference between a stranger and her own flesh and blood," an effacement that, because it is self-consciously undertaken, does not suppress racial and class difference but rather puts it into play—the play of a "game." The difference in question is the difference between the abstract, "white" liberal citizen and the historically specific, racially marked "flesh and blood" of a black descendant; it is the difference that divides civic status from genealogy in principle while organizing political membership on the basis of ascription in practice. DeMott's liberalism would efface this difference in a way that privileges "whiteness" as the (non)mark of citizenship; Auggie's story engages this difference in an altogether different way. This is what a "good" story can do. The clear implication, of course, is that the founding fiction of liberalism can be reappropriated in such a way, in contradistinction to the way in which it is typically appropriated by the Hollywood tradition of interracial friendship film. Rather than excoriating, with DeMott and Berlant, the mythography that transforms the liberal story of universal citizenship into an ideological reinscription of racial hierarchy, *Smoke* deconstructs the narrative possibilities that organize, without necessarily predetermining, this mythography.

How does Paul know that Auggie's Christmas story is "bullshit"? It is perhaps *too* coherent—Paul knows that "true" stories always contain elements of the implausible or the improbable, that they *surprise* and *exceed* reason and logic, and that they do not "push all the right buttons." The hallmark of falsehood, ironically, is verisimilitude. But Paul still insists that Auggie's is "a good story" and compliments him for being "among the masters" of blowing smoke. If Paul's story of the bet contains the film in embryo, Auggie's Christmas story recapitulates the elements of the film in a new narrative that is not "true," but "good"—and linked explicitly to friendship and exchange. It is "good" not only because in it Auggie does something nice for—gives a gift to—a stranger, and not only because the story itself is a gift to a friend (offered "in exchange" for lunch), but, perhaps more important, because it is an example of the way a "good" story works: by reappropriating the chance, smoke-like, ambiguous remainders[64] of "reality" and by forming, thematically and performatively, the substance of friendships, relationships conditioned on and secured by debt, faith, credit, and the trust inherent in the sharing of secrets, most notably the secret that the stories that bind may not be true but are good—in just the way both "true" and "counterfeit" money is good so long as it continues to function as a principle of sociality. In just this way, the story liberalism tells about the origin of the social contract is a good story, even though it is purely speculative and knows itself to be so. The fictive or speculative nature of this story is linked directly to the structure of the contract it describes through the figure of the bet offered in the film's opening story, the sense of which is mirrored in Auggie's story. Closing the quotation marks around the main narrative—and reediting a selection of its elements—this scene, paired with the story of the bet, not only summarizes the thematic concerns of the film, but also re-marks the *iterability* of narrative.

"If you can't share your secrets with your friends, then what kinda friend are you?" Auggie asks. The act of sharing secrets is what defines friendship—but what is the secret in question? Is it the content of the story (Auggie's theft) or the fact that the story is fictional? This is undecidable within the film, and this undecidability is the film's point: the grandmother is blind, so she acts "as if" her "vision" of the world comports with a "reality" she knows she cannot know; this is what Auggie tells Paul we must do—it makes the content of his story "true" even if it is "false." In the form of a gift offered during the "season of giving," Auggie "gives" counterfeit coin that can nonetheless profitably be put to use just as "real" money can.

Auggie's comment seems almost designed to function as a response to Kant's counterintuitive insistence that friends should shield one another from the burdens imposed by the confession of secrets. The emblematic representative of practical reason whose philosophical speculations are intimately related to the logic of liberalism—for example, the Rawlsian logic of distributive justice-through-calculation or the Habermasian logic of communicative rationality—Kant, for whom friendship is of central importance, also cautions that "we should so conduct ourselves towards a friend that there is no harm done if he should turn into an enemy."[65] Friends must behave *as if* they *will have become* enemies—in effect, as enemies in advance. That is, for both ethical and practical reasons, friends ought not share secrets; indeed, this nonsharing is among the highest (non)acts of friendship. Kant would have friends "give" each other the gift of nongiving or nonsharing. Friendship, which Kant conceives as "an association of two persons through equal and mutual love and respect," must be strictly reciprocal, and this reciprocity would be violated by confession, by the gift of the secret's burden, which would unbalance the scales of respect.[66] It is the *withholding* of credit or faith that would safeguard Kantian friendship, which would *consist* in protecting the other from the burden of one's secret and in protecting oneself from the speculatively projected betrayal by the other. Leaving aside the complex problems posed by this conjunction of "love" and "respect"—which, for Kant, are heterogeneous faculties of, respectively, affect and reason—how is this equality to be measured or calculated?[67] For Auggie—and for *Smoke*—friendship would be the relation that propels its subjects beyond calculation and beyond the order of the calculable. And it is the shared secret, the credit extended in the form of its burden, the irreducible risk that the friend will perhaps become an enemy, that is the necessary condition of friendship.

As Bonnie Honig explains, "Teleological self-respect (and the self-control, concealment, and discipline it implies) is what the members of Kant's community look for in others; it is the basis of their inclusion or exclusion of others from their moral and juridical arrangements."[68] A necessary condition of this respect is the nongiving that would secure reciprocity, and it is reciprocity of respect that secures "juridical arrangements." In order to render his political theory—given, in terms of an economy of reason, as universal reciprocal obligation—consistent with his speculative psychology, Kant must surmount the obstacle of friendship, which threatens to unbalance his account by introjecting excess in the form of the nonreciprocal, unaccountable obligation imposed by the gift. His solution is to recharacterize friendship in direct opposition to the conventional apprehension of it as a thoroughly intimate mode of attachment founded on irreducible partiality and only partly constrained by reason and moral law. Given that he finds it necessary to locate this detour through friendship at the heart of his account of moral law, this account in effect depends on this reconfiguration of the figure of friendship. Consequently, it is the expenditure-without-return figured by gift/exchange in *Smoke* as the irreducible condition of sociality that haunts the liberal imaginary.

Conclusion

On the other hand, could it be that, in *Smoke,* via the figure of circulation, *abstraction itself fails* to sustain its demand and collapses into particularity? Judith Butler, Ernesto Laclau, and Slavoj Žižek all maintain that this conflation is a basic feature of discourse—that is, the abstract Universal (for example, formal rights-based citizenship) always involves a particular content whose particularity is disavowed (for example, white, heterosexual, male).[69] But with Derrida we may be thinking something else. *In the very drive of abstraction,* it turns out that what circulates is incalculable, untotalizable debt as the principle of "total" sociality. This circulation actively underscores the incapacity of, say, money, to remain—or even fully become—abstract (Louise to Thelma: "That money was our future!" Rashid to Paul: "This money is my whole future") and to secure *purely* (or merely) calculative reciprocity. Is this, then, a "failure" of liberal universalization, or is such failure *rhetorically staged as the legitimating postulate* of liberal discourse itself? Does this "failure" of exchange-based sociality reproduce liberalism by reinscribing disavowed particularity to supplement abstraction, thereby sustaining it? Or does it interrupt and suspend the relentless régime of dis-incorporation? The gift of smoke unblocks the flow of signs, the capacity to narrate, by decentering or de-valorizing the distinction between (the demand to produce) truth and (the excess of idiosyncrasy implicit in) fiction. It is the circulation of undecidable narration—not the integrative force of shared norms or hegemonic "empty signifiers" of social totality—haunted by radical debt that installs relays of obligation among the broken subjects in the film without "suturing the gaps" between them. Indeed, this circulating undecidability mediates a normative refusal of integrative force, a refusal that paradoxically implies and betokens infinite responsibility heterogeneous to any sort of signifying totality.

Consequently, these gaps do not collapse to produce pure, intimate "community"—just the reverse. What is suspended is *the demand to produce one's own abstraction* through dis-incorporation (the demand that mutes Paul and exiles Rashid). In its place is introduced a moment of negative self-relation, an inner distance that, far from reinscribing alienation, affirms the excessiveness of sociality over its "ideological" determination(s). The subjects of debt do not begin magically to coincide with themselves or to commune with each other; instead, they learn to "look awry" at the signifying machine within which they are caught. It is perhaps this gesture that embodies the signal achievement of liberal discourse as a deconstructive rhetoric.

From another direction, it may be argued that capitalism installs itself into the gap between the abstract (universal) and the particular sustained by radical debt, appearing as the law of exchange that secures sociality by universalizing a particular content (for Marx, "labor") as the measure of all things. From this vantage, what is dissimulated in ideology is not (only) that a particular content has been installed as universal (not, that is, that heterosexual white males are the transparent subjects of liberalism) but that *this gesture is itself impossible* because of a radical interruption structuring the opposition itself. The critique of ideology that presumes the accomplishment of this gesture reproduces ideology by "granting" to it that the absence of which it functions to conceal. Demanding to expand the abstract/universal to make it genuinely inclusive (Rawls, Habermas) or rejecting the abstract/universal to insist on particularity as the condition of social belonging (communitarians, feminists, multiculturalists) are two obverse strategies that both fatally concede the actuality of the distinction.

From the deconstructive perspective so resonant in the film, the circulation of money should appear not simply as the violent *erasure* of particularity to produce abstraction (a common and problematic reading of Marx), nor, conversely, as the covert *smuggling in* of particularity as that which makes money circulate as the substance of sociality (a common and problematic reading of Mauss). Instead, as the "empty signifier" that sutures social totality, money should be recognized as the site where the opposition is *suspended* (like smoke) or undecidable: how do we know money is not counterfeit? Only social convention sustains its authenticity, and only the possibility of authenticity sustains the socius. Thus what circulates is the impossibility of the socius—as a condition of its possibility.

To be sure, the misrecognition this circulation produces is the idea that I owe someone a determinable quantity, that debts can and ought to be settled, and that the total system of exchange is what holds the social together. What I actually owe is my assent, my acknowledgment of irredeemable debt. But since this debt is, as it were, *given* and thus impossible either to refuse or endorse, I cannot acknowledge it. My acknowledgment itself takes the form of operational blindness: I keep on owing and paying. I am he who pays, and my desire to belong to the socius must appear to me to be the result of my own rational calculation regarding the benefits to be derived from belonging, from obeying the law, which will in turn recognize me.

In *Smoke,* however, the friends lie to each other in a way that foregrounds the impossibility of authentication and thereby keeps in circulation not the forcible, clandestine universalization of particularity but the structuring gap between them. In this way, radical mutual indebtedness is *thematized* as the impossible/necessary condition of the "total social fact": communication is *systematically exposed* as presupposing an impossible presocial moment of conventional agreement, that is, the Law of law. This "agreement" is painstakingly depicted by the narrative as purely spectral even if unmistakably forceful, producing material consequences and materiality as such. It is *credited with giving* rise to the appearance of an opposition between the universal and the particular, insofar as the convention implies universality even as its demand is always on me in my specificity (which is nothing other than *my* singular responsibility before the call of this debt). This opposition—and not particularity—is the fictional object of liberal critique; it is what, in the allegorical mode exemplified by *Smoke,* liberal discourse refuses in order to establish itself. Here, citizenship as friendship is neither the fulfillment of abstract universal law nor the radically particular love of another; instead, it is the scrupulous fidelity to the failure of this distinction.

Conclusion

The Friendship Supplement and the Rule of Allegory

Beginning with Marx, the most trenchant critiques of liberal democracy have focused on its disabling effects. For Marx, liberalism was to be understood as the benign ideological mask concealing and facilitating the ruthless colonization of social life by capital. It was the false promise of individual autonomy, a form of freedom construed in such a way that its exercise would produce the illusion of self-determination while leaving untouched the actual mechanisms of subordination. It was a depoliticized, depoliticizing politics, insofar as it systematically excluded from its purview the operation of the market, the logic of commodification, and, most important, the forms of alienation these produced. The theme of alienation is common to most of the subsequent critiques of liberalism. Thus, for example, communitarians decry the liberal valorization of the fictive pre-social individual as the basic atom of democracy, while civic republicans insist on the priority of political relations in the cultivation of citizenship.

The forms of alienation liberalism is said to produce multiply energetically: liberal subjects are alienated from themselves by the commodification of their productive capacities in labor; they are alienated from one another by the myth of autarky, able to enter into only precarious, provisional, and superficial relations of contractual exchange; they are alienated from their capacity for collective political action by individuating liberal concepts such as "rights" and "liberty." And it gets worse: for feminists, queer theorists, and multiculturalists, liberal universalism tacitly encodes the white heterosexual male as its model of the autonomous, rational, rights-bearing subject of liberty and contract. By contrast, women, nonwhites, and sexual minorities appear in its optic as inadequately embodying this model. Moreover, those who find themselves alienated from the polity in this way find their capacity to combat their relegation circumscribed by the very mechanism that produces it: minoritized and disempowered by group ascription, they are enjoined from marshalling their group membership and marginalization against this denial.

In addition to such forms of depoliticizing alienation, liberalism is accused of fostering a weak political bond. The contractual model, the notion of individual rights, and the restriction of the government's sphere of influence mean that citizens fail to experience a strong commitment to the polity, requiring such supplementary forms of attachment as nationalism and racism. One of the consequences is the periodic eruption of crises of legitimacy, which only intensify the sense of social fragmentation, further undermine the will to and capacity for collective action, and either catalyze internal strife or provoke the abdication of liberal principles to de facto forms of oligarchy or autocracy.

Notwithstanding the inconsistencies among these various critiques (for instance, liberalism is styled as somehow both politically quiescent *and* politically volatile; its citizens are both uninterested in politics *and* actively prevented from participating; it is a counterfeit promise *and* one inadequately fulfilled; it fails abjectly *and* succeeds diabolically; and so forth), some notion of alienation is central to them all. Yet we have seen that liberal theorists themselves envisioned the sphere of private intimacy made possible under liberal régimes to be a heaven of sociability. And we have attended to the proliferation of popular narratives devoted to imagining strong affective bonds. It is possible, of course, to reconcile these observations. Liberal theorists were ideologues or they were simply mistaken, and the saturation of popular culture with narratives of friendship is compensatory in nature. From this perspective, the sociological analysis proffered by Robert Bellah or Robert Putnam could be linked to friendship films in a straightforward way: American subjects of a late modern liberal régime are living in profound alienation, lacking even an adequate language in which to articulate the full depth and breadth of their anomie and only dimly aware of its true causes, but their fervent desire for community is partially satisfied through collective experiences of publicly circulating fictional narratives. It matters somewhat less whether this supplementary relation is understood as a cynical project of the capitalist "system" to profit, opportunistically or programmatically, from the very pain it inflicts, or if it is understood more benignly as a kind of cultural symptom, a "reaction formation" aimed at meeting the actual needs of alienated citizen-consumers.

Either way, the figure of friendship would have to be conceived as a supplement to liberal citizenship. So understood, this figure would not be a secondary stylistic addition to an otherwise self-sufficient liberalism; rather, like any supplement, it would prove indispensable for securing this self-sufficiency, in effect sustaining the very coherence of liberal discourse. I have endeavored to demonstrate the rhetorical productivity of this supplement by attending to the ways in which it sustains the liberal imaginary by functioning as a contradictory figure of antipolitical citizenship, as well as by mediating a series of familiar controversies regarding liberalism's apparent deficiencies that in fact serve to consolidate liberal citizenship as the privileged solution to the obstacles confronting democracy.

This analysis could be construed as eventuating in a critical choice. On the one hand, friendship might be regarded as a compensatory prosthesis for a perennially failing liberalism; on the other hand, friendship might be regarded as a cunning instrument of a diabolical liberalism. In either case, a politically transformative critical intervention might consist in depriving liberalism of this device. However, I have tried to suggest that these are neither the only nor the best options available. Instead, I propose that the rhetorical power of liberal discourse itself constitutes an opportunity incipient in the friendship supplement and in the allegorical mode it imposes on the liberal imaginary. Rather than redeploying this supplement to disarm or subvert liberal hegemony, it is possible to recover the democratically productive potential made available by liberalism's reliance on this supplement. Indeed, having discerned the major rhetorical implications of the friendship fiction, it is possible to find such a rhetorical possibility, impelled precisely by the friendship supplement, taking place within liberal discourse itself.

In *The Big Chill,* an apparent dispute between communitarianism and liberalism turns out to be the discursive manifestation of liberalism itself, which generates the nostalgic fantasy of disappearing community in order to secure the priority of elective attachment as the proper locus, form, and medium of political obligation and agency. The narrative's rhetoric resignifies philia so as to reinscribe, in the very mode of communitarian critique, the logic governing liberal citizenship. Accordingly, the film's republicanism must rely on the self-evidence of liberal culture for its own discourse to attain minimal coherence: the assertion that friendship can reinvigorate the political within the social depends on the continuing, untroubled hegemony of affective attachment as the form assumed by private elective sociality. The "friends" who are to develop faculties of judgment remain liberal subjects engaged in contractual relations with one another, as if outside any wider polity and without purchase on the institutions of either the state or capital. Indeed, the very possibility, significance, and utility of their friendship depend on this abdication.

The politics of intimacy whose effect is to subvert what Arendt called "action in concert" ratifies the rejection of emancipatory politics as itself a symptom of personal naïveté. The concomitant staging of egaliberté as "lost" politics prepares the way for the "solution" of interpersonal micropolitics. It thus becomes clear that forms of critique centered on the claim that liberalism "displaces" politics tend to obscure the way this gesture (of displacement) functions rhetorically to posit, retroactively, the private as such. It is not simply that liberalism *has* an answer to such critiques; it is itself this answer. Far from *lacking* a civic bond because it privatizes politics, the liberal imaginary promulgates a mode of sociality aimed at *supplanting* one polemically overdetermined conception of politics with another. The object is not simply to disable political engagement—or to suppress the "ontological" antagonism constitutive of the social—for strategic purposes, but to *configure the horizon* within which the very ("ontic") meaning of politics is to take shape.

In this way, *The Big Chill* proves emblematic of a pivotal rhetorical maneuver transacted, for reasons mandated by the logic of the liberal imaginary, by the trope of friendship. So understood, the efficacy of this maneuver implies a new frame for understanding certain prevalent critical approaches to questions of democratic citizenship and its articulation in the popular imaginary. Yet if friendship "displaces" politics in the act of appearing to salvage it, what happens when the problem of power "returns" to erupt at the midst of private life—say, in the context of a friendship between two women? Surely such an event would pose a genuine challenge to the liberal model of citizenship as private affective attachment? This is the question raised by *Thelma & Louise,* where the female friends' inadvertent but inevitable rebellion seems clearly to menace the liberal privatization of politics.

Like *The Big Chill, Thelma & Louise* stages a popular critique that seems to correspond uncannily with familiar academic objections to the phallocentrism of the juridical and state apparatuses, tacitly sanctioned pervasive social practice, and cultural norms of representation. In consonance with the axiomatics advanced by feminist and queer critics, the film undertakes a reflexive interrogation of various friendship film genres in order to challenge the barely concealed and ubiquitous sexualization of agency. Here, friendship mediates not the depoliticized politics of affective sociability as articulated within the liberal partition, but the avowedly antithetical project of rebellious (de)sexual(izing) solidarity aimed at subverting this partition from its own constitutive margins. Implicit in the film's narrative strategy is the feminist/queer psychoanalytic articulation of the putative heterosexism of the contemporary symbolic order. Thelma and Louise appear reflexively to politicize their very illegibility as a way of refusing to endorse or embody it.

Yet this gesture turns out to produce the fictive coherence of patriarchy as a violation of liberal principles, which the narrative labors energetically to secure. In effect, friendship as the figure of subversive rebellion functions to reinforce the distinctive liberal construction of political subjectivity. In grasping the prefigured failure of friendship to exit the cul-de-sac of patriarchal representation, it becomes clear that the very unity of patriarchy is a rhetorical postulate whose efficacy is consolidated, rather than weakened, by feminist recourse to friendship as the figure of rebel-citizenship. In the mode of popular controversy it assumes in the film, the problem of patriarchy, without ceasing to persist and engender pernicious effects, turns out to be a presupposition of, rather than an obstacle to, the hegemony of liberal discourse. By the same token, and like its academic counterpart, the feminist and queer politics of resistance and subversion staged by the film is a vehicle for the production of liberal citizenship, and not any less so when it appears to reject liberal principles as phallocentric or heteronormative. This is because the film is emblematic of the liberal determination of power as domination and therefore as a normatively empty place, the occupant of which is per se suspect. As the figure of extrapolitical solidarity that serves as a bulwark against power, the friendship that mediates the narrative's feminism confers coherence on this liberal metadiscourse, while determining gender privilege as the anachronistic residue of a now delegitimated model of authority.

This, in turn, means that feminist critiques of patriarchy are hampered by their indifference to the liberalism that enframes them, while feminist critiques of liberalism are hampered by their indifference to its specifically rhetorical, rather than institutional, ideological, or normative, efficiency. If critics such as Judith Butler were right that improper bodies and sexualities subvert the binary code of phallocentrism by their very excessive existence, then phallocentrism would have to be conceived less as an obdurate social fact and more as a nostalgic fantasy. It may be prevalent as an aspiration, but those invested in it would of necessity always be fighting a rearguard action. The familiar critical gesture here is to invoke reflexive rhetorical modes—such as irony, parody, or camp—as strategies for denaturalizing phallocentric premises supposed to inhere in the universalism on which liberalism relies. But this view overlooks the degree to which the liberal imaginary is itself constituted through a rhetoric of reflexivity—as well as the critics' own integral function as bearers of this reflexivity.

Accordingly, the notion that performative denaturalization of ideological premises is the privileged path toward emancipatory ends turns out to be a retrospective product of reflexivization that has come to characterize the very modality of power. Inspired but insufficiently influenced by the insights of Jacques Derrida, this line of thinking attempts to apply them to the internal functioning of the symbolic order. Yet when Derrida speaks of a "precomprehension" conditioning both the social bond and the exclusions generated in its name, he is certainly not speaking of anything like conventional or tacit social agreement, but rather of its conditions of possibility—conditions that must be considered as radically exceeding the symbolic order itself. The distinction is decisive, and the failure to grasp its full implications results, as we have seen in the case of *Thelma & Louise,* in a dead-end politics.

By contrast, *Lost in Translation* confronts precisely the impasse that *Thelma & Louise* can only construe as the terminal cunning of patriarchy—the impasse of social reflexivity itself. The liberal imaginary's signature capacity to put in question its own conditions of possibility may serve to immunize it to the array of autocritiques it thereby generates, but this capacity itself becomes an obstacle to the social and individual autonomy it is supposed to facilitate. The film's protagonists find themselves disabled by a hyperreality that seems perfectly capable of functioning without them, a form of social organization perversely indifferent to the autonomous persons it addresses and purports to serve. The rhetoric of social reflexivity produces a social reality deprived of both sociality and reality. As a result, there appears to be no form of action that is not already programmed and therefore utterly inconsequential, altogether deprived of its status as action. The more the protagonists pursue the forms of life promised to and expected of them, the more pointless these forms become. The predicament is a cogent allegory of the political reflexivity animating the liberal imaginary: here the problem is no longer reducible to power as the key political stake, but now becomes the evacuation of reality and agency as a consequence of the discursive modality devised to redescribe and resolve the problem of power.

Returning yet again, friendship serves as the vehicle for negotiating this impasse, becoming the figure of a sociality imagined to exceed the paradox of reflexivity. Yet the narrative only supplants the feedback loop of hyperreality with that of friendship, which itself turns out to be nothing other than a relay for the self-referential circuit of an observation that reenters and thereby constitutes the relation it observes. The film's observation is that, within the liberal imaginary to which this style of observation belongs, the friendship relation is rhetorically programmed to be the paradigmatic domain of unprogrammed relations; as a result, the critical intervention this figure mediates can only mark its own futility. Thematizing the debilitating effects of an increasingly self-referential and thus hyperreal social imaginary, all the narrative can do is reproduce self-reflection as the paradigm of sociability. The film thus becomes an iteration of the rhetorical dilemma it attempts to describe and supersede, and the solution it proposes—friendship—turns out to be indistinguishable from the problem it postulates.

Put another way, this friendship narrative registers (even as it must helplessly repeat) the artifice of reflexivity as the privileged rhetorical mode of the liberal imaginary; but because this very exposure must itself take the form of reflexive observation—instated in the film by Bob's "act" of friendship toward Charlotte—any possibility of exiting the self-perpetuating circuit of this rhetorical mode is forestalled. Here, then, friendship seems to have passed from functioning as a malleable supplement to liberal citizenship to constricting the efficacy of liberal rhetoric. The liberal project of reflexivity eventuates in a discursive apparatus that must rely on friendship to escape its recursivity, but finds in friendship only the recursivity it has already installed there. Yet this situation should not be understood as the final ironic revenge of the supplement or the ultimate self-destruction of liberal autonomy. This sort of intrinsic failure of rhetorical reflexivity, while it marks a crucial limit to the hegemony of the liberal imaginary, falls short of suggesting a plausible transformation of this imaginary. There would seem to be no way forward except to repeat what is now clearly a hollow and futile gesture of self-reference. So the discovery of constitutive limits is not, by itself, critically or politically productive.

It is here that the rhetorical and political significance of deconstruction becomes apparent. With the conceptual and critical tools found in the work of Jacques Derrida and deployed in the speculative fiction that forms at once the theme and the rhetorical strategy of *Smoke,* it becomes possible to envision a dislocation of liberal hegemony. For the aporetic structure of friendship itself unbalances the scales of contractualist reciprocity and belies the fantasy of elective attachment underpinning the promise of liberal sociability. It is only because we can never know, let alone decide, who our friends will have been that friendship—or citizenship—is possible at all. If liberalism endeavors to capitalize on friendship, the aporia of debt at the heart of reciprocity will always have been the condition of im/possibility of liberal social logic.

Ultimately, *Smoke* demonstrates the way friendship, rhetorically determined as an extrapolitical relation of reciprocity in order to cement liberal citizenship, simultaneously encodes a certain irreducible excess for which liberalism cannot account, but which does not for this reason simply subvert the liberal imaginary. Figured in the film in terms of the fortuitous circulation of unremunerable gifts, this excess manifests within the discursive space the quasi-transcendental condition of all sociability. That is, it marks the operation of a certain "friendship" beyond (but not antithetical to) choice, autonomy, equality, contract, or reciprocity. This excess founds and conditions an unbreakable bond that makes liberal social logic possible, including the overdetermination of the friendship supplement. Indeed, it is for this reason that friendship is neither a contingent nor simply a strategic metaphor within liberalism but is positively required by it. If, however, friendship is always usurping that which it supplements, this is itself possible not because friendship as it is conceived by either liberalism or its critics is simply to be opposed or preferred to liberal alienation, but rather because *this alienation itself is already conditioned* by the virtual yet unbreakable bond figured by the gift of friendship.

Politically, the excess thematized by this gift destabilizes the dichotomy of equality/power, so that it turns out to be misleading to speak, on the one hand, of an inherent tendency within friendship toward democratic equality and, on the other hand, of friendship as the crucible of revolutionary solidarity. Both temptations are to be rigorously avoided if the radical political entailments of friendship's constitutive excessiveness are to be fully grasped. If friendship supplies a political model, this model remains an incipient effectivity within the alienating recursive circuit of liberalism itself. Rather than asserting friendship within or against liberalism, a radical democratic rhetorical invention must capitalize on the irreducible gift of "friendship" already conditioning this imaginary itself.

When a text such as *Smoke* stages the deconstruction of liberalism by elucidating the speculative indeterminacy unexpectedly underpinning the social contract, does it thereby locate itself at or beyond the margins of the liberal imaginary? Or is the deconstructive rhetoric of *Smoke* finally no less liberal—and no more hostile to liberalism—than that of *The Big Chill*? If so, then the capacity for self-deconstruction is not only inherent within the liberal imaginary—since the discursivity of every social formation renders it deconstructible—but is integral to its rhetorical efficacy. From this vantage, the productivity of its limits should be respected as the precondition for its transformation, which in turn is to be thought of not as a wholesale destruction or replacement of the hegemonic formation but as its dislocation. Such a dislocation will not, however, be easily graspable as a clear departure from the dislocated structure. Put another way, a "post-"

liberal imaginary will not be easy to distinguish from liberalism "itself," since what dislocates liberalism is nothing other than (a certain tendency within) liberalism. This is the most provocative rhetorical lesson of *Smoke,* in which a series of liberal legitimating myths return in allegorical form as narratives of their own productive impossibility. These allegories both are and are not liberal, and thus at once reproduce and modify the imaginary that makes them possible. Indeed, they reproduce it in dislocated form, not simply as rejection or autocritique, but as the active deferral of its own hegemonic closure. Is this deferral the end of liberalism or yet another cynical ruse? Perhaps both.

Liberalism and the Rule of Allegory

There is a fairly obvious irony to the line of reasoning I have been pursuing. If the self-revisionism integral to liberal discourse requires the production of critiques of liberalism, then these must of necessity postulate the possibility of dislodging liberalism, which they must also misrecognize as a doctrine, institutional framework, ideology, or culture to which they are in some important sense external. Consequently, such critiques are not simply mistaken; on the contrary, the misrecognition of liberalism they produce and sustain is constitutive. This, in turn, means that such critiques cannot simply be dismissed; yet it also means they are, in a sense, beside the point I am trying to make. Internal to the liberal imaginary, they persistently raise but cannot deliver the possibility of superseding it. On the contrary, they tend to immunize liberalism against this possibility.

If the marking of liberalism's limits is integral to the liberal imaginary, this marking need not impede the reproduction of liberal discourse and institutions; on the contrary, it accounts for their resilience. Indeed, this is already implicit in the signature narratives of liberal theory, which construct citizenship as a hypothetical and provisional solution to an intractable problem, the paradox of collective self-rule. That is, from a liberal vantage, it should hardly be surprising that democracy is endlessly failing and that liberal institutions are inherently inadequate to the task of sustaining it. The constitutive impossibility of a fully integrated society—the kind that would seem necessary for the effective practice of democratic self-rule—is *itself* a key topos and trope of liberal discourse, at least from Hobbes onward. This impossibility is not the recent discovery of "postmodern" social theory but a long-standing, if unsettling, presupposition of such liberal innovations as the separation of powers, freedom of speech, state secularism, and constitutional allegiance.

If the deconstruction of liberal categories does not undermine the liberal imaginary, it is because this imaginary is not reducible to the articulation of these categories but includes the eventuality of their deconstruction. Put differently, liberalism is not only one among several possible solutions to the "democratic paradox"; rather, it is *nothing other than the discursive production of this paradox as an organizing political trope*—to which friendship lends a prevalent cultural form because this trope troubles the citizenship it would underwrite. This does not mean, of course, that the paradox is sheer myth; rather, it acquires visibility and political salience in its own right, as a paradox, in a determinate way, and with observable consequences. But its reality is not that of an antecedent logical or empirical impediment that liberalism encounters or to which it responds; nor is it, like the Lacanian Real, a constitutive gap or inadvertent side effect liberalism inevitably produces but cannot master. Rather, the liberal imaginary *cultivates* this paradox as an obstacle that functions rhetorically as an enabling condition within a historically novel discursive politics that productively defers, rather than pursuing or promising, its eventual resolution. The distinctiveness of this trope lies in the fact that it does not only legitimate concrete institutions and practices—since it can just as easily undermine or modify them—but that it renders necessary and launches a *public rhetorical culture* within which these will have to be embedded. The democratic paradox must appear, it must be made visible and articulate, it must return again and again in the official guise of public controversy and in the popular guise of cultural politics, and the liberal imaginary inheres and consists precisely in the efficient reflexive reproduction of such "hegemonic struggle."

Insofar as the liberal imaginary reproduces itself by means of staging such struggle, the unity of liberal discourse is not contravened but rather supplied by its internal heterogeneity—that is, by the rigorous and explicit disavowal of integration. This disavowal is not, as some would have it,[1] antithetical to liberalism, even if it contradicts a well-known strand of liberal theory determined to fill the gap this disavowal opens up.[2] Understood as a rhetorically constituted imaginary, liberalism mobilizes but is not reducible to its universalist claims—just as it includes, but is not thwarted by, various critiques of universalism. Even a brief glance at everyday practices of liberal culture should suffice to demonstrate this, and I have tried to make the case more systematically in this study. As a result, it is crucial to see that there is neither a Hegelian "sublation" of internal differences that would account for the hegemonic efficacy of liberal discourse, nor a failure of this discourse to "master" these differences that would in turn open the way to its replacement. Homogeneity and heterogeneity—integration and its failure—overlap or coincide in a novel rhetorical formation whose very principle is deconstruction.

Ernesto Laclau has argued vigorously and at length that this overlap is constitutive of discursivity as such, supplying the conditions of possibility for politics generally and indicating the shape of democratic politics as the form that would acknowledge its own discursive limits.[3] My sense, grounded in the foregoing analyses, is that Laclau has mistaken the emergent discourse of liberal democracy for the ontological conditions of politics as such. Such conditions lack either empirical or ideal existence; they are themselves always postulated from within a rhetorical formation—in this case, the liberal imaginary—as its own presuppositions. It is not democracy as such, but the liberal imaginary in its specific rhetorical configuration that, not at all contingently or coincidentally, "incarnates" the ontological conditions Laclau describes. This incarnation is the rhetorical source of these conditions as hegemonic discursive postulates, not their more or less faithful ontic manifestation.

Perhaps the point can be clarified if we turn briefly to Paul de Man's concept of allegory as a heuristic device. In a now canonic passage, de Man stipulates:

> The paradigm for all texts consists of a figure (or a system of figures) and its deconstruction. But since this model cannot be closed off by a final reading, it engenders, in its turn, a supplementary figural superposition which narrates the unreadability of the prior narration. As distinguished from primary deconstructive narratives centered on figures and ultimately always on metaphor, we can call such narratives to the second (or the third) degree *allegories.* Allegorical narratives tell the story of the failure to read whereas tropological narratives . . . tell the story of the failure to denominate. The difference is only a difference of degree and the allegory does not erase the figure. Allegories are always allegories of metaphor and, as such, they are always allegories of the impossibility of reading.[4]

A modification or extension of de Manian allegory may be useful here, enabling us to conceive of liberalism not only as an efficaciously self-reflexive political discourse—that is, a discourse "about" politics integral to the politics it appears only to describe—but also, in virtue of all that is implicit in this feedback loop, as primarily a discourse about the politics of discourse. If for de Man allegory narrates the impossibility of metaphorically secured closure, it testifies to the failure of the discourse of modernity—the failure de Man believes is the latent theme of Romanticism as the literary mode emblematic of modernity. But the impossibility of closure—that is, the inevitable failure of discursive hegemony—is only a problem for a discourse whose efficacy postulates closure as a requirement. Yet, as de Man himself so ably demonstrates, allegory can supply the rhetorical form of a discourse that disavows this possibility, even if the disavowal amounts to a performative contradiction, styled by deconstruction as "undecidability." Accordingly, the allegorical maneuvers on display in *Smoke* can be understood as performing just such a disavowal, which must also be implicit in liberal discourse generally. In effect, friendship fictions sustain liberal citizenship, but they do so neither as ideological tropes nor as recuperated cultural symptoms of ideological failure; rather, their efficacy derives from their allegorical capacity *to stage the problems of language, representation, and rhetoric as political problems* par excellence. From this vantage, the discourse of "liberalism" amounts to an allegory about the rhetoricity of language and its centrality for democracy. The liberal imaginary corresponds to a kind of "rule of allegory."[5]

It is easy to see, then, why critiques of liberalism and its discursive operations—such as the ubiquitous deployment of friendship narratives—tend to miss their mark. For the decisive political concern is not, despite everything, the sheer hegemonic force of liberal discourse, but the often surprising consequences of its allegorical staging of rhetoricality itself—consequences that cannot be regarded as in any sense peripheral to the liberal imaginary that, apparently despite itself, gives rise to them. No doubt these can prove formidable in preempting the emergence of alternative political imaginaries; yet they can just as easily, and not at all accidentally, evince the liberal imaginary's own utopian potential, which inheres in liberalism's irreducible difference from itself and its promises. If liberal rhetoric inevitably subsumes and constricts the surplus of discursive play—say, by styling democracy as a paradox that calls for reflexively fictive elective reciprocity as the signature social bond—it also preserves and offers access to this surplus, demonstrating that things are always already otherwise than they are. In marshaling friendship as a focal metaphor of citizenship, liberalism also produces itself as an allegory of this metaphorization, postulating the rhetorical contingency of the discursive limits it would set for itself and offering a glimpse of a democratic bond beyond all limits, one available only by virtue of this allegory. In short, it may be that the most radically utopian alternative to liberalism is simply another liberalism, one that is with us right now, right here, today.

Notes

Introduction

1. E.g., Hannah Arendt, *The Human Condition* (Chicago: University of Chicago Press, 1958); Alisdair MacIntyre, *After Virtue* (Notre Dame: Notre Dame University Press, 1981); Michael Sandel, *Liberalism and the Limits of Justice* (New York: Cambridge University Press, 1982); Robert Bellah, *Habits of the Heart* (Berkeley: University of California Press, 1985); Charles Taylor, *The Ethics of Authenticity* (Cambridge: Harvard University Press, 1992); Robert Putnam, *Bowling Alone* (New York: Simon & Schuster, 2000).

2. E.g., Iris Marion Young, "Polity and Group Difference: A Critique of the Ideal of Universal Citizenship," *Ethics* 99 (January 1989): 250–74; Nancy Fraser, "Rethinking the Public Sphere: A Contribution to the Critique of Actually Existing Democracy," and Michael Warner, "The Mass Public and the Mass Subject," both in *The Phantom Public Sphere,* ed. Bruce Robbins (Minneapolis: University of Minnesota Press, 1993); Wendy Brown, *States of Injury* (Princeton: Princeton University Press, 1995).

3. This is Marx's well-known and often rediscovered thesis. See especially Karl Marx, *Capital* (New York: Vintage, 1977): 1:280.

4. E.g., Carl Schmitt, *Crisis of Parliamentary Democracy,* trans. Ellen Kennedy (Cambridge: MIT Press, 1988); Jürgen Habermas, *The Structural Transformation of the Public Sphere,* trans. Frederick Lawrence (Cambridge: MIT Press, 1989); Bonnie Honig, *Political Theory and the Displacement of Politics* (Ithaca: Cornell University Press, 1993); Jacques Rancière, *Disagreement* (Minneapolis: University of Minnesota Press, 1998); Douglas Kellner, *Media Spectacles and the Crisis of Democracy* (New York: Paradigm, 2005).

5. E.g., Jürgen Habermas, *Legitimation Crisis,* trans. Thomas McCarthy (Boston: Beacon, 1973); Chantal Mouffe, *The Democratic Paradox* (London: Verso, 2000).

6. For a cogent recent rearticulation of these problems of liberal citizenship, see Charles Taylor, "Cultures of Democracy and Citizen Efficacy," *Public Culture* 19 (Winter 2007): 117–50.

7. E.g., Will Kymlicka, *Liberalism, Community and Culture* (Oxford: Oxford

University Press, 1989). Kymlicka argues that a marginalized tradition within liberal theory can be marshaled to solve the major problems confronting liberal institutions. Jürgen Habermas tries to salvage the key liberal concepts of universality, neutrality, equality, and rights from antifoundationalist critique by grounding them in the normative dimension of communication practices. See *The Theory of Communicative Action,* trans. Thomas McCarthy (Boston: Beacon, 1985). Richard Rorty stipulates that liberalism cannot be sustained philosophically but defends it on the putatively pragmatic grounds that it constitutes the predominant robust tradition of political reflection and practice available to us. See *Contingency, Irony and Solidarity* (New York: Cambridge University Press, 1989). Kwame Anthony Appiah turns to John Stuart Mill for an alternative derivation of liberalism compatible with a form of identity politics. See "Liberalism, Individuality and Identity," *Critical Inquiry* 27 (Winter 2001): 305–32. Many other examples can be adduced.

8. Here I am using "discourse" in Foucault's sense: see Michel Foucault, *Archaeology of Knowledge,* trans. Rupert Swyer (New York: Pantheon, 1972): 31–39; Jim McGuigan, "The Cultural Public Sphere," *European Journal of Cultural Studies* 8.4 (2005): 427–43.

9. On the rise and structure of imagined communities, see Benedict Anderson, *Imagined Communities* (London: Verso, 1983). On the mediatized publicness of liberal polities, see Michael Warner, *Publics and Counterpublics* (New York: Zone Books, 2002). On the visuality of liberal-democratic public culture, see Robert Hariman and John Louis Lucaites, *No Caption Needed* (Chicago: University of Chicago Press, 2007).

10. All three views have their origin in Frankfurt School–style ideology critique. See Theodor Adorno and Max Horkheimer, *The Culture Industry* (New York: Routledge, 1991); Jürgen Habermas, *The Structural Transformation of the Public Sphere,* trans. Frederick Lawrence (Cambridge: MIT Press, 1989); Stuart Hall, "Notes on Deconstructing 'the Popular,'" in *People's History and Socialist Theory,* ed. Raphael Samuel (London: Routledge & Kegan Paul, 1981), 228.

11. An obvious and important exception is Toby Miller, although his work centers on larger-scale institutional aspects of contemporary media culture, determining the influence of liberalism as the political economy comprising the production, circulation, and consumption of media discourses.

12. For an extended discussion of the political function of an extra- or antipolitical public, see Charles Taylor, *Modern Social Imaginaries* (Durham: Duke University Press, 2004), 83–101.

13. The view that Hollywood cinema is ideological has had enormously influential exponents, including Noël Burch, *To the Distant Observer* (Berkeley: University of California Press, 1979); Colin MacCabe, "Realism and the Cinema: Notes on Some Brechtian Theses," *Screen* 15.2 (1974): 7–27; Robert Ray, *A Certain Tendency in Hollywood Cinema* (Princeton: Princeton University Press, 1985).

Under the influence of cultural studies, the notion of popular culture as a site of hegemonic struggle has become pervasive both within and beyond film studies.

Among the tentative early steps toward this view from a Frankfurt School direction is Douglas Kellner and Michael Ryan, *Camera Politica: The Politics and Ideology of Contemporary Hollywood Film* (Bloomington: Indiana University Press, 1988).

14. For war, see, e.g., *1969,* dir. Ernest Thompson (Los Angeles: Atlantic Entertainment, 1988); *The Deer Hunter,* dir. Michael Cimino (Burbank, CA: EMI / Universal, 1978); *Flashback,* dir. Franco Amurri (Burbank, CA: Paramount, 1990).

For gender politics, see, e.g., *Rich and Famous,* dir. George Cukor (Burbank, CA: MGM, 1981); *Nine to Five,* dir. Colin Higgins (Burbank, CA: IPC / 20th Century Fox Film, 1980); *Fried Green Tomatoes,* dir. John Avnet (Los Angeles: Universal Pictures, 1991); *Private Benjamin,* dir. Howard Zieff (Los Angeles: Warner Bros., 1980); *G.I. Jane,* dir. Ridley Scott (Los Angeles: Buena Vista, 1997); and countless films organized around male friendship.

For homosexuality and heterosexism, see, e.g., *Boys on the Side,* dir. Herbert Ross (Los Angeles: Warner Bros., 1995); *The Adventures of Priscilla, Queen of the Desert,* dir. Stephan Elliott (Los Angeles: Gramercy Pictures, 1994); *Philadelphia,* dir. Jonathan Demme (Los Angeles: TriStar Pictures, 1993); *Peter's Friends,* dir. Kenneth Branagh (London and Los Angeles: BBC / Channel 4 / Samuel Goldwyn, 1992).

For class anxiety, see, e.g., *The Outsiders,* dir. Francis Ford Coppola (Los Angeles: Zoetrope / Warner Bros., 1983); *The Full Monty,* dir. Peter Cattaneo (London and Los Angeles: Channel 4 / 20th Century Fox Film, 1997); *Metropolitan,* dir. Whit Stillman (Los Angeles: New Line Cinema, 1990); *Friends with Money,* dir. Nicole Holofcener (Los Angeles: Sony Pictures, 2006).

For the "crisis" of the family, see, e.g., *Best Friends,* dir. Norman Jewison (Los Angeles: Warner Bros., 1982); *Muriel's Wedding,* dir. P. J. Hogan (Los Angeles: Miramax, 1995).

For the power and impotence of the presidency, see, e.g., *My Fellow Americans,* dir. Peter Segal (Los Angeles: Warner Bros., 1996).

For racial tensions, see, e.g., *The Defiant Ones,* dir. Stanley Kramer (Los Angeles: MGM / United Artists, 1958); *White Men Can't Jump,* dir. Ron Shelton (Los Angeles: 20th Century Fox Film, 1992); *Grand Canyon,* dir. Lawrence Kasdan (Los Angeles: 20th Century Fox Film, 1992); and others too numerous to list.

For immigration, see, e.g., *My Beautiful Laundrette,* dir. Stephen Frears (London: Channel 4 / Working Title, 1986); *Lone Star,* dir. John Sayles (Los Angeles: Castle Rock Entertainment / Columbia Pictures, 1996).

For ethno-cultural diversity, see, e.g., *Mississippi Masala,* dir. Mira Nair (Los Angeles: Samuel Goldwyn, 1992); *Bend It Like Beckham,* dir. Gurinder Chadha (Los Angeles: Fox Searchlight, 2003); *Bulletproof Monk,* dir. Paul Hunter (Los Angeles: MGM, 2003).

For globalization, see, e.g., *Die Hard: With a Vengeance,* dir. John McTiernan (Los Angeles: 20th Century Fox Film, 1995); *Ronin,* dir. John Frankenheimer (Los Angeles: United Artists, 2003); *The Terminal,* dir. Steven Spielberg (Los Angeles: Dreamworks, 2004).

15. Aristotle, *Nichomachean Ethics,* trans. Terence Unwin (Indianapolis: Hack-

ett, 1985); Aristotle, *Politics,* trans. R. F. Stalley and Ernest Barker (Oxford: Oxford University Press, 1995); Arendt, *The Human Condition;* Arendt, "On Humanity in Dark Times: Thoughts about Lessing," trans. Clara Winston and Richard Winston, in *Men in Dark Times* (New York: Harvest Books, 1955); Giorgio Agamben, *The Coming Community,* trans. Michael Hardt (Minneapolis: University of Minnesota Press, 1993); Hardt, "Friendship," *Contretemps* (December 2004): 2–7.

16. See Horst Hutter, *Politics as Friendship* (Waterloo: Wilfrid Laurier University Press, 1978).

17. On the role of friendship in Aristotle's political philosophy, see Suzanne Stern-Gillet, *Aristotle's Philosophy of Friendship* (Albany: SUNY Press, 1995), 147–70. On the cultivation of friendship by liberalism, see Allan Silver, " 'Two Different Sorts of Commerce'—Friendship and Strangeship in Civil Society," in *Public and Private in Thought and Practice,* ed. Jeff Weintraub and Krishan Kumar (Chicago: University of Chicago Press, 1997).

18. I am thinking here of Habermas's sophisticated articulation of Parsonian-Luhmannian systems theory to Rawlsian liberalism. Jürgen Habermas, *Between Facts and Norms,* trans. William Rehg (Cambridge: MIT Press, 1998).

19. This line of attack is pursued by Sandel, *Liberalism and the Limits of Justice;* Charles Taylor, *Sources of the Self* (Cambridge: Harvard University Press, 1992); Michael Walzer, *Spheres of Justice* (New York: Basic Books, 1983); Bellah, *Habits of the Heart;* Putnam, *Bowling Alone.*

20. My use of the phrase *democratic paradox* differs from that of Chantal Mouffe, *The Democratic Paradox* (London: Verso, 2000). Whereas Mouffe has in mind the relation of simultaneous mutual dependence and limitation of freedom and equality, I have in mind the Derridean insight that collective self-rule must presuppose the forms of agreement it purports to produce (Jacques Derrida, "Declarations of Independence," *New Political Science* 15 (Summer 1986): 7–15.) By the same token, because this presupposition cannot have been democratically produced, it becomes an obstacle to the democratic cooperation it would facilitate.

21. The project of "historical poetics of cinema" has been forcefully advocated by David Bordwell and remains powerfully influential in contemporary film studies. See his "Historical Poetics of Cinema," in *The Cinematic Text,* ed. R. Barton Palmer (New York: AMS, 1989), 369–98. As a "neoformalism," historical poetics would subsume questions of ideology, such as the ones pursued by Burch, MacCabe, Ray and, more recently, the armies of scholars working on the "politics of representation" in film and other media.

22. Noël Burch, *Theory of Film Practice,* trans. Helen R. Lane (New York: Praeger, 1973).

23. Without wishing to become embroiled in the old debate concerning the specificity of film as a medium, I will simply note that only the most extravagantly popular novels enjoy audiences comparable to those of moderately successful films; that theater is highly localized and does not circulate the way films can; that pop songs seldom reference friendship and rely far less than movies do on more or

less coherent and fully elaborated narratives; and that television series, while they commonly center on friendship and frequently thematize citizenship, rarely link the two as a sustained narrative principle—and when they do (as, for example, in *NYPD Blue* or *The West Wing*), the results appear quite similar to what happens in film (a hypothesis worth investigating separately).

Robert Ray borrows the concept of "path dependence" from economics to use as an explanatory category. See *How a Film Theory Got Lost and Other Mysteries in Cultural Studies* (Bloomington: Indiana University Press, 2001), 7–14.

24. John Fiske offers a particularly lucid summary of this argument, drawing on the now-standard sources: Gramsci, Foucault, and Stuart Hall. John Fiske, *Media Matters: Race and Gender in U.S. Politics* (Minneapolis: University of Minnesota Press, 1996).

25. Nancy Fraser's well-known notion of counterpublicity in fact names the normative liberal conception of citizenship, and not, as she thinks, a form opposed to this conception.

26. I borrow the term *autological* from Elizabeth Povinelli, *The Empire of Love* (Durham: Duke University Press, 2006).

Chapter 1

1. Chantal Mouffe, Ernesto Laclau, and others claim the appellation "radical democracy" for their project of rendering the putatively weak, abstract, "negative," and purely formal construction of citizenship regnant in liberal régimes compelling precisely by insisting on its "empty" form, which they argue reproduces at the level of political allegiance the late modern hyperreflexive model of personal sociability. It should come as no surprise that these theorists attempt to enlist the antithetical theses of Oakeshott and Schmitt into their version of liberalism.

2. Hutter, *Politics as Friendship,* 2.

3. Ibid., 176, 10. Hutter is innocent of the problematics instituted by poststructuralist thought, and he does suggest that friendship can be defined rigorously enough to exclude many kinds of relationships that those involved would call by that name. The idea that the meaning of "friendship" is itself determined by historical and cultural context does not vex his analysis. However, although it sounds naïve as theory, it does comport with the facile assumption that people always and everywhere need to be involved with others in a way that can safely be termed "friendship." Certainly this is the view implicit in popular culture narratives that repeatedly juxtapose the inescapable call of friendship with the distensible world of politics.

4. Ibid., 2–3.

5. Silver, "'Two Different Sorts of Commerce,'" 46.

6. Ibid., 44, 45.

7. Ibid., 46, 47–48, 55.

8. Habermas, *Between Facts and Norms.*

9. See, e.g., Chantal Mouffe, *On the Political* (London: Verso, 2005); Jacques Rancière, *Disagreement* (Minneapolis: University of Minnesota Press, 1998).

10. On this point, see Mouffe, *The Democratic Paradox*.

11. Chantal Mouffe, "Democratic Citizenship and the Political Community," in *Dimensions of Radical Democracy: Pluralism, Citizenship, Community*, ed. Chantal Mouffe (London: Verso, 1992), 235.

12. See Jürgen Habermas, "Political Culture in Germany since 1968," in *The New Conservatism: Cultural Criticism and the Historians' Debate*, ed. and trans. Shierry Weber Nicholsen (Cambridge: MIT Press, 1989), 193.

13. Mouffe, *On the Political*, 20–21.

14. Danielle S. Allen, *Talking to Strangers* (Chicago: University of Chicago Press, 2006).

15. This is, of course, one of the most common definitions of ideology. But it is also what Laclau identifies as the fundamental procedure of political hegemony—and thus constitutive of politics tout court. For Laclau, political practice consists precisely in the equivalential articulation of diverse interests—"demands"—into a chain held together by one of them, which thereby assumes universal status. From this vantage, Marx's famous thesis that liberal rights are a cynical fiction whose function is to underwrite the capitalist contractualism that facilitates the commodification of labor should be reread: far from indicting the notion of rights as an ideological ruse, Marx is simply identifying the operation of an "empty signifier" that secures the liberal solution to the problem of voluntary cooperation, linking a heterogeneous plurality of possible demands under the "abstract" rubric of individual liberty encoded by the concept of rights. Liberal citizens can be both political and extrapolitical "friends" precisely because they regard even their most antagonistic differences in adversarial terms. Rights belong to the algorithm by means of which liberalism transforms antagonism into cooperation (often in the form of competition). Given that such a transformation is the sine qua non of democratic politics, it is simply incoherent to claim that liberalism ignores, denies, suppresses, subverts, or otherwise displaces antagonism.

16. It is worth recalling that, for Marx, the "class struggle" refers to the inevitable conflict over the apportionment of the collectively produced surplus. Though every mode of production results in its own corresponding class division, no form of social cooperation—other than communism—can escape such division, for the simple reason that any conceivable distribution of the surplus inevitably and quite rationally appears unjust and illegitimate to at least some members of the social whole. Despite numerous differences, this account of the political ontology of the social is continuous with that offered by Hobbes two centuries earlier, as well as the one offered by Laclau most recently (Thomas Hobbes, *Leviathan* [Indianapolis: Hackett, 1994]; Ernesto Laclau, *On Populist Reason* [London: Verso, 2005]). Hobbes's insight was that voluntary cooperation is highly improbable, since its incentive structure will produce prisoners' dilemmas. In the absence of coercive unifying

authority, the paradox of cooperation will produce sheer unremitting antagonistic struggle. Laclau's argument is structurally homologous: the irresolvable tension between the basic logics of difference and equivalence ensures that no ultimate integration of the social totality will be possible and generates a permanent antagonism concerning the universal categories—or "empty signifiers"—essential for maintaining hegemonic order. In sum, all three theorists recognize that, as Derrida often puts it, the conditions of possibility for social cooperation are also its conditions of impossibility. This aporia is of acute urgency in any régime that purports to secure cooperation on purely voluntary grounds. This, contra Mouffe, is the real "democratic paradox."

17. Among the noteworthy implications of such a view is that liberalism does not implacably entail either full social integration (i.e., the more or less violent reduction of assorted "differences") or utter disintegration (i.e., the various forms of alienation, disempowerment, or suspicion). Critics of liberal rationalism and abstract universalism, as well as critics of its supposedly corrosive effects on community and political solidarity, are in effect knocking on an open door: the emptiness of liberal categories is key to their efficacy, and in fact facilitates precisely the quests for both inclusion and agentivity it appears to inhibit.

18. Silver describes how, in the classical liberal view, commercial society demands a separation between commercial and personal relations in order to facilitate market efficiency. Accordingly, individuals are "freed" from obligations deriving from prior existing relations or statuses, and meet in the market as equals. This freedom has a counterpart in intimate relations as well, where it is commercial or contractual obligations that are removed or suspended in favor of "sympathetic," "sentimental," or "moral" attachments. What classical liberalism thus offers as a way of organizing social relations superior to that necessitated by feudalism is just as plausibly described by Marx and others as a form of alienation, whereby a particular mode of being situated within a community or socius is undone. While this mode undoubtedly produced considerable problems for individuals subject to it, commercial society succeeds only in disembedding them, substituting "strangeship" as a key new mode of social relation. While Silver takes pains to specify that strangeship is only a kind of friendship-yet-to-be, this massive reordering of social space delineates a specific new relationship between politics and friendship that Silver does not see.

19. Sheldon Wolin, "Democracy and the Political," in *Hannah Arendt: Critical Essays,* ed. Lewis Hinchman and Sandra Hinchman (Albany: SUNY Press, 1994), 290.

20. For example, the privileged status Arendt grants friendship receives virtually no attention in the following: John McGowan, *Hannah Arendt: An Introduction* (Minneapolis: University of Minnesota Press, 1998); John McGowan and Craig Calhoun, eds., *Hannah Arendt and the Meaning of Politics* (Minneapolis: University of Minnesota Press, 1997); Hinchman and Hinchman, *Hannah Arendt;* George Kateb, *Hannah Arendt: Politics, Conscience, Evil* (Totowa, NJ: Rowman &

Littlefield, 1983); George Kateb, "Arendt and Individualism," *Social Research* 61 (1994): 765–94; Maurizio Passerin d'Entrèves, "Hannah Arendt and the Idea of Citizenship," in Mouffe, *Dimensions of Radical Democracy,* 149–68.

The role of friendship in Arendt's thought has not gone entirely unnoticed, of course. There are useful discussions in Ronald Beiner, *Political Judgment* (Chicago: University of Chicago Press, 1983), and Honig, *Political Theory,* as well as essays devoted to the topic: Shin Chiba, "Hannah Arendt on Love and the Political: Love, Friendship and Citizenship," *Review of Politics* 57 (Summer 1995): 505–35; Martha Stortz, "Geographies of Friendship: Arendt and Aristotle," *Dialog* 41.3 (2002): 225–30; Margaret Canovan, "Friendship, Truth, and Politics: Hannah Arendt and Toleration," in *Justifying Toleration,* ed. Susan Mendes (Cambridge: Cambridge University Press, 1988), 197; Lisa J. Disch, "On Friendship in 'Dark Times,'" in *Feminist Interpretations of Hannah Arendt,* ed. Bonnie Honig (University Park: University of Pennsylvania Press, 1995), 285–312.

21. Craig Calhoun, "Plurality, Promises, and Public Spaces," in McGowan and Calhoun, *Hannah Arendt and the Meaning of Politics,* 233.

22. Hannah Arendt, "What Remains? The Language Remains: A Conversation with Günter Gaus," in *Essays in Understanding, 1930–1954,* ed. Jerome Kohn (New York: Harcourt Brace, 1994), 10–11.

23. It goes without saying that, for Arendt as for most others seeking to understand the Holocaust, explanations grounded in rational choice theory are inherently suspect. So while the diabolical conundrum of the prisoners' dilemma might offer a powerful explanatory mechanism, a certain a priori investment in moral critique weighs strongly against recourse to it. Ironically, the perverse or "irrational" outcomes produced by many rational forms of collective behavior can be enormously useful for the emerging theories of "radical democracy" and their revival of Hobbes's and Schmitt's theories of social antagonism.

24. Canovan, "Friendship, Truth, and Politics"; Disch, "On Friendship in 'Dark Times.'"

25. Arendt, "On Humanity in Dark Times."

26. Disch, "On Friendship in 'Dark Times,'" 304.

27. Canovan, "Friendship, Truth, and Politics," 185; Disch, "On Friendship in 'Dark Times,'" 302.

28. Canovan, "Friendship, Truth, and Politics," 191.

29. Disch, "On Friendship in 'Dark Times,'" 305.

30. Canovan, "Friendship, Truth, and Politics," 191–92.

31. Ibid., 191.

32. Arendt, "On Humanity in Dark Times," 27.

33. Eli Zaretsky, "Hannah Arendt and the Meaning of the Public/Private Distinction," in McGowan and Calhoun, *Hannah Arendt and the Meaning of Politics,* 217–18.

34. While on the one hand the term is polysemic and historically malleable, and while, on the other hand, Arendt would be right to claim that a modern view of

friendship is precisely what her determination is meant to resist or revise, the fact is that affect and intimacy are consistently attributed to friendship across the centuries, from the ancients to the moderns.

35. Arendt, *The Human Condition* 242–43.

36. Arendt, "On Humanity in Dark Times," 29; emphasis in the original.

37. Disch, "On Friendship in 'Dark Times'" 307.

38. Jacques Rancière, "Ten Theses on Politics," *Theory and Event* 5.3 (2001): thesis 1.4.

39. Ibid., thesis 2.6.

40. Bonnie Honig, "Declarations of Independence: Arendt and Derrida on the Problem of Founding a Republic," *American Political Science Review* 85.1 (1991): 97–113.

41. Rancière, "Theses," theses 6.19, 7.20.

42. This is what Honig generously attributes to Arendt under the appellation "*vírtu* politics," even though it is an implication Arendt herself seems deliberately to refrain from drawing.

43. Rancière, "Theses," thesis 7.21.

44. While Arendt herself turns to Kant's aesthetics for a model of judgment not reducible to the application of rules, and though her notion of "natality" resonates strongly with Derrida's analyses of the radical performativity of language and the correlative madness of reason, the worldliness of friendship effectively takes the place of a priori necessity in grounding social cooperation. It is here that communitarians have found support in her work: friendship implies a community that I am not simply free to exit when it suits me; it is the precondition of "my own" interests and motives; it provides the sole possibility of their enactment; etc. The community may not have the transcendental status of moral law, but it nonetheless forms the horizon of possibility for any conceivable project of the self. This acceleration of Arendt's thought from Kantian aesthetic judgment toward Hegelian *sittlichkeit* is made possible by her turn to friendship—despite her unmistakable hostility to sentimentalism and insistence on the radical freedom of invention constitutive of politics. Put simply, Arendt seeks in friendship a model of social attachment capable of grounding "natality." Derrida's intervention, though not aimed directly at Arendt, evinces her error, which consists in her reluctance to take the final step necessitated by her own theory. If politics is ultimately nothing other than natality, then it can have no ground—in either theory or practice. Or, as Derrida tirelessly reminds the reader of *Politics of Friendship,* "O my friends, there is no friend" means that friendship can be what it would be only because it is never secure. The bond of friendship—and thus the democratic bond—binds by failing to bind; the obligation it imposes is not that of a moral or pragmatic requirement, or even that of a promise in the ordinary sense (as a performative that engages established protocols of promising and obligates in virtue of the rules these encode, since such a model of promising only defers the problem of the genesis of the *force* of obligation). A friendship sustained by either (moral) duty or (prag-

matic) calculation—even if this calculation pertains to the "world" of "political facts" rather than a given individual or collectivity—is not a friendship, just as, for Arendt, a friendship sustained by sentimental attachment is not a friendship either. The latter, for Arendt, is a symptom of what Schmitt calls the friend/enemy distinction, the solidarity of those who find themselves opposed to some threat to their collective way of life. Such a solidarity has no inner vitality; it is reactive and will disintegrate along with the threat—hence Schimtt's insistence that only through an enemy is there politics at all. But for this very reason, the enemy himself is a kind of friend who cooperates with "us" in making "us" possible. By the same token, the friend, as Kant knows, can always become an enemy—indeed, the most dangerous kind—and this possibility means that my friend is already my worst enemy. This paradox is not a dialectic; it has no resolution in a "higher" synthesis of the opposing options. It is an aporia constitutive not only of friendship, but of social ontology tout court. It is, in other words, the aporia that opens politics as such. Conceived in this precise sense, the aporia of friendship does indeed "ground" politics, albeit not in any sort of attachment but precisely in the impossibility of one. Like friendship, citizenship is an "impossible" mode of attachment, and it is this very impossibility that makes it a *democratic* one. This is the step Arendt's theory forecasts and compels, but Arendt herself stops short of taking.

45. Geoffrey Bennington, "Politics and Friendship: A Discussion with Jacques Derrida" (paper presented at the Center for Modern French Thought, University of Sussex, Falmer, UK, December 1, 1997), http://www.sussex.ac.uk/Units/frenchthought/derrida.htm (accessed May 3, 2005).

46. Michael Walzer, "The Obligation to Live for the State," in *Obligations: Essays on Disobedience, War and Citizenship* (Cambridge: Harvard University Press, 1970); Walzer, "What Does It Mean to Be an 'American'?" *Social Research* 71 (Fall 2004): 633–54.

47. This is where Hutter's assertion that friendship tends toward democracy is tautological: only once we posit the democratic values of equality and unconstrained mutual election as irreducible features of friendship does friendship self-evidently appear as a paragon of democratic membership.

48. Niklas Luhmann, *The Reality of the Mass Media* (Stanford: Stanford University Press, 1996).

49. Cf. Bonnie Honig, "The Myth of an Immigrant America," in *Democracy and the Foreigner* (Princeton: Princeton University Press, 2003).

50. In his most recent book, Laclau argues at length that "the impossible fullness of the community" constitutes a lack for which some proxy must constantly be invented, and that the rhetorical struggle over such proxies is what is called politics. Accordingly, politics concerns chiefly the catachrestic production of metonyms of "the people" as placeholders for the missing social totality. See *On Populist Reason.* One might venture, however, that such metonyms need not be synonyms. In other words, there is no a priori reason why the name of a singular, intersubjective rela-

tion cannot function as a proxy for the impossible social totality. Indeed, this possibility could account for the supposed deferral or displacement of political struggle in liberal polities: in place of antagonistic struggle over the "structurally necessary" name(s) of "the people," liberal discourse institutes fables of friendship in which the "missing" social totality circulates in the guise of an excess marking reciprocal elective attachments. I will address this strategy in detail in chapter 5.

51. See, e.g., Richard Beardsworth, *Derrida and the Political* (London: Routledge, 1996); Alex J. P. Thomson, *Deconstruction and Democracy* (London: Continuum, 2005); Geoffrey Bennington, *Legislations: The Politics of Deconstruction* (London: Verso, 1994); Martin McQuillan, *The Politics of Deconstruction: Jacques Derrida and the Other of Philosophy* (London: Pluto, 2007).

Chapter 2

1. Anthony Giddens, *Modernity and Self-Identity* (Palo Alto: Stanford University Press, 1991), 209–31.

2. E.g., by Terry Eagleton, Fredric Jameson, and Slavoj Žižek.

3. Brown, *States of Injury*, 3–29.

4. On the one hand, in order to register as historically novel and more democratic, radically reflexive politics must explicitly differentiate itself from the "older," more naïve or insidiously oppressive form. On the other hand, this disavowal, according to which nothing (of value) is surrendered, is experienced as deprivation.

5. A survey of the relevant literature would be interminable, but would surely include Marx's analysis of the ideological saturation of social relations; Habermas's analysis of the transformation of the public sphere; Arendt's critique of "the social"; Rancière's excoriation of political theory's effort to "police" the political; feminist efforts to rethink the public/private distinction; various and multiplying accounts of micropolitics; the "culturalization" thesis derived from the Frankfurt School and the Birmingham Center for Critical Cultural Studies; and an expansive literature on modern liberal "displacement(s)" of politics.

6. The list of noteworthy others is quite short but includes *Grand Canyon* (Kasdan's quasi-sequel to *The Big Chill*), *1969, Small Circle of Friends, American Graffiti, Flashback,* and *Forrest Gump.*

7. For example, Vincent Canby ("*The Big Chill,* Reunion of 60's Activists," *New York Times,* September 23, 1983) writes, "'The Big Chill' is a somewhat fancy variation on John Sayles's 'Return of the Secaucus Seven,'" while Cynthia Rose observes that "[a] direct line can be traced from [*Secaucus 7*'s] script to Lawrence Kasdan's *The Big Chill*" ("The Urbane Gorilla: John Sayles, Maverick Film Director, Is Turning to Television," *Independent* [London], August 24, 1990, 12). John Barron quotes Kasdan coyly admitting to the similarities ("Warming Up to the Big Chill," *Milwaukee Sentinel*, September 30, 1983, 18).

8. Timothy Noah ("The Big Massage," *Washington Monthly,* February 1984,

39–44) and Pat Aufderheide ("The Way We Were," *In These Times* 7.38 (1983): 15–16) are emblematic of leftist criticism, while Isidor Silver ably stands in for the Right ("Big Chill, Big Deal," *Society* 21 (March/April 1984): 90–91).

9. James Jasinski, "(Re)Constituting Community through Narrative Argument: *Eros* and *Philia* in *The Big Chill*," *Quarterly Journal of Speech* 79 (1993): 467.

10. E.g., Benjamin DeMott, *The Trouble with Friendship* (New Haven: Yale University Press, 1998); Lauren Berlant, *The Queen of America Goes to Washington City* (Durham: Duke University Press, 1997).

11. For a rich, systematic, and sympathetic account of the emergence of this hierarchy, see Silver, "'Two Different Sorts of Commerce.'"

12. Fredric Jameson, "The Vanishing Mediator: Narrative Structure in Max Weber," *New German Critique* 1 (Winter 1974): 52–89.

13. Giddens, *Modernity and Self-Identity.* Though Giddens's account functions heuristically here, it is later complicated by the suggestion that the very transition from emancipatory to life politics comes into view only from the perspective of late modern liberal culture. Emancipatory politics is posited as a presupposition of fully individualized life politics, so that if it is apprehended as collective struggle, this collectivity is not opposed to, but rather conditions, later forms of "private" citizenship. Giddens should not be (mis)read as endorsing, for example, an account of the shift from the polis to the liberal welfare state or from authentic community to narcissistic atomism.

14. Jasinski, "(Re)Constituting Community," 467, 470.

15. Ibid., 468.

16. Arendt's conception of politics is both exquisitely elaborated and notoriously difficult to pin down. Simply put, commentators continue to disagree as to what "counts" as politics for her, given that the examples she offers are frequently at odds with one another, as well as with her descriptive accounts and normative pronouncements. Lisa Disch usefully distinguishes between readings advancing either "agonal" or "associative" interpretations of Arendt. While Jasinski seems to fall within the latter camp, Disch's thesis is that among Arendt's central concerns was cross-contaminating the two in order to curb the latent narcissism of the former and the oppressive majoritarianism of the latter: "Where the agonistic reading celebrates differentiation and plurality over publicity [which, according to Disch, is *the* criterion of politics for Arendt], the associative reading emphasizes public consensus over contestation and difference . . . at the cost of domesticating the public space by reinstating the norm of mutual understanding" (Lisa Disch, *Hannah Arendt and the Limits of Philosophy* [Ithaca: Cornell University Press, 1994], 87). Taking issue with both interpretive strategies, Disch argues that "Arendt makes solidarity conditional on publicity" (89). In other words, the "associative" dimension of Arendtian politics presupposes and derives its character from the principle of plurality, which in turn is not reducible to "agonism" but indicates the status of reality as an irreducibly social artifact. Among the consequences flowing from such an interpretation is a radical transformation of the concept of "action," which

now becomes social through and through, to the point of decentering the locus of agency from a subject to the social process of reception, interpretation, and (re)production.

17. Jasinski, "(Re)Constituting Community," 469.

18. Ibid., 470, 483.

19. Ibid., 483. "Liberalism" is far from univocal, and the term can simultaneously and ambiguously refer to several sometimes divergent strands of political theory, a set of institutional and juridical arrangements, as well as what Anne Norton describes as "the common sense of the American people, a set of principles unconsciously adhered to, a set of conventions so deeply held that they appear (when they appear at all) to be no more than common sense" (*Republic of Signs* [Chicago: University of Chicago Press, 1993], 1). In Marxian terms, Norton's is a description of ideology, a term some recent theorists, in an effort to disown some of its unwieldy epistemological and polemical baggage while retaining the sense of the collective imaginary mediation of reality, have supplanted with "social imaginary." See, e.g., Cornelius Castoriadis, *The Imaginary Institution of Society* (Cambridge: MIT Press, 1998); John Thompson, "Ideology and the Social Imaginary: An Appraisal of Castoriadis and Lefort," *Theory & Society* 11 (September 1982); Thompson, *Ideology and Modern Culture* (Stanford: Stanford University Press, 1990); Taylor, *Modern Social Imaginaries;* Dilip Parameshwar Gaonkar and Benjamin Lee, eds., *New Imaginaries* (Durham: Duke University Press. 2002). Consequently, a "characteristically liberal" feature is, here, one that has been "vindicated" by history by becoming doxa (though it may in fact have appeared in theoretical accounts only after emerging historically). Theorists may differ, as, say, Locke and Mill emphatically do, concerning the precise meaning and institutional implications of "liberty"; yet the notion remains constitutive for liberal theory, public discourse, and quotidian practice. Grasping what "liberty" effectively means today entails triangulating among these sites and the traffic between them, which therefore together comprise what I am calling the liberal social imaginary. Such is the case, too, for the very notion of "politics," since liberal theory and practice commence with the effort and constitute the project of producing a radically new partition of social life, one in which a new zone of privacy is to emerge in contradistinction to the market and the state from which it is to be defended. What all liberal theorists share, irrespective of what may otherwise be irreconcilable differences among them, is the commitment to found the public political order on the basis of consensual relations among at least notionally "private" individuals, a commitment that has, in fact, become inextricable "common sense." Insofar as this project is inherently contradictory, the proper locus of politics has remained a constitutive liberal concern that is reflected in, but by no means restricted to, theoretical debates. A pivotal feature of liberal cultural logic, then, is the establishment, policing, and continual renegotiation of an imaginary frontier between the private self girded by its affective attachments and the impersonal, "alienating" demands of the market and the state.

20. Jasinski, "(Re)Constituting Community," 472.

21. Ibid., 475.

22. Ibid., 472. The allegorical reading of the film relies on the fact that Harold's faculty of judgment evolves throughout the narrative, so that it may seem unjust to hold him responsible for repugnant judgments made early on. Yet there is never any diegetic indication that Harold comes to revise this particular judgment. Moreover, the scene functions quite systematically to dissipate the guilt which, though voiced by Meg, is clearly attributable to the group as a whole—as well as, if we are speaking allegorically, the cohort for which it stands. The origins, character, and implications of this guilt are complex and controversial, and a reading arguing that the film advises abandoning the polemical exploration of this guilt in favor of a transpolitical search for optimal communal norms effectively accepts the thoroughly ideological notion that nothing relevant to the practice of citizenship can be learned from either this guilt or from the polemics surrounding it. The "allegorical" shift of emphasis from political guilt to the cultivation of judgment, construed as a "faculty" and cultivated among friends, is itself eminently polemical.

23. In fact, the notion of "action" is inadequate here, for the demand imposed upon the "authentic" subject is to *emit signs* of authenticity, where action is only one way of doing so.

24. The systematically uneven distribution of power within a society such as ours poses what may be an insurmountable challenge to Arendt's politics of plurality. While the latter notion is meant to indicate the irreducibly social or intersubjective character of reality by emphasizing the heterogeneous variety of perspectives constitutive of the "web of relationships" making up what Arendt calls "the world," it fails to take into account the way in which power overdetermines the very field of heterogeneity. In other words, one of Marx's basic lessons concerning ideology is that not all differences of perspective or ways of being socially situated are equivalent, since some differences exercise decisive influence over what all the others will mean. It does not suffice, then, to acknowledge the situatedness of each perspective; it is also necessary to grant that some perspectives structure both the character and the salience of the others in advance. Once this is understood, democratic politics can no longer simply strive reflexively to thematize plurality; if it is to remain democratic, it must commit itself to dislodging ideological overdetermination. One of the main obstacles to such a project is that it would entail what would be experienced as the destruction—rather than valorization—of the very plural perspectives whose character is inextricably linked to the undemocratic cunning of ideological distortion. From this perspective, Arendt's poignant call to reinvent collective agency in the modern world is both tantalizingly close and infinitely removed from Marx's own revolutionary project. They agree on everything but the essentials. Moreover, the contour of this particular dilemma changes only marginally in light of "postmetaphysical" accounts of power that dispense with the notion of ideological overdetermination. Even once it is granted that no single structural feature (e.g., relations of production) can explain the power dynamics

shaping a historical conjuncture, it remains the case that the dramatic differences in the agentive capacities of various social actors cannot be understood as arbitrary or idiosyncratic differences of perspective but indicate the operation of systematic and obdurate—if incoherent or incompatible—logics in "the imaginary institution of society."

25. The feeling of guilt at once masks and betokens a range of ultimately impersonal political phenomena. The political effect of guilt is that it produces evasive strategies; its analytic usefulness is that it marks the site where the political and the personal actually intersect. Simply put, the sixties generation had nothing to be guilty about: on the one hand, many of its projects met with considerable success; on the other hand, if these successes did not amount to a wholesale transformation in the relations of power, this is not because of failures attributable to particular persons or groups. The very fact that this nonoccurrence of revolution came to be experienced subjectively and collectively as a failure meriting guilt betokens the cunning of the liberal logic that facilitated shifting the ground of political engagement in first place.

26. Even if it were possible to secure the claim that by the film's conclusion Harold adequately embodies Arendtian judgment, it remains the case that Arendt's model of judgment in light of what she calls "plurality"—the model exemplified, not simply analogized, by friendship—fails to take into account the possibility that plurality is itself always already overdetermined by systematically unequal relations of power and/or ideological "distortion." From this perspective, the confusion, ambivalence, and downright incoherence everywhere marking her account—effaced in Jasinski's version of it—is the product of a basic ruse of liberal social logic. In effect, *friendship is paradigmatic of the form capitalist depoliticization takes,* so that if we are to turn friendship into a means of repoliticization, this can transpire only if and when the "faculty" and practice of judgment is radically socialized—conceived as operating at the level of the collectivity and directed not at members of the polity but toward the conditions structuring the polity as such. In fact, Arendt can be read as advocating something like this step (cf. Disch) in her recommendation of "storytelling." Yet because she tends to denigrate and renounce, rather than learn from, liberal/capitalist (or "modern") "alienation" of agency, her efforts to imagine its restoration remain internally inconsistent. Once again, the "reflexivity thesis" is a useful foil here: where Arendt argues that alienation of agency in "the social" entails the misguided surrender of reflexive control over "political facts," Beck and Giddens demonstrate that, on the contrary, late modern "alienation" is an effect of reflexivity itself, so that what causes political helplessness is the very effort to direct social life on the basis of what we learn about it. That is, even collective, multiperspectival judgment cannot produce, and in fact inhibits, the transparency of "political facts" presupposed by Arendtian politics.

Relatedly, her view that the heterogeneity of perspectives on the world, while entailing disagreement, testifies to the commonality of that world (without implying anything determinate about its attributes) does not admit of the possibility that, for example, Harold and the "scum" effectively live in *different* worlds. That is, ideological overdetermination means that some perspectives enjoy the status of self-evident fact while others appear illegitimate, disingenuous, perverse, antisocial, pathological, incoherent, or simply illegible, so that it is either irrational or downright impossible to entertain them as instances of plurality. Among the resulting differences is that Harold's early judgment, while ill advised and in principle open to revision, is permitted to appear in the guise of a communicative act subject to interpretation and contestation, while the scum are from the start burdened by the self-evident fact that they have failed to engage in similarly legible communicative practices. Their criminal acts can charitably be described as uncivil yet political disobedience, but for this very reason are inadequate as civic practices. Whatever perspective on the world such acts encode must be disarticulated from the acts themselves and given exclusively linguistic form. Of course, the burden of qualifying for inclusion in this sort of political activity rests entirely on those whose criminality is an artifact, at least in part, of their exclusion.

27. In a peculiar sense, Harold is quite right: neither Meg nor any of the friends is guilty of any personal lapse. Their guilt has an enigmatic character insofar as it gives psychic form to a thoroughly impersonal phenomenon—the resignification of politics itself. If Meg and the others took steps inconsistent with their political commitments, it was because the ground shifted beneath their feet, as it were. Thus, for example, it must have become impossible for Meg to generate a rationale—a "story," in Arendt's parlance—according to which continuing her work with the "scum" still had a meaningful political dimension. From this perspective, her sense of guilt is misplaced: she experiences as a personal failure of political imagination her acceptance of a forced bargain in which no real alternative ever existed. The experience to which Meg's guilt testifies is therefore precisely the experience of alienation decried by Arendt. Yet it is an experience that appears only obliquely in the film, in a scene that actively endorses the notion that guilt is misplaced, while simultaneously—and by the same, highly condensed rhetorical token—discouraging any investigation of this guilt's actual genesis. Meg is acquitted not because a structural transformation made what had seemed like political agency magically disappear, but because she had been mistaken all along.

28. The point is not that the Hollywood "mode of representation" is univocally liberal or that it systematically trumps pragmatic constraints or polemical aims in specific films. Rather, it is simply that while the aesthetic form of *The Big Chill* meticulously serves its narrative strategy, this strategy, which is independent of any medium, is consistent with a normatively liberal framework for imagining viable forms of citizenship and sociality.

29. This is one of Arendt's chief complaints regarding the "rule of no one" characteristic of "the social"—what Tocqueville calls the "benign despotism" to which American—that is, liberal—democracy is prone. Implicit in this complaint is the "agonistic" Arendt, for whom politics is not confined to negotiation over communal norms but presupposes irreducible differences no set of norms can fi-

nally mediate. It is only on condition of this irreducibility that action, power, and a durable public world are possible at all. See Arendt, *The Human Condition.*

30. Significantly, the lesson Harold learns when Nick rejects his offer and Sarah upbraids him for this misguided act of generosity has nothing to do with the political implications—however bourgeois—of the juridico-economic trespass involved. Rather, it concerns the breach of Nick's autonomy and the risk to the merger itself. That is, Harold's error consists in pursuing what could become a self-defeating course of action; it is a pragmatic miscalculation, not an ethico-political one.

31. See Disch, "On Friendship in 'Dark Times.'"

32. Though Karen has a different instance of symmetry in mind, her comment applies equally well here.

33. This is not to say Sarah does not feel goodwill toward Meg. On the contrary, Sarah's love for Meg is precisely the alibi securing her misrecognition of her own motives.

34. Though the term was famously coined by Oneida commune founder John Humphrey Noyes, as a lay philosophy and political project of the sixties counterculture, the doctrine of "free love" derives from interpretations of Freud by such figures as Herbert Marcuse and, notably, Wilhelm Reich. In *The Sexual Revolution: Toward a Self-Governing Character Structure* (completed around 1930 but appearing for the first time in English in 1945) and *The Mass Psychology of Fascism* (1933), Reich took Freud's account of the libidinal structuration of the psyche to indicate that the behavioral norms expressed in moral strictures and social institutions presuppose the repression of an otherwise spontaneous sexuality. (Wilhelm Reich, *The Sexual Revolution,* trans. Theodore P. Wolfe [New York: Farrar, Straus & Giroux, 1963]; *The Mass Psychology of Fascism,* trans. Vincnet Carfagno [New York: Farrar, Straus & Giroux, 1980].) A communist until his expulsion from the German Communist Party in 1933, Reich argued that the capitalist structures that produced, and were reproduced by, bourgeois morality constituted an ongoing threat to psychic and social health and psychic freedom. Bourgeois sexual repression produced widespread neurosis, and true revolutionary emancipation could be achieved through the cultivation of an active, guilt-free sex life. Pursuit of sexual pleasure outside the confines of bourgeois norms would result in the dismantling of the socioeconomic structures that relied on the sublimation of libidinal drives. If Reich is a father of the sixties' "sexual revolution," it is in this explicitly political sense.

35. The silent interlocutor evoked by the effort to sharpen the distinction between eros and philia is Herbert Marcuse, perhaps the most prominent theorist and a vocal advocate of the "new social movements" of the sixties. It was Marcuse who identified the peculiar form of libidinal blackmail by means of which "total administration" came to assume the form of apparently total personal freedom. The key to "one-dimensional" or postdialectical society is the advent of "repressive desublimation," or the gradual removal of various prohibitions aimed not at liberating the individual but at enslaving her all the more effectively. See Hebert Mar-

cuse, *Eros and Civilization* (Boston: Beacon, 1955), and *One-Dimensional Man* (Boston: Beacon, 1964).

36. Notable here is the homology between the ideologically deceptive desire to experience "pure" pleasure in the absence of a supporting "perverse" substrate and the desire to experience a "pure" relationship untinged by "pathological" cathexis. Both are dialectical responses to an ideological constraint that they only reproduce, since the very promise of purity generates the desire it proposes to fulfill.

37. Silver, "'Two Different Sorts of Commerce.'"

38. Jasinski, "(Re)Constituting Community," 478.

39. See Lauren Berlant, "The Theory of Infantile Citizenship," in *The Queen of America.*

40. "Objective" is, for Marx, not a positivist category but rather the designation of the way certain features (say, of the commodity) actually or effectively appear to subjects even when the subjects do not think that these features appear this way. This form of objectivity has a structure homologous to that of Arendt's "world," which we cannot directly locate "out there" but which also is not reducible to our own subjective fantasy or illusion.

41. Jasinski, "(Re)Constituting Community," 478.

42. See Jacques Derrida, *Politics of Friendship,* trans. George Collins (London: Verso, 1997).

43. Appiah, "Liberalism, Individuality."

44. See Dana Cloud, *Control and Consolation in American Culture and Politics: Rhetorics of Therapy* (London: Sage, 1998); Micki McGee, *Self-Help, Inc.: Makeover Culture in American Life* (London: Oxford University Press, 2005).

45. Berlant, "Infantile Citizenship."

46. When Harold haughtily defends this friendship by insisting that the cop "happens to be one heck of a guy," his warrant for this claim is that "he's twice kept this house from being ripped off." Nothing in the film more clearly evinces the logic of "selling out": here is a cynical pseudo-friendship rationalized as necessary to protect one's private property from "scum." It is a textbook example of bourgeois ideology as Marx described it, from the subjective investment in property sustained by the distorting capitalist system of incentives through its self-deluding rationalization and the endorsement of antidemocratic state policies all the way to the paradoxical consequences—the debasement of the very forms of sociability supposed to be secured by private autonomy founded on property. The cop appears to be a friend only insofar as both he and Harold are entangled in a system of relations distorted by capital. Yet even within this system both sense their unsurpassable mutual alienation, an alienation bound to push them toward hysterical overinvestment in the system that creates it: Harold comes to see the underclass as "scum" and financial success as responsible social membership; the cop develops paranoia toward strangers and a naïve identification with television detective-heroes.

47. For a discussion of mediated intimacy-at-a-distance, see John Thompson, *Political Scandal* (Cambridge: Polity, 2000), 39–40.

48. At issue here is the problem of distance within intimacy. As Arendt imagines the intercession of "the world" formed by the friendship relation into this intimate space, this raises the question of the always already mediated (linguistically, socially, ideologically, juridically, etc.) nature of any intimacy—as well as the equally pressing question of mass-mediation posed by the reflexivity thesis (Luhmann, Beck, Giddens). That is, when Arendt imagines restoring distance to a space that appears to lack it—and thereby fails to achieve the spaciousness (openness, publicness, etc.) proper to it—she is asserting a counterfactual model of intimacy as it exists in the modern world she critiques. The erotic(ized) closure of intimacy is itself a (late- or post-) modern *fantasy,* sustained by the mediatized "in-between" as a promise of its own collapse.

This, in turn, brings us to the numerous (re)markings of mediation within the filmic diegesis: Michael, the writer for *People* magazine (we might linger briefly over the apt choice of *People,* a "respectable" gossip rag vaguely appropriating the visual rhetoric of news weeklies and named for the indeterminate mass subject to which it is devoted and to whom it addresses itself—the "people" it is about and the "people" who read it: a more perfect emblem of the reflexive circuit of modern mediated stranger sociability could not have been adduced), has even reflected in print about his friend Alex; Sam, the actor whose image as fictional detective circulates on TV and in magazines, is thereby able to mediate a juridical conflict between Nick and a diegetically real policeman into a sociable relation; Nick, the former radio therapist, is disgusted with the misprision of stranger sociability in the context of (already reflexively staged) psychotherapeutic intimacy; the repeated use of the video camera as a diegetic device for staging self-consciously ironized confessions; Sarah's comparison of Harold to the fictional TV character John Beresford Tipton; and even the very genesis of political disappointment. When Meg reflects on her disillusionment with the "scum" she once defended in court, the very possibility of this disillusionment is a function of the source of her initial political motivation—mass-mediated images and narratives of social injustice and its victims. No wonder that when asked if she thought she'd be defending Grumpy and Sneezy, Sam jumps in with "No—Huey and Bobby." These names indicate not only the political nature of the group's erstwhile orientation but also the mediated nature of their political imaginary. The latter can be glossed by citing two first names as if they are brand logos on a conceptual par with fictional characters—which, of course, they are.

49. For an astute discussion of this temptation, see Michael Walzer, "The Communitarian Critique of Liberalism," *Political Theory* 18.1 (1990): 6–23.

Chapter 3

1. Jean Bethke Elshtain, *Public Man, Private Woman: Women in Social and Political Thought* (Princeton: Princeton University Press, 1981); Seyla Benhabib, "The Generalized and the Concrete Other," in *Women and Moral Theory,* ed. E. F. Kittay and D. T. Meyers (Totowa, NJ: Rowman & Littlefield, 1987); Carole Pateman,

The Disorder of Women (Cambridge: Polity, 1989); Nancy Fraser, "Rethinking the Public Sphere: A Contribution to the Critique of Actually Existing Democracy," *Social Text* 25/26 (1990): 56–80; Young, "Polity and Group Difference"; Kathleen Jones, "Citizenship in a Woman-friendly Polity," *Signs* 15 (Summer 1990): 781–812; Wendy Brown, "Liberalism's Family Values," in *States of Injury.*

2. For a cogent summary of these debates, see Mary Dietz, "Current Controversies in Feminist Theory," *Annual Review of Political Science* 6 (2003): 399–431. See also Martha Nussbaum, "The Feminist Critique of Liberalism," in *Sex and Social Justice* (New York: Oxford University Press, 1999), 55–80, for a representative argument in defense of liberal feminism.

3. Brown, "Liberalism's Family Values," 137; emphasis in original.

4. Though outnumbered by sympathetic reviews, hostile critics were prominent and influential. The most widely cited are Joe Bob Briggs, "Mantrack," *Playboy,* February 1994; Fred Bruning, "A Lousy Deal for Women—and Men," *Maclean's,* August 12, 1991; Margaret Carlson, "Is This What Feminism Is All About?" *Time,* June 24, 1991; Richard Grenier, "Killer Bimbos," *Commentary,* September 1991; Richard Johnson, *New York Daily News* columnist, quoted in Richard Schickel, "Gender Bender," *Time,* June 24, 1991; John Leo, "Toxic Feminism on the Big Screen," *U.S. News & World Report,* June 10, 1991; Terrence Rafferty, "Outlaw Princesses," *New Yorker,* June 3, 1991; John Robinson, "The Great Debate over *Thelma and Louise,*" *Boston Globe,* June 14, 1991; John Simon, "Movie of the Moment," *National Review,* July 8, 1991.

5. Schickel, "Gender Bender."

6. The scrutiny prompted screenwriter Callie Khouri to aver artfully that "[t]he issues surrounding the film are feminist, but the film itself is not" (Lizzie Francke, "Interview with Callie Khouri," *Guardian,* July 9, 1991, 17). The film was only the most recent, and not the most provocative, entry in a long roster of popular texts challenging the social, cultural, and political marginalization of women. An exhaustive list would be lengthy, but earlier television hits such as *That Girl* and *The Mary Tyler Moore Show,* and films such as *Alice Doesn't Live Here Anymore* (1974), *Woman Under the Influence* (1974), *An Unmarried Woman* (1978), *Norma Rae* (1979), and *Working Girl* (1988) presented no less audacious visions of female agency than the campy violence of *Thelma & Louise.* Indeed, Susan Faludi's list of eighties "backlash" films attests to the consolidation of Hollywood feminism years prior to the release of *Thelma & Louise* (*Backlash* [New York: Anchor, 1992]). Moreover, the theme of sexual violence as a symptom of structural patriarchy had become a staple of media feminism, reaching a kind of apex with *The Accused* (1988).

7. Walter Benjamin, "Critique of Violence," in *Reflections,* ed. Peter Demetz (New York: Schocken, 1986).

8. Jacques Derrida, "Force of Law: The Mystical Foundations of Authority," in *Deconstruction and the Possibility of Justice,* ed. Drucilla Cornell, Michael Rosenfeld, and David Gray Carlson (London: Routledge, 1992), 33.

9. Ibid., 34–35.

10. Marita Sturken, *Thelma & Louise* (London: BFI, 2000); Jack Boozer, "Seduction and Betrayal in the Heartland: *Thelma and Louise,*" *Literature-Film Quarterly* 23 (July 1995); Steven Cohan and Ina Rae Hark, introduction to *The Road Movie Book,* ed. Steven Cohan and Ina Rae Hark (London: Routledge, 1997); Manohla Dargis, "The Roads to Freedom," *Sight and Sound* 1 (July 1991); Marsha Kinder, "*Thelma & Louise* and *Messidor* as Feminist Road Movies," *Film Quarterly* 4 (Winter 1991–92): 29–30; Leo Braudy, "Satire into Myth," *Film Quarterly* 4 (Winter 1991–92): 27–28; Peter N. Chumo II, "At the Generic Crossroads with *Thelma and Louise,*" *Post Script* 13 (Winter/Spring 1994). Similarly, for Yvonne Tasker the film revises the masculinism of action cinema (*Spectacular Bodies: Gender, Genre and Action Cinema* [New York: Routledge, 1993], 134–52), and for Marleen Barr it verges on feminist science fiction ("*Thelma and Louise:* Driving toward Feminist SF," *Foundation* 53 [Autumn 1991]: 80–86).

11. Cohan and Hark, introduction, 11.

12. Glenn Man, "Gender, Genre and Myth in *Thelma and Louise,*" *Film Criticism* 18 (Fall 1993): 36–53. Sustained analyses of the gaze in the film is offered by Ann Putnam, "The Bearer of the Gaze in Ridley Scott's *Thelma and Louise,*" *Western American Literature* 27 (October 1992): 291–302, and Brenda Cooper, "'Chick Flicks' as Feminist Texts: the Appropriation of the Male Gaze in *Thelma & Louise,*" *Women's Studies in Communication* 23 (Fall 2000): 277–306.

13. Cohan and Hark, introduction, 3.

14. Timothy Corrigan, *A Cinema without Walls* (New Brunswick: Rutgers University Press, 1991): 137–62.

15. Other critics situate the film within genres they see as already more congenial to women. Carol Clover, Linda Williams, Jacinda Read, and Hilary Naroni view it as a rape-revenge film (Carol J. Clover, *Men, Women and Chainsaws* [Princeton: Princeton University Press, 1992], 234; Linda Williams, "What Makes a Woman Wander," *Film Quarterly* 4 [Winter 1991–92]: 28–29; Jacinda Read, *The New Avengers: Feminism, Femininity and the Rape-Revenge Cycle* [Manchester: Manchester University Press, 2000]; Hilary Naroni, *The Violent Woman: Femininity, Narrative and Violence in Contemporary American Cinema* [Albany: SUNY Press, 2005]); Susan Morrison regards it as a woman's film ("Pearl, Hilda, Thelma, and Louise: The Woman's Film Revisited" *Cineaction* 30 [Winter 1993]: 48–53); and James Maxfield finds in it elements of noir (*The Fatal Woman* [New York: Fairleigh Dickinson University Press, 1996]). The strategy of such readings is to contest the masculinism of some genres by marshaling a countervailing series of others.

16. Cathy Griggers, "Thelma and Louise and the Cultural Generation of the New Butch-Femme," *Film Theory Goes to the Movies,* ed. Jim Collins, Hillary Radner, and Ava Preacher Collins (New York: Routledge, 1993).

17. Lynda Hart, *Fatal Women* (Princeton: Princeton University Press, 1994). In addition to Hart and Griggers, Barbara Johnson attempts a "disappointing" queer reading ("Lesbian Spectacles: Reading *Sula, Passing, Thelma and Louise,* and *The Ac-*

cused," in *Media Spectacles,* ed. Marjorie Garber et al. [New York: Routledge, 1993], 160–66). Yvonne Tasker observes that *Thelma & Louise* was routinely appropriated as a lesbian film (*Spectacular Bodies,* 29, 134). Noting that many critics commented on its lesbian subtext, Marita Sturken argues that the film openly accommodates both straight and queer readings (*Thelma & Louise,* 77).

18. Sharon Willis, "Hardware and Hardbodies; or, What Do Women Want? A Reading of *Thelma and Louise,*" in Collins, Radner and Preacher Collins, *Film Theory Goes to the Movies,* 127.

19. Judith Butler, *Gender Trouble* (New York: Routledge, 1990), 38–39, 5–6.

20. E.g., Seyla Benhabib, "Feminism and Postmodernism: An Uneasy Alliance," in *Feminist Contentions: A Philosophical Exchange,* ed. Seyla Benhabib et al. (New York: Routledge, 1995), 17–34; Catharine MacKinnon, "Points against Postmodernism," *Chicago Kent Law Review* 75 (2000): 687.

21. On this point, she is especially clear in her exchange with Žižek. See Judith Butler, Ernesto Laclau, and Slavoj Žižek, *Contingency, Hegemony, Universality* (London: Verso, 2000).

22. Ibid., 149.

23. Butler has recently begun to take up a version of this problem. In particular, see *Antigone's Claim: Kinship between Life and Death* (New York: Columbia University Press, 2000). Even here, however, she is more interested in the politics of kinship than in the possibility of decentering "defiance" as the privileged mode of political agency (see 1–2).

24. Butler would likely deny that her work authorizes such claims advanced on behalf of *Thelma & Louise.* Yet her focus on epistemic exclusion tends to accelerate (appropriations of) her work in the direction of a structuralism from which she seeks to distance herself.

25. Hart, *Fatal Women,* 76.

26. Ibid., 79.

27. In a variation on this theme, David Russell locates this compulsion in the popular media's dismissal of the film as "too lesbian" ("'I'm Not Gonna Hurt You': Legal Penetrations in *Thelma and Louise,*" *Americana* 1 [Spring 2002], http://www.americanpopularculture.com/journal/articles/spring_2002/russell.htm [accessed June 1, 2009]). Russell argues that the charge of lesbianism betokens popular anxiety about the women's ascension to what Lauren Berlant calls "diva citizenship" (*The Queen of America*). Yet while he maintains focus on the rhetorical instrumentality of the film's lesbian subtext and is the only critic to give any prominence to the question of citizenship, he too praises the film in exuberantly liberal terms: "Thelma and Louise become patriots in a new revolution, that of activating and celebrating various identity positions outside the law."

28. The most sustained analysis of this issue is Sarah Projansky, *Watching Rape: Film and Television in Postfeminist Culture* (New York: New York University Press, 2005), 121–53. The subject also figures prominently in Clover, *Men, Women and Chainsaws;* Martha McCaughey and Neal King, "Rape Education Videos: Present-

ing Mean Women Instead of Dangerous Men," *Teaching Sociology* 23 (October, 1995): 374–88; Naroni, *The Violent Woman;* Read, *The New Avengers;* Elizabeth Spelman and Martha Minow, "Outlaw Women: An Essay on *Thelma & Louise,*" *New England Law Review* 1281 (Summer 1992); Sturken, *Thelma & Louise,* 61–69; Shirley Wiegand, "Deception and Artifice: Thelma, Louise and the Legal Hermeneutic," *Oklahoma City University Law Review* 22 (Spring 1997): 25–49.

29. Projansky, *Watching Rape,* 9. While only a few critics center their attention on the question of sexual violence, most critics writing about the film understand the sexual victimization of its protagonists as a synecdoche of systematic subordination of women (see Dana Cloud, "The Therapeutics of Feminism: From Self-Esteem to Suicide," in *Control and Consolation,* 119). Despite numerous differences among them, most commentators understand Louise's shooting of Harlan as a response to his assertion of masculine prerogative, which she regards as validated by law enforcement, legal procedure, and the "kind of world" the women inhabit.

30. The main exponent of this view is Faludi.

31. Willis, "Hardware and Hardbodies"; Griggers, "New Butch-Femme." Both films were actually released earlier, in 1987.

32. Projansky, *Watching Rape,* 125. See note 29 above for a list of critics who express versions of this view. See also Cooper, "'Chick Flicks.'" Claiming that hers is one of only three "analyses of *Thelma and Louise* that directly address the sexual violence in the film" (152), Projansky argues that Harlan's assault of Thelma is rendered inconsequential in most other readings. She maintains that critics largely seek to identify forms of feminist pleasure in the film, at the cost of de-emphasizing the role of rape in facilitating such pleasure (123–24). Yet this line of argument, while not lacking for evidentiary support, overstates its case. Harlan's assault commonly provokes discussion of women's predicament in relation to the law and/or the sexist discursive régime of contemporary American culture. Such discussions invariably presuppose that Louise's culpability is mitigated by the assault (and her own experience of rape), so this event is hardly marginal to them. At the same time, the film ambiguates the issue by having Louise interrupt the rape and by having her shoot Harlan for reasserting masculine prerogative. The effect is to shift the narrative focus from the *fact* of violence to its *inscription* within a larger social, juridical, and discursive framework. This is why so much ink is expended on questions of law, language, and representation, which are indispensable to grasping what the film has to say about the persistence of women's subordination, as well as the crucial but not dispositive role of violence in that subordination.

33. Carol Clover makes a similar point regarding the deployment of "redneck" stereotypes in horror films as "a kind of universal blame figure . . . held responsible for all manner of social ills" (*Men, Women and Chainsaws,* 135).

34. If, as Projansky has it, the film has a "postfeminist" dimension (*Watching Rape,* 133–37), the rhetorical function of rendering patriarchy as anachronistic is not to devalue or "post" *feminism,* which must, given the film's overall trajectory, remain politically salient. Rather, it is to advocate the liberal model of citizenship

as fundamental to any democratic project, including feminism. It is this strategic function of feminism in the film that, in requiring *both* the continuity and relegation of patriarchy, prompts Projansky to read it as "ambivalent," both feminist and postfeminist at once. An analysis that situates the film's thematic concern with gender in relation to its rhetoric of citizenship makes it possible to account for what otherwise remains an opaque and terminal ambiguity—a critical impasse that mirrors the one reached by the protagonists.

35. Wiegand is unusual in arguing that Louise performs a vigilante act of preemptive law enforcement: "Harlan is not killed because Thelma was in danger; he was killed because other women were and those women had no more legal protection than Thelma and Louise. Many viewers recognized this, many women viewers felt it, and they were therefore happy to see him dead" ("Deception and Artifice"). This reading directly positions the women—and the audience—as good liberal citizens, ones who abide by the rationale legitimating the law even when the law itself fails to do so.

36. As Projansky observes, "the film not only offers self-defense/revenge as a viable response to sexual assault, but defines such actions as potentially pleasurable" (*Watching Rape,* 129). Yet the very possibility of audience pleasure presupposes that its members are not themselves under indictment for complicity in patriarchal oppression. This tacit exemption is one of the key indices of the film's presumptive liberalism.

37. Two canonic versions are Pateman, *The Disorder of Women* and Fraser, "Rethinking the Public Sphere." The standard multiculturalist version is Young, "Polity and Group Difference."

38. Cf. Nussbaum, "Feminist Critique." Nussbaum accepts the liberal bargain, arguing that women gain more than they give up by pressing claims for rights and equality (e.g., 69–71).

39. Butler, *Gender Trouble;* Warner, "Mass Public and the Mass Subject," 239.

40. However, the stipulation according to which the power of speech always belongs to the (masculine) Other consigns rhetoric to the endless task of "subverting" this power—a task whose political counterpart is the liberal trope of "vigilance," such that the vigilante and the outlaw unexpectedly overlap in the liberal rebel-citizen.

41. Luce Irigaray, *Speculum of the Other Woman,* trans. Gillian C. Gill (Ithaca: Cornell University Press, 1985), 68.

42. The theme of fantasy figures prominently in Hart, *Fatal Women;* Griggers, "New Butch-Femme"; and Barr, "Driving toward Feminist SF." Despite notable differences in the way they develop this theme, each critic tends to treat the two women as subject to the same fantasy.

43. Griggers, "New Butch-Femme," 137; emphasis added.

44. Eschewing deception is, of course, essential for maintaining audience identification with the women, and comports perfectly with their enduring civility. This is another way the rhetorical imperatives organizing the film preclude options left open by the logic of the narrative.

45. Slavoj Žižek demonstrates that social membership is *nothing but* this appearance of an obdurate social bond, sustained by the rules of etiquette (*Looking Awry: An Introduction to Lacan through Popular Culture* [Cambridge: MIT Press, 1991], 72–75).

46. Žižek distinguishes the "passage to act" from "acting out" as "entail[ing] . . . an exit from the symbolic network, a dissolution of the social bond" (ibid., 139). The point is that it is a fundamental error to invoke the rules of the social game in order to call violators to account, since the violations are inherent to the rules themselves. Thus when Thelma and Louise rely on the norms of civility to practice critical citizenship, this reliance vitiates the critique it appears to support.

47. Karen Hollinger, *In the Company of Women* (Minneapolis: University of Minnesota Press, 1998), 120; Cooper, "'Chick Flicks'"; Patricia Mellencamp, *A Fine Romance: Five Ages of Film Feminism* (Philadelphia: Temple University Press, 1995), 117.

Chapter 4

1. See Niklas Luhmann, *Observations on Modernity* (Stanford: Stanford University Press, 1998).

2. Cf. Nicolas Royle, "Déjà Vu," in *Post-Theory,* ed. Martin McQuillan (Edinburgh: Edinburgh University Press, 1999). Through a deconstructive reading of Freud, Royle determines déjà vu as "nothing other than supplementarity-as-experience, the experience of a supplement without origin" (11). One would hasten to add that, given the incessant and explicit re-marking of contingency in the cultural public sphere as well as in the most "intimate" spaces, this experience is no longer to be understood as merely intrapsychic and transient, but rather as constitutive of modern social reality tout court. The disconcerting sense of repetition has itself become endlessly repetitive.

3. Peter Krapp, *Déjà Vu: Aberrations of Cultural Memory* (Minneapolis: University of Minnesota Press, 2004). Krapp links the proliferation of these effects to media technologies, but while the peculiar temporality of the mediascape undoubtedly engenders "aberrations" of cultural memory, the distinctively modern experience of déjà vu should also be grasped in terms of the basic cognitive structure of the modern episteme.

4. See Jean Baudrillard, *Simulations* (London: Semiotext(e), 1983).

5. See Anthony Giddens, *The Consequences of Modernity* (Stanford: Stanford University Press, 1990).

6. Luhmann, *Observations on Modernity.*

7. As William Rasch observes in his exceptionally lucid discussion of Luhmann's work, "The challenge [is] understanding how every critique of modernity extends modernity, whether that extension is desired or not." *Niklas Luhmann's Modernity: The Paradoxes of Differentiation* (Stanford: Stanford University Press, 2000), 10.

8. This is the central point of contention between Luhmann and Habermas on the one hand and Lyotard on the other. For systems theory, Habermasian ratio-

nalization is a reaction-formation aimed at circumscribing the contingency proliferating in modernity; while Lyotard's valorization of Wittgensteinian language games as radically incommensurable in view of the *differend* ends up in a kind of discursive monadism. (On the latter point, see Gunther Teubner, "Economics of Gift—Positivity of Justice: The Mutual Paranoia of Jacques Derrida and Niklas Luhmann," *Theory, Culture & Society* 18.1 [2001]: 35.) From this vantage, the semantics of "postmodernity" is hopelessly confused, since Habermas is, ironically, "post-" modern in effectively seeking to surpass modern contingency and Lyotard is a premodern metaphysician in disguise. In sum, neither the (Habermasian project or anti-Habermasian accusation of) rationalization nor radical incommensurability gets modern reflexivity right.

9. See Castoriadis, *The Imaginary Institution of Society;* and Niklas Luhmann, *Social Systems* (Stanford: Stanford University Press, 1996). Both derive their notions of autopoiesis from the biological theories of Varela and Maturano. (For a lucid discussion of autopoiesis in Castoriadis, see Suzi Adams, "Castoriadis and Autopoiesis," *Thesis Eleven* 88.1 [2007]: 76–91.)

10. This is a point of unexpected convergence between Niklas Luhmann's antihumanist theory of modernity (*Observations on Modernity*) and the humanist narrative of modernity offered by Charles Taylor (*Modern Social Imaginaries*).

11. Ironically, precisely because such practice is itself a form of social-scale reflexivity.

12. Scott Durham, *Phantom Communities: The Simulacrum and the Limits of Postmodernism* (Stanford: Stanford University Press, 1998), 21, 62.

13. See note 35 below for a discussion of Slavoj Žižek's version of this thesis. What Žižek regards as the corrosive effect of pervasive commodity fetishism Luhmann sees as inherent in the logic of modern autopoietic systems, of which the economy is but one instance.

14. Durham, *Phantom Communities,* 22.It is crucial to keep in mind—and easy to forget—that the liberal emphasis on individual autonomy is supposed to secure social cooperation. The problem being highlighted here is not that such autonomy is fictive, impossible, or ideologically duplicitous, but, on the contrary, that it is self-defeating. This is so not because, as communitarians and republicans fear, too much autonomy weakens the social bond and undermines collective agency, but because the fully autonomous liberal citizen would, paradoxically, be nothing other than a supplementary posit of the liberal order, "a rebel without a cause."

15. The debate concerning postmodernity, whether as an aesthetic, economic, historical, or epistemological development, repeatedly generates figures of the conundrum of social cybernetics identified by Luhmann and Giddens. Simply put, the problem is that steering social processes on the basis of systematic knowledge about them eventually integrates this knowledge into the processes themselves, so that, as Borges famously has it, it becomes impossible to distinguish the map from the territory. Explicitly drawing on Borges's metaphor, Baudrillard calls this situation "hyperreality." The challenge posed by hyperreality is on dramatic display in

Fredric Jameson's attempt to trace Baudrillard's insight to the cultural logic of late capitalism as it manifests itself in aesthetic features such as pastiche, ironic self-reference, and nostalgia for the present. Finding it impossible to distinguish cause and effect, he does not fully recognize the tautological epistemology of reflexive modernity and can only lament the collapse of critical distance, incoherently recommending the practice of "cognitive mapping" as the implausible solution to the integration of the map into the territory. And while the postmodernity debate has cooled with the institutional prominence of cultural studies and its hostility to "theory," the problem continues to return forcefully across the critical humanities and social sciences. James Carrier and Daniel Miller call the economic version of the conundrum of simulation "virtualism" (*Virtualism* [London: Berg, 1998]). Marilyn Ivy identifies it in the "discourse of the vanishing" characteristic of modernization in Japan (*Discourses of the Vanishing: Modernity, Phantasm, Japan* [Chicago: University of Chicago Press, 1995]). Ackbar Abbas brings into relief the "culture of disappearance" that results when contingency becomes the organizing principle of a social formation (*Hong Kong: Culture and the Politics of Disappearance* [Minneapolis: University of Minnesota Press, 1997]). In a different context but with strikingly similar results, Serguei Oushakine analyzes the aphasia that results from the collapse of the metadiscursive framework—i.e., the cognitive "map" ("In the State of Post-Soviet Aphasia: Symbolic Development in Contemporary Russia," *Europe-Asia Studies* 52.6 [2000]: 991–1016).

16. The song's lyric makes explicit the stakes of their relationship, linking the theme of self-commodification to the ambivalent gesture of abject yet paternalistic sacrifice (one thinks here of the unexpected coincidence of powerlessness and violence in "cute" aesthetics):

> Listen to the girl
> As she takes on half the world
> Moving up and so alive
> In her honey dripping beehive (beehive)
> It's good, so good,
> It's so good, so good
> Walking back to you
> Is the hardest thing that
> I can do
> That I can do for you
> For you
> I'll be your plastic toy
> I'll be your plastic toy
> For you
> Eating up the scum
> Is the hardest thing for
> Me to do.

17. Guy Debord, *The Society of the Spectacle,* trans. Donald Nicholson-Smith (London: Zone, 1994).

18. In an account that bears a striking and not at all coincidental resemblance to Derrida, Luhmann explains that every system achieves its systematicity by first distinguishing between itself and its environment, a distinction that can in turn be observed. When the contingency of this distinction is marked "inside" the system, the reference to exteriority appears as an artifact of internal operations. One effect of acknowledging the interior determination of the exterior is the effective disappearance of exteriority as such, at the very moment when the integrity of the system most urgently demands it. Derrida and Baudrillard can thus be understood as highlighting mutually contingent, if obverse, phenomena: the destabilization of every sovereign self-identity on the one hand and the disintegration of all referential reality on the other. The general point is that the proliferation of contingency is the direct, if paradoxical, effect of a historically unprecedented development: the socialization of social processes through functions-systems. Counterintuitive though it seems, system autonomization produces, rather than working to master or preclude, contingency—and it does so by instituting reflexive processes of observation that mark its own determinations as merely operational. It is against this background that the endlessly repeated "demonstrations" of contingency in cultural studies should be understood.

19. Recall that for Luhmann, society consists not of persons but of systems.

20. It is not a question of simulation displacing a more authentic sociability, but of a sociability constituted by simulation through and through. Information and entertainment technology is neither the cause nor a symptom; it is the synecdoche of fully reflexive sociability constituted by its "mediation" through complex and abstract social systems, techniques, and forms of knowledge—in sum, a cybernetic sociability of which machine interaction is but one, aptly representative mode.

21. Mark Seltzer, "The Crime System," *Critical Inquiry* 30 (Spring 2004), 570.

22. It is this logic that generates the short-circuit between the film's rhetorical project and the internal logic of its rhetoric. Psychoanalysis is, of course, a paradigmatic form of the sort of reflexive knowledge typical of simulation. Indeed, its aspiration toward scientific status overlaps with its literary origins and deployments in a way that makes it impossible to decide whether it is a mode of knowledge appropriated by literature or a literary mode functioning as a form of expert knowledge. The conflation is inevitable, given that literary fiction and social science are, as evidenced by the competition between them, two modes of modern social reflexivity—or, as Niklas Luhmann has it, two mutually contingent social systems (Luhmann, *Social Systems*). The psychoanalytic relationship is exemplary of modern cybernetic sociability: the very possibility of a subject-supposed-to-know is irreducibly modern, for what this subject would instate is the knowledge of the social totality. In a traditional society, such a knowledge would be unthematizable. It is only the would-be modern subject that reflexively gauges itself against a generalized Other with access to objectively observable social facts—as opposed to revealed moral truth.

23. This self-citation is also an intertextual one, an amusing reprise of a similar gesture in *Groundhog Day,* where Bill Murray's character mimes his own weatherman shtick. It's simulacra all the way down.

24. If, for Luhmann, "people don't communicate; only communication communicates," here the communication system thwarts its own functioning.

25. This is among the paradoxes identified by Luhmann and registered less explicitly by Giddens.

26. Refusal and acquiescence paradoxically overlap: for the hyperreflexive sujet suppose savoir, to play his part means refusing to play it. As a result, both knowing and not knowing how to play his part produce the same result—the refusal to play it. It makes no difference whether Bob refuses because he knows how transference works or because he fails to recognize it altogether. And since refusal is what is called for, he cannot but succeed. This is because the cybernetic function of the analyst consists in miming knowledge. Whether he knows it or not, the analyst is compelled by the cybernetic structure of the psychoanalytic relationship to *act as if* he knows. The cybernetic system thus "knows" through him, irrespective of his subjective participation. In this sense, Bob the professional simulacrum is the perfect candidate for the job: after all, simulation proceeds by means of him but without him.

27. I cannot resist calling attention to the explicitness with which the lyric highlights the mutual contingency of the self-producing individual and the mediating other. The Hegelian coincidence of narcissism and hysteria described by authors such as Richard Sennett or Slavoj Žižek might be seen as the song's main theme.

28. Christine Yano, "The Floating World of Karaoke in Japan," *Popular Music & Society* 20 (Summer 1996), 12, 13, 3–4; emphasis in original.

29. Ivy, *Discourses of the Vanishing,* 224–26. On the vicissitudes of "primordialism" in the context of globalization, see Arjun Appadurai, *Modernity at Large* (Minneapolis: University of Minnesota Press, 1996), 139–57.

30. In this, they correspond precisely to Bob's own ambivalent position as the subject who effectively knows even when he refuses to participate in the metadiscursive game of transference.

31. Significantly, despite the pervasive irony in their repartee throughout the film, Bob and Charlotte exhibit very little of it in their singing. They may not aspire to embody the attitudes conveyed by their songs, but the songs are brilliantly selected to reflect back on their (always already) surrogate performers. (Indeed, a separate analysis of the film's soundtrack would be a worthy undertaking.) In brief, various versions of reflexive self-distance already characterize the songs themselves, their form as well as their thematic content and the enunciative modes they stage and demand. Elvis Costello's bitterness in his frontal attack on the depoliticizing misanthropy of punk irony may be earnest, but as in all pop music the earnestness—and the demand for a return to humane authenticity—is artful, or reflexively performed. The protagonist portrayed by Chrissie Hynde cautiously aspires to embody the persona she narrates—a stereotype supposed to succeed so-

cially in a way that has eluded her unscripted self—and thus only underscores both her inability to do so and the cost of failure. Finally, Roxy Music's innovation consisted precisely in the complex and studiously ambiguous reflexivity of the pop pastiche that Bryan Ferry and Brian Eno cultivated *sous rature,* or under erasure, as if condemned to life in the convergence of nostalgia, irony, and techno-utopianism but willfully committing to their predicament.

32. Durham, *Phantom Communities,* 65, 21, 62.

33. J. K. Gibson-Graham, *The End of Capitalism (As We Knew It): A Feminist Critique of Political Economy* (Minneapolis: University of Minnesota Press, 1996); Gibson-Graham, *A Postcapitalist Politics* (Minneapolis: University of Minnesota Press, 2006).

34. Laclau, *On Populist Reason;* Mouffe, *On the Political.* I have analyzed this limitation of Laclau's project in Michael Kaplan, "Capitalizing on the Dialectical Economy of Hegemony: Laclau, Populism and the Liberal Wager," *Cultural Studies* (forthcoming).

35. Taylor, *Ethics of Authenticity;* Richard Sennett, *The Fall of Public Man* (New York: W. W. Norton, 1974).

36. It is here that I think Giddens's insights concerning the paradoxes of modern self-construction and Seltzer's observations on the mutual contingency of popular fiction and reflexive modernity should be pushed a critical step further. Recall Žižek's argument that commodity fetishism inaugurates a historical objectivity in which people regard themselves as contingent tokens of an abstract, universal type, as well as his frequent recourse to the example of a hooligan who openly deploys the language of therapy to give an account of his own (mis)behavior. Žižek's point is that liberal-capitalist culture is "objectively" ideological, in that mundane social reality itself is "distorted." Here Žižek is closer than he would like to admit to Baudrillard's invocation of Borges: to claim that social life itself, and not only its discursive representation, is distorted in being constituted by a kind of immanent, objective abstraction presupposes that no distinction can any longer be pretended to exist between reality and representation—and that this state of affairs amounts to a *loss.* Thus when skinheads can explain themselves in the expert idiom of social workers without experiencing the cognitive dissonance of performative contradiction and without feeling compelled to modify their behavior, the critical efficacy of reflexive knowledge is lost. Indeed, reflexivity would now appear to belong to the logic of contemporary culture itself, and Žižek unreservedly blames commodity fetishism for this unwelcome development. Yet, beyond the fact that Žižek can offer no justification for singling out capitalism as the discrete cause of our predicament, he must also concoct a convoluted and improbable account of "postmodern" ideology as "practical fetishism," which is characterized by a loss of symbolic efficiency such that, as he is fond of putting it, "we know what we are doing, yet we continue doing it." Clearly, in *Lost in Translation* as in many other recent films, "knowing what we are doing" is precisely the problem under examination (which of course raises the specter of reflexivity's infinite regress). But here,

such reflexive knowledge is not simply an inadequate solution—to be supplanted, as Žižek follows Badiou in recommending, by revolutionary action—but precisely itself the crux of the problem. That is, it is not that "we continue to do it" *despite* knowing (better); on the contrary, knowing is, perversely, what compels us to do it—or, rather, renders us powerless to do otherwise. Put another way, "knowing" *is* what we are "doing," with the effect that it is no longer "we" who do it. To return to Seltzer: yes, the contradiction between "self" and "society" is itself a product of social cybernetics; but this is not a neutral historical or sociological fact. It remains to ask how this contradiction directly facilitates, rather than symptomatically indicating, the distinctively modern solution to the problem of cooperation—that is, modernity's (liberal) political structure. Žižek's language of ideological distortion, while it effectively focuses attention on the political labor done by reflexivity, is ultimately unhelpful in explaining this labor. Precisely because the imagined moment of irreducible opacity "solves" the predicament of autopoiesis, it facilitates the project of social cybernetics. Only if we continue to believe in the possibility of our own secret singularity will we continue to pursue the projects of the self that sustain modernity's structures of cooperation, including its expert systems and social imaginaries.

Chapter 5

1. Carol Horton, "Liberal Equality and the Civic Subject: Identity and Citizenship in Reconstruction America," in *The Liberal Tradition in American Politics,* ed. David F. Ericson and Louisa Bertch Green (New York: Routledge, 1999), 115–25.

2. In the present context, the citizen is still determined as essentially male.

3. This is the central implication of Iris Young's argument in "Polity and Group Difference."

4. See, for example, Jonathan Rosenbaum's condemnation of the film's view of race in *Movies as Politics* (Berkeley: University of California Press, 1997), 159–65.

5. And here we can perhaps push Rashid's choice of words toward "ideological."

6. Paul Auster, *Smoke & Blue in the Face* (Los Angeles: Miramax, 1995), 19.

7. The credits at the conclusion of the film identify them as OTB Men as well, but the only direct reference to their status as gamblers in the scene itself is Auggie's comment that the only thing they ever read is the racing form. By way of a marginal detour, one may speculate regarding the connotations of "off-track" betting within a story where economic rationality's condition of possibility is the nonrational detour of credit, faith, or speculation.

8. An entirely different essay can and should be written elaborating an analysis of the phallogocentrism articulated—not without considerable, and perhaps even decisive, irony—in the film. By way of a gloss, it should be noted that the problematic of gift/exchange that figures so prominently in *Smoke* is coextensive, in Lévi-Strauss, with the problematic of the incest taboo. In the process of resolving the lat-

ter with the aid of the former, Lévi-Strauss situates women as tokens of exchange among men—in a sense, as the money of male sociality. In this early scene, we already witness such an exchange among men rendered in terms of, on the one hand, conspicuously absent women and, on the other, the humorously overdetermined social token of the cigar. Moreover, this exchange is suggestively linked to philosophy and, in the next moment, to the history of capitalism, liberal democracy, and the seat of phallogocentric power occupied by a woman.

9. Kenneth Burke includes synecdoche among the "basic" figures of speech; as one of the forms of metonymy, it is a "master trope" (*The Philosophy of Literary Form* [Berkeley: University of California Press, 1974], 26). Both tropology and mastery (as well as their relation to the structure of the name) are part of what is at stake in the film.

10. Jacques Derrida, *Given Time I: Counterfeit Money,* trans. Peggy Kamuf (Chicago: University of Chicago Press, 1992),94. Derrida is discussing the paradoxical effects of the position of the title as both inside and outside the narrative. These effects have to do with the operation of law as both social convention and that which underwrites all such conventions. The consequences of this operation are put in play by this scene.

11. It is not clear, at least within the film "text," whether the story is apocryphal. However, that of all possible stories concerning tobacco the one chosen concerns "real" historical personages is suggestive.

12. Charles Hatch, America's Oldest Legislative Assembly & Its Jamestown Statehouses (Washington: U.S. Dept. of the Interior, National Park Service, 1956). Lisa Rein, "Mystery of Va.'s First Slaves Is Unlocked 400 Years Later," Washington Post, Sunday, September 3, 2006, p. 1.

13. See Jacques Derrida, "Declarations of Independence," *New Political Science* 15 (1986): 7–15.

14. For example, Raleigh's status as the subject of a monarchy; the form of natural law citizenship that arises in the United States beginning with the Declaration of Independence; and the political status of slaves and, ultimately, the entry into citizenship of free African Americans.

15. The name Thomas Jefferson Cole will return to occupy us at some length.

16. Derrida, *Given Time,* throughout.

17. The economic cycle of tobacco production involves the transformation of human beings into labor, labor into tobacco, and tobacco into a multitude of other commodities, including, and especially, money. Despotism and democracy, mercantilism and capitalism, freedom and enslavement depend, at least in part, on this alchemy.

18. This one of the major axes that relate this story of the bet, which opens the film, to Auggie's Christmas story, which closes it.

19. It is to this function of the gift that Jerry inadvertently refers when he mentions the coupon inside each box of Raleigh cigarettes.

20. Derrida, *Given Time,* 7 and throughout.

21. Ibid., 13.

22. Jacques Derrida, "Women in the Beehive," in *Men in Feminism,* ed. A. Jardine and P. Smith (New York: Methuen, 1987), 14.

23. Derrida, *Given Time,* 14.

24. Ibid., 11.

25. For a discussion of the far-reaching implications of starting from this "book of nature" metaphor as the foundation of knowledge, see Jacques Derrida, *Of Grammatology,* trans. Gayatri Chakravorty Spivak (Baltimore: Johns Hopkins University Press, 1976).

26. See Jacques Derrida, "Devant la Loi," trans. Avital Ronell, in *Kafka and the Contemporary Critical Performance: Centenary Readings,* ed. Alan Udoff (Bloomington: Indiana University Press, 1987): 128–67.

27. This is the conclusion at which Mauss himself arrives: "One can also see how this concrete study can lead not only to a science of customs, to a partial social science but even to moral conclusions, or rather, to adopt once more the old word, 'civility', or 'civics', as it is called now days. . . . the various aesthetic, moral religious, and economic motivations . . . which are the basis of society and constitute our common life, the conscious direction of which is the supreme art, *Politics*" (*The Gift,* 83).

28. Ibid., 1. 85n4, 1–2; emphasis added.

29. Ibid., 81.

30. Mary Douglas, foreword to Mauss, *The Gift,* x.

31. Derrida, *Given Time,* 44.

32. Mauss, *The Gift,* 5, 72.

33. Ibid., 65, 13.

34. Claude Lévi-Strauss, *Introduction to the Work of Marcel Mauss,* trans. Felicity Baker (London: Routledge, 1987), 47–59.

35. Mauss, *The Gift,* 71. It is noteworthy that the speech Mauss cites at this point refers repeatedly to the interchangeability of "humans," "ancestors," and "spirits." From these "archaic" rituals to the history of modern political economy to the film *Smoke,* tobacco is linked to the logic of haunting.

36. Derrida, *Given Time,* 17.

37. Auster, *Smoke & Blue in the Face,* 13.

38. Mauss, *Given Time,* 13.

39. Marilyn Friedman, "Feminism and Modern Friendship: Dislocating the Community," in *Friendship: A Philosophical Reader,* ed. N. K. Badhwar (Ithaca: Cornell University Press, 1993), 293.

40. As we find out soon afterward, this interruption is re-marked by Auggie's photography project, a hobby explicitly tied to the thematic exploration of the relation between necessity and chance, history and abstraction, and the speculative function of narrativity.

41. Here, again, we are faced with speculation: Paul loses his future, a loss no less powerful, and in fact more so, for being, like any future, radically unknowable.

When, early in the film, Auggie recounts the events of the day when Paul's wife fell victim to a stray bullet during a robbery shootout outside the cigar store, he speculates what might have happened had his financial transaction with her taken a bit longer. She was buying Paul cigars, and had Auggie made change more slowly, she might have lived. Here again, we witness the tropological chain connecting tobacco, economic exchange, speculation, temporal deferral, and narrative.

42. Genealogy cuts both ways here: "Merely a concrete test of the underlying principles of the great republic is the Negro Problem, and the spiritual striving of the freedmen's sons is the travail of souls whose burden is almost beyond the measure of their strength, but who bear it in the name of a historic race, in the name of this the land of their fathers' fathers." W. E. B. DuBois, *The Souls of Black Folk* (New York: Bantam, 1989), 8–9.

43. Jefferson inherited his slaves from his father and uncle, a patrilineal legacy intimately linked with the history of democracy.

44. Here is another hint of the complexity of the dynamic of haunting at work in the logic and history that links these names: "[T]here are to-day no *truer* exponents of the pure human *spirit* of the Declaration of Independence than the American Negroes" (DuBois, *Souls of Black Folk,* 8; emphasis added).

45. Since Virginia, the cradle of presidents, derives its name from the Virgin Queen, Jefferson and the American Republic are in a sense the progeny of a dissemination of royal (tobacco) seed: a virgin female who occupies the ultimate place of privilege in the phallogocentric system of monarchy exercises her imperial powers to join with one of her subjects in cultivating a luxury crop; i.e., the disseminated locus of the origin of power nonetheless produces and reproduces, generating as its quasi-legitimate offspring the political entity that ultimately comes to usurp its power precisely through a process of deconstruction, that is, by delinking the *arché* from the father and from the father's seed, by disseminating or diffusing the unitary locus of power and replacing the fictions of origin and filiation that theretofore endorsed political legitimacy—in short, by blowing the system up in smoke.

46. There are several instances of literal and metaphorical haunting thematized in the film: Cyrus is clearly referring to both possession and liquor when says he was under the influence of "spirits" when he got behind the wheel of a car with Thomas's mother; he describes his artificial limb as a kind of phantom of his missing arm that serves to re-present that previous possession; the story Paul tells Thomas about the skier who finds his long-dead—and younger—father frozen in the snow is a story of the return of the dead and the paradoxes of temporalization it engenders; Thomas is, in one sense, haunted by the absence of his biological father and the death of his mother; Paul is haunted by the death of his pregnant wife.

Derrida links the structure of haunting to speculation through the movement of différance: as the value of the present is determined through the future anterior, the future haunts the present as its past; the present emerges as such as a function of the interplay between a speculative future and memory speculatively produced by it. The substantial textual evidence of haunting in part underwrites the reading developed here of speculation as the aporetic structure organizing the contractual configuration of citizenship.

47. "[T]he Negro is a sort of seventh son, born with a veil, and *gifted* with second-sight in this American world,—a world which yields him no true self-consciousness, but only lets him see himself through the revelation of the other world. It is a peculiar sensation, this double-consciousness, this sense of always looking at one's self through the eyes of others. . . . One ever feels his twoness,—an American, a Negro; two souls, two thoughts, two unreconciled strivings; two warring ideals in one dark body. . . . And yet it is not weakness,—it is the contradiction of double aims." DuBois, *Souls of Black Folk,* 3; emphasis added.

48. One of DuBois's key insights is that rhetorical performance is self-authorizing, that stylistic accomplishment transforms into ethos by becoming evidence of its own presumed origin in the way that a son is evidence of a father.

49. Can anyone authorize oneself to name oneself? On the other hand, doesn't one always authorize one's name, like a story authorizes its title by way of the infinite abyss that joins and separates the name and its subject/object? And isn't it precisely the authority to tell stories that he confers upon himself by the very act of naming himself, exactly in the manner the Declaration of Independence functions in Derrida's analysis?

50. Once again, the script provides information not available in the filmic text (and one is forced to speculate as to its value in determining the meaning of that text). Aunt Em is the wife of Thomas's mother's brother, and therefore not a "blood" relative but one whose relationship to the boy is "purely" conventional rather than, in any sense, "natural." She is also a female witness to a familial conflict among men: Cyrus is responsible for the death of Thomas's mother, Louisa, and is therefore persona non grata with her brother, Henry (Auster, *Smoke & Blue in the Face,* 60–61).

Aunt Em tells Paul—and this is in the film—that Thomas himself said, "I don't have a father. As far as I'm concerned, the son of a bitch is dead." The would-be natural order of filiation is here thoroughly dysfunctional and patriarchy self-destructive. The "truth" about patrilineal names comes down behind the back, as it were, of this order, in the figure of (a) woman who marks the place of convention, agreement, or contract in its apposite relation to "nature." Both external and internal to this "family of man," Aunt Em can testify to its internal contradictions.

51. It is the convention for the parents to name, under the law; interestingly, there is no legal requirement that a person have a name.

52. For a suggestive discussion of the relation between these themes and the structure of drawing or painting, see Jacques Derrida, *The Truth in Painting,* trans. Geoffrey Bennington and Ian McLeod (Chicago: University of Chicago Press, 1987).

53. Derrida, *Given Time,* 169–70.

54. This is why the *valence* of tobacco/smoke must be subjected to a measurement, or the disciplining principle of a calculation: the indeterminable must be made determinable and determinate. The irreducible ambivalence of the trope necessitates, however, that the calculation that would efface it is itself the subject of, on the one hand, speculation and, on the other, the excessiveness of the measurement itself: not only is it a question, literally, of measuring an excess, but it is a contradictory excess and a contradictory measurement, because the smoke is not "in" the cigar even as it is the "essence" of the cigar. Recording and calculating the change in the cigar's weight would yield the desired result only if smoke were that which is itself subtracted from the cigar, which it obviously is not. This difference is itself premised upon an indeterminacy, or upon an unanswerable question: "What is the relation between the smoke and the cigar?" The calculation that would discipline radical indeterminacy only dissimulates its deferral.

The bet is therefore a ruse that symbolically performs the imaginary vindication of value. Determinacy of value depends upon the speculative temporal movement of the "will have been" which the bet can reenact by giving itself as an example of the procedure whereby existing uncertainty is settled at a specific moment in time. If bets can be settled, then indeterminacies are only provisional, not radical. Paul's story shows, however, that the bet is an alibi, not a solution, to radical indeterminacy. As an alibi, it is at the same time the trace—ash or cinder—of this indeterminacy.

55. In this particular case, the illegality of the cigars is the result of a political judgment concerning Cuba's status as a democracy, a judgment predicated upon the presumed inextricability of democracy and capitalism: is Cuba's political organization unacceptable because Castro is not a democratically elected leader or because communism is anathema to capitalism?

56. Again, the favor involves tobacco and economic exchange, and again, we can only *speculate* what *would have been* had Auggie not recovered the camera when he did.

57. Derrida, *Given Time,* 100.

58. Ibid., 59. Forgiveness: Auggie forgives Thomas and Ruby; Thomas forgives Cyrus; Paul forgives Thomas (or does he repay him?).

59. The coincidence of time and place that is the sine qua non of the metaphysics of presence is repeatedly linked in the film to chance on the one hand (the death of Paul's wife, the death of Thomas's mother, Thomas's involvement with the robbery, etc.) and to speculation (the "perhaps" or the "would have been") on the other. The only way the conditions of presence appear to be satisfied are by chance—that is, beyond either agency or intentionality—and then only imaginatively; the right place and the right time never actually coincide because of the ineluctable operation of différance.

60. There remains to be written an essay on homosocial desire in *Smoke*—perhaps the same essay, suggested in an earlier note, that would address the film's imbrication with phallogocentrism.

61. I refer the reader to the analysis of money offered in Derrida, *Given Time,* an analysis that, for lack of time and space, cannot be faithfully reproduced here.

62. Paul's answering lines, "It doesn't have to be true. It just has to be good," are on p. 137 of the script, but are absent from the film. Their appearance in the script conveniently supports the present reading, but, more important, serve as evidence that Auster and Wang were astute enough to have realized that including the lines in the film would have compromised its perfectly calibrated ambiguity.

63. That is, the beginning of the story coincides with the anniversary of the beginning of the nation.

64. "Remainder" would indicate the irreducible coimplication of unassimilated excess and intended product. If smoke is both the essence and the excess of tobacco and stands for the ambiguity of the opposition between "truth" and "fiction," "reality" generated through narrativization produces remnants—in Derrida's parlance, ashes or cinders (see, for example, *Glas,* a work that offers a graphic model of the way *Smoke* and *Given Time* ought to be read together)—that attest to the nonnatural nature of this production. In remaining available to new appropriations, they serve to deconstruct the logic that produced them and liberate from its potentially totalizing grip those elements that had been assimilated. Auggie's Christmas story, framed explicitly as "the story of how I got my first camera," thus thematizes the relation of the remainder to the process of narrative production exemplified by his photographic hobby.

65. Immanuel Kant, *Lectures on Ethics,* trans. Louis Infield (New York: Harper & Row, 1963), 208.

66. Immanuel Kant, *The Doctrine of Virtue,* trans. Mary J. Gregor (New York: Harper & Row, 1964), 469.

67. Interestingly, Kant describes respect in terms of excessive economic obligation: "Respect is a tribute we cannot refuse to pay" (*Critique of Practical Reason,* trans. Lewis White Beck [Indianapolis: Bobbs-Merrill, 1956], 77). In effect, there is no reciprocity of respect; there is only infinite duty to give it. This means, of course, that mutual respect cannot be secured by social convention or rational choice.

68. Honig, *Political Theory,* 32

69. Butler, Laclau, and Žižek, *Contingency, Hegemony, Universality.*

Conclusion

1. E.g., feminists, multiculturalists, Laclau, Mouffe, Rancière, etc.

2. Today, mostly Rawlsian rationalists and Habermasian deliberativists.

3. Most recently in *On Populist Reason.*

4. Paul de Man, *Allegories of Reading: Figural Language in Rousseau, Nietzsche, Rilke, and Proust* (New Haven: Yale University Press, 1982), 205.

5. I am adapting a formulation coined, in a significantly different context, by Paul Ricoeur, *The Rule of Metaphor: The Creation of Meaning in Language* (Toronto: University of Toronto Press, 1977).

Index

Characters from screenplays are in italics and are alphabetized by first name.